When Dead Tongues Speak

AMERICAN PHILOLOGICAL ASSOCIATION

CLASSICAL RESOURCES SERIES

Justina Gregory, Series Editor

NUMBER 6
WHEN DEAD TONGUES SPEAK
TEACHING BEGINNING GREEK AND LATIN

Edited by
John Gruber-Miller

When Dead Tongues Speak

TEACHING BEGINNING
GREEK AND LATIN

Edited by John Gruber-Miller

OXFORD
UNIVERSITY PRESS

2006

OXFORD
UNIVERSITY PRESS

Oxford University Press, Inc., publishes works that further
Oxford University's objective of excellence
in research, scholarship, and education.

Oxford New York
Auckland   Cape Town   Dar es Salaam   Hong Kong   Karachi
Kuala Lumpur   Madrid   Melbourne   Mexico City   Nairobi
New Delhi   Shanghai   Taipei   Toronto

With offices in
Argentina   Austria   Brazil   Chile   Czech Republic   France   Greece
Guatemala   Hungary   Italy   Japan   Poland   Portugal   Singapore
South Korea   Switzerland   Thailand   Turkey   Ukraine   Vietnam

Copyright © 2006 by The American Philological Association

Published by Oxford University Press, Inc.
198 Madison Avenue, New York, New York, 10016

www.oup.com

Oxford is a registered trademark of Oxford University Press

Library of Congress Cataloging-in-Publication Data
When dead tongues speak : teaching beginning Greek and Latin /
edited by John Gruber-Miller.
p. cm.—(Classical resources series / American Philological
Association ; no. 6)
ISBN-13 978-0-19-517494-6; 978-0-19-517495-3 (pbk.)
ISBN 0-19-517494-1; 0-19-517495-X (pbk.)
1. Classical philology—Study and teaching.   2. Greek language—
Study and teaching.   3. Latin language—Study and teaching.
I. Gruber-Miller, John.   II. Classical resources series; no. 6.
PA74.W47 2006
480.071—dc22   2005026643

omnibus magistris
qui discipulos discipulasque colunt
et amorem discendi alunt.

Preface

This book has been long in the making. The idea for this volume arose at a meeting of classicists from small classics departments at the APA who wanted to reflect on the theory and practice of teaching and to share the fruits of their experience teaching Greek and Latin with other teachers, both experienced and in training. I want to express my gratitude to all the contributors who were able to blend research and practical advice with their own personal passion for teaching in each chapter. I want to acknowledge the University of North Carolina Press for permission to include sample oral scripts from Paula Saffire and Catherine Freis, *Ancient Greek Alive*, third edition. Thanks also go to thank Joel Lidov, the APA Textbook Committee, and the anonymous reviewers for their constructive comments that greatly improved this book. Finally, I also want to express my appreciation to my wife, Ann, and my children, Stephen, Timothy, and Theresa, for their support, understanding, and patience.

Contents

Contributors

Kathryn Argetsinger (Ph.D., Princeton University) recently returned to teaching Latin, Greek, and ancient history at the University of Rochester after several years as a middle school Latin teacher in Pittsford, New York. At the University of Rochester, she has helped to develop a program to certify secondary school Latin teachers, as well as a "Latin Skills" course that emphasizes an active four-skills approach to Latin, including listening, speaking, and writing. When not teaching Latin, she practices Zen meditation at the Rochester Zen Center.

Laurie J. Churchill (Ph.D., University of California, Santa Cruz) held faculty positions at Texas Tech and Ohio Wesleyan Universities before reinventing her life in New Mexico. Her research and publications have focused on representations of gender, sexuality, and misogyny, especially in Latin literature, and on the gendered dimensions of Latin education. She is the lead editor of *Women Writing Latin: From Roman Antiquity to Early Modern Europe* (Routledge 2002). Recent endeavors include fiber art and a collection of essays and photographs—in progress—on *West Texas Women Artists: From the Panhandle to Big Bend* (co-authored with Kippra Hopper).

Andrea Deagon received her Ph.D. from Duke University in 1984. She directs the classical studies program at the University of North Carolina at Wilmington. In addition to her work in Latin pedagogy, she has published on such diverse topics as the Gilgamesh epic, representations of Salome, and the history of oriental dance. She is currently developing course materials centered on natural history for elementary Latin students.

John Gruber-Miller (Ph.D., Ohio State University) is a one-person classics section within the Department of Classical and Modern Languages at Cornell College in Mount Vernon, Iowa. As a result, his research interests in Greek and Roman comedy, language pedagogy, and technology frequently intersect with his teaching: his intermediate Latin students have staged bilingual productions of Roman comedy on eight occasions. He has developed websites for teaching the ancient world, most recently *Ariadne: Resources for* Athenaze (http://cornellcollege.edu/classical_studies/ariadne/). He has also published articles on reading and speaking Latin, using the VRoma MOO in beginning Latin, and teaching Cicero's *de Amicitia*.

Barbara Hill's experience in the area of teaching Latin to students with learning difficulties has come through a career-long involvement in Latin pedagogy. She served as the Latin Program coordinator for the Department of Classics at the University of Colorado at Boulder for nearly two decades, and she still serves as the program coordinator of Modified Foreign Language at that institution. As MFL coordinator, Hill is responsible for counseling and placing students with learning disabilities or a history of failure in foreign language classes into self-contained modified classes and for training and supporting the instructors who teach these classes. Hill received her B.A. and M.A. from the University of Michigan at Ann Arbor.

Daniel V. McCaffrey has taught at Randolph-Macon College in Ashland, Virginia, since 1975 and now holds the rank of professor of classics. He received an A.B. from Fordham University (1968) and a Ph.D. from the University of Michigan (1974). His interests include Latin elegy, Latin language and pedagogy, computerized language processing, and the psychology of reading. His e-mail address is dmccaffr@rmc.edu.

Kenneth Scott Morrell is associate professor of Greek and Roman studies at Rhodes College in Memphis, Tennessee. He received his B.A. degree in German literature and classics from Stanford University in 1982 and his M.A. and Ph.D. in classical philology from Harvard University in 1989. Before joining the faculty at Rhodes in the fall of 1993, he taught at St. Olaf College in Minnesota. His research interests include Homeric poetry, Greek and Latin pedagogy, the archaeology of Lycia, and cultural informatics.

Paula Saffire received her Ph.D. from Harvard University in 1969 and is associate professor of classics at Butler University. She has been using classroom conversation to teach ancient Greek since 1971. She is coauthor, with Catherine Freis, of the textbook *Ancient Greek Alive*. She has developed a "performance-lecture" in which, wearing ancient Greek costume, she sings the songs of Sappho in English and in Greek to musical accompaniment, with commentary, personal anecdotes, and slides. Her newest work, in progress, is *Singing Sappho*, a book on what she has learned about Sappho's songs through performance. For more information see http://blue.butler.edu/~psaffire/.

Standards for Classical Language Learning

Goal	Standard
1. Communication *Communicate in a classical language*	1.1 Students read, understand, and interpret Latin or Greek. 1.2 Students use orally, listen to, and write Latin or Greek as part of the language learning process
2. Culture *Gain knowledge and understanding of Greco-Roman culture*	2.1 Students demonstrate an understanding of the perspectives of Greek or Roman culture as revealed in the practices of the Greeks or Romans 2.2 Students demonstrate an understanding of the perspectives of Greek or Roman culture as revealed in the products of Greeks or Romans
3. Connections *Connect with other disciplines and expand knowledge*	3.1 Students reinforce and further their knowledge of other disciplines through their study of classical languages 3.2 Students expand their knowledge through the reading of Latin or Greek and the study of ancient culture
4. Comparisons *Develop insight into own language and culture*	4.1 Students recognize and use elements of the Latin or Greek language to increase knowledge of their own language 4.2 Students compare and contrast their own culture with that of the Greco-Roman world
5. Communities *Participate in wider communities of language and culture*	5.1 Students use their knowledge of Greek or Latin in a multilingual world 5.2 Students use their knowledge of Greco-Roman culture in a world of diverse cultures

Source: From Richard C. Gascoyne et al., *Standards for Classical Language Learning* (Oxford, OH: American Classical League, 1997).

Introduction

Many changes, both in and out of the classroom, are challenging us to reexamine how we teach Latin and Greek: the rapid pace of communication, new technologies, the explosion of new knowledge, the growing diversity in our schools and communities. Educators and employers recognize the need for graduates who have good communication skills, who understand diverse cultures, who can work with people from different backgrounds, who can solve problems, and who can work collaboratively. The language classroom is one place where all these skills can be taught. It is in the Latin and Greek classroom that we can teach students how to communicate, how to synthesize new knowledge, how to respond to other cultures, how to solve problems, and how to collaborate.

This book is the beginning of a conversation about teaching Latin and Greek, about how we as Latin and Greek teachers can respond to the changes in our classrooms so that we can help our students achieve these goals. It summarizes the research that linguists, psychologists, and language teachers have done over the past thirty years and puts this research into practice with classroom activities that give teachers the tools to be creative in the classroom, to go beyond textbooks. It makes a case that recognizing learners' diverse needs—their various cognitive and affective learning styles—encourages us to and perhaps even demands that we transform our classrooms into places where communication and collaboration take place within meaningful contexts. My fellow contributors and I view this volume as an introduction to current trends—national standards, learner needs, collaboration, cultural context, meaning-based instruction—in teaching languages. Just as each contributor has grappled with how to make use of this research to change his or her classroom practice, the essays in this collection challenge classicists to reenvision how they teach beginning languages and how to reach a wider and more diverse group of students than ever before.

Each contributor has not only reviewed the research relevant to the chapter's topic but has also evaluated it in the light of his or her own experience in the classroom. A review of the research, therefore, provides a theoretical framework for each chapter. At the same time, each chapter includes specific techniques, advice, and activities that teachers can take with them into the classroom. The result, then, is that each chapter is grounded in both research and practice. Although some chapters are written with either Greek or Latin as the primary focus, most of the theoretical perspectives presented and many of the activities are applicable to both languages. Furthermore, while many of the contributors are writing with the college classroom in mind, it is our hope that many of the concepts and classroom activities in each chapter are of value to middle and high school teachers, too.

Part I, "Setting the Scene," sets out some of the theoretical background for the rest of the book. "Communication, Context, and Community: Integrating the *Standards* in the Greek and Latin Classroom" situates the five goals of the *Standards for Classical Language Learning* (Gascoyne et al.) into a model of language learning that centers on communication, contexts, and communities. The chapter begins by defining "communication" and "communicative competence" and then shows that the exchange of meaning is at the heart of communication. Communication is not only the first goal of the *Standards* but is also the best way to learn a language. For language learners need to integrate form with meaning to transfer knowledge to long-term memory. Communication, however, cannot take place without contexts. Language learners need to pay attention to Culture (goal 2) and rhetorical structure in order to understand extended discourse. Two other goals—Connections to other disciplines (goal 3) and Comparisons (goal 4)—also provide additional contexts for understanding texts and for extending students' knowledge of the ancient world to the modern world. The final goal, Communities (goal 5), provides an audience for the exchange of meaning and an opportunity for students to share their understanding of the Greek and Roman world with others. This goal also puts student learning and learners' needs at the center of the language classroom.

The second part of the volume, "Focus on the Learner," explores the many factors that influence how people learn a second language and how we can make the classroom a place where language learners can learn most effectively—in other words, context and community. In chapter 2, "Cognitive Style and Learning Strategies in Latin Instruction," Andrea Deagon provides an introduction to the many cognitive factors that determine how adolescents and adults learn a second language. She also offers reasons for a more learner-centered approach to teaching classical languages, and provides specific examples of how to teach vocabulary and intermediate reading in a way that is attentive to different cognitive styles. Finally, she presents ways for teachers and students to diagnose their different cognitive styles and to make use of the learning strategies best suited to help them learn more efficiently and autonomously.

In chapter 3, "Latin for Students with Severe Foreign Language Learning Difficulties," Barbara Hill continues the discussion of cognition and learning strategies presented in chapter 2 by defining the specific cognitive difficulties that put students at risk for learning a foreign language. It is characteristic of high-risk foreign language students to have linguistic coding difficulties—most often with the sound system, secondarily with syntactic and semantic coding—but otherwise they are on par with their peers in intelligence. Hill explains how learning-disabled (LD) students learn best, and recommends concrete strategies for making the Latin learning process for these students more effective. In particular, she discusses the effectiveness of utilizing a multisensory approach that integrates the auditory, visual, and kinesthetic elements of language so that learners hear, see, and act out language in meaningful contexts.

Chapter 4, "Peer Teaching and Cooperative Learning in the First Year of Latin," by Kathryn Argetsinger, addresses the learner's need for variety and for opportunities to use the language with two solutions: near-peer teaching and cooperative learning. Near-peer teaching utilizes undergraduates who are somewhat more experienced in the language as assistants or tutors in the first-year language course. Cooperative learning involves structured interaction with fellow classmates in small groups working toward a common goal. Not only do these classroom designs respond to learner's cognitive needs, Argetsinger argues, but they also address affective and social concerns by creating a low-anxiety, noncompetitive atmosphere and providing students with new strategies for learning language as a community.

In chapter 5, "Is There a Woman in This Textbook? Feminist Pedagogy and Elementary Latin," Laurie Churchill continues the discussion of social and affective factors that influence how our students learn Latin, exploring the implicit gendered assumptions our textbooks make about the Latin language and Roman culture. In particular, she asks us to reevaluate the *how* and *what* we teach in the Latin classroom so that we might respond to the change in demographics in our classrooms and engage more students in the study of Latin. She argues that it is important to look at how gender socialization affects learning and how to be more inclusive by using a wider range of teaching and learning strategies, especially collaborative learning strategies. She then offers a variety of specific classroom activities: journals to help students reflect and compare Roman attitudes to gender with our own, vocabulary activities to help students gain insights about Roman women, and readings on Camilla and Boudica from Vergil and Tacitus to introduce participles in authentic Roman contexts.

While part II focuses on learner needs, classroom contexts, and community, part III, "Focus on the Language," explores discourse, cultural contexts, and communication. In chapter 6, "Reading Latin Efficiently and the Need for Cognitive Strategies," Dan McCaffrey provides an introduction to reading theory and then focuses on strategies—known as bottom-up reading strategies—that help readers process the linguistic code more automatically. The Latin (and Greek) noun system has many ambiguous forms: *-ae* (genitive and dative singular and nominative plural), *-o* (dative and ablative singular), and so on. By examining the texts of Vergil, Ovid, and Livy, McCaffrey uncovers some of the ways that Romans may have resolved the ambiguities of identical case endings as the sentence unfolded in natural Latin word order. In particular, he shows several strategies for disambiguating the nominative and accusative plural of the third, fourth, and fifth declensions, and then he offers exercises for students to make these strategies more automatic. In short, he demonstrates how to read Latin in Latin word order. The end result is more fluent readers of Latin who pay attention to meaning because the linguistic code has become more automatic.

In chapter 7, "Language Acquisition and Teaching Ancient Greek: Applying Recent Theories and Technology," Kenny Morrell makes a case for integrating all four skills—listening, reading, speaking, and writing—in the elementary Greek classroom so that students of Greek become better readers. In particular, he stresses the importance of context and background knowledge (top-down reading strategies) in helping students read for meaning, and argues that listening to Greek helps students develop many of the same skills that they need for reading fluently. Finally, he presents a model for integrating authentic Greek texts in beginning-level courses, which includes prereading activities that help students activate relevant prior knowledge (linguistic, rhetorical, and content schemata) before they read, strategies for comprehending the text, and postreading activities to consolidate new knowledge and information. He then applies these principles, giving a specific lesson plan for a passage from Lysias 1, *On the Murder of Eratosthenes*.

Chapter 8, "Ancient Greek in Classroom Conversation," by Paula Saffire, returns to the issue of listening and speaking in beginning Greek introduced by Morrell in chapter 7. Although she recognizes that few of us have been trained to speak Greek conversationally, she argues that there are psychological, social, and cognitive reasons that make conversational ancient Greek a good choice to use in the classroom as a complement to reading and writing activities. Many of her arguments are rooted in the learner variables discussed by Deagon in chapter 2. Saffire stresses that for conversation to work, it must be used for genuine communication—that is, to convey ideas, establish relationships, and gather information. In order to make conversation in ancient Greek feasible for those who have never done it, she provides sample scripts that she and others have used successfully over the years and offers practical advice on how to use conversation in the classroom.

Like Saffire, John Gruber-Miller in chapter 9, "Teaching Writing in Beginning Latin and Greek: *Logos, Ethos, and Pathos*," speaks of the need for learners to produce the language and interact with others in order to become proficient in the language. He argues that writing simply to translate sentences from English to Latin or to practice grammar is a limited view of writing. He suggests that we return to a classical view of writing that involves *logos, ethos,* and *pathos* (roughly text, writer, and audience) and shows how teachers can sequence writing activities that lead from controlled, carefully structured assignments to more open-ended, creative ones. Like McCaffrey, who is concerned that students use case morphology automatically, Gruber-Miller demonstrates that writing helps students master the basic linguistic code. Like Morrell, who argues for integrating all four skills, Gruber-Miller explains how writing reinforces reading. Like Argetsinger, Churchill, and Saffire, he stresses the importance of audience and community to give speaking and listening, writing and reading a purpose and a context.

The volume ends with an annotated bibliography. The bibliography does not pretend to be complete but, rather, is designed as a good place to begin further reading on particular topics. Items were chosen for inclusion because they provided either a good summary of current research or practical activities for classroom use. Typically, when there were several works on a topic, the more recent work was chosen so that the research and references would be most up to date.

PART I

Setting the Scene

CHAPTER 1

Communication, Context, and Community

Integrating the *Standards* in the Greek and Latin Classroom

John Gruber-Miller

Latin is a language,
Dead as dead can be:
First it killed the Romans;
Now it's killing me.

—Anonymous

The Forum and the Agora were alive with the sounds of commerce, the speeches of politicians, the noise of gossip.

—Richard Gascoyne et al., *Standards for
Classical Language Learning*

Anyone who has studied Latin long enough has heard the first quotation. For those of us who teach Greek and Latin, it sets off a little voice inside of us that says, How can anyone think that Latin or Greek is dead? What could be more interesting than exploring the cultures, history, politics, and society of the Greeks and Romans through their own words? We might respond with words similar to those of the second quotation. Latin and Greek were heard and spoken, read and written. They were languages in which people expressed their deepest emotions: joy, fear, anger, love, satisfaction, grief. They were languages in which people talked about relationships with family members, obligations to friends, interactions with strangers, and duties to the gods. In fact, they are languages that still communicate ideas, feelings, thoughts, and arguments. After all, isn't that why we fell in love with Latin and Greek—so that we could understand the people whose lives fascinate us and respond to the texts they wrote?

When I was first teaching, I was more concerned to "cover the grammar" and "finish the book," and then, I thought, my students would know Latin and Greek. After all, time is short, so it was best, I thought, to focus on what the book had to offer. There were paradigms to be memorized, vocabulary to be studied, exercises to be completed, and passages to translate. Once my students completed these hurdles, I assumed (or at least hoped) that they understood the new grammar well enough and had learned enough vocabulary to move on to the next chapter. Somehow, I expected my students, after memorizing forms, studying vocabulary, and practicing sentences, to be able to read and understand—almost magically—Latin and Greek. And if they could not read yet, I usually gave them more of the same: exercises that focused on sentence-level syntax rather than the strategies needed for reading chunks of discourse. Instead of helping my students learn to read, understand, and interpret Greek and Latin within their cultural contexts, I was focusing on accuracy at the sentence level, only one aspect of what linguists call communicative competence. In short, I was practicing a theory of language teaching and learning that did not fit with my goal of helping students to read Greek and Latin fluently and accurately, of appreciating it as a "living" language. What I needed to do was to reexamine these assumptions in the light of what I hoped my students would be able to do after they had studied beginning Latin or Greek.[1]

Many sources are challenging us to rethink our basic assumptions about teaching Greek and Latin, from research in linguistics about what it means to be competent in a language, to research in psychology about how people learn languages, to the deeper realization in the humanities and social sciences of the way that culture and language intersect. In addition, the emphasis on communicative approaches by our colleagues in modern languages and the push for national standards for foreign language learning are already changing the way that teachers of Latin and Greek view their classroom practices (e.g., Abbott; Abernathy et al.; Sienkewicz et al. 1999; Wills). In what follows, I explore three areas that are necessary for language learning: communication, context, and community. I argue that with the incorporation of meaning-based instruction and communication in the classroom, students can more easily reach higher levels of proficiency in Greek and Latin. By attending to context, whether the context of extended discourse or the cultural context, students establish a framework for understanding Greek and Roman texts. And with communities, students have more opportunities for testing hypotheses about language, negotiating meaning, interpreting discourse, or presenting their ideas. Throughout this discussion of communication, context, and community, I delineate how the five goals of the *Standards for Classical Language Learning*—Communication, Culture, Connections, Comparisons, and Communities—fit into this model of language learning.[2]

Communication

Defining Communication

There is a tendency among some language educators to divide the world between oral skills and written texts. Traditionally, modern language students speak and converse in the target language; Greek and Latin students focus on reading texts, or more typically, translating them. This dichotomy, of course, is an exaggeration, based on the assumption that communication is primarily speaking (VanPatten 1998b) and that reading a text in Greek and Latin is primarily translation, not communication.

Over the last thirty or more years, a deeper, richer sense of what it means to communicate has evolved. Communication is something we do every time we read a text, write a letter, or discuss a problem. Communication helps us establish our individual identities, develops our relationships with others, allows us to create communities, and shapes our view of the world. It is not limited to speaking, but more often than not involves several, if not all, modes of communication:

listening, speaking, reading, and writing. In the introductory chapter of her book *Communicative Competence, Theory and Classroom Practice*, Sandra Savignon defines communication as "a continuous process of *expression, interpretation, and negotiation of meaning*" (8, emphasis in original).

Significantly, goal 1 of the national *Standards for Foreign Language Learning* and the *Standards for Classical Language Learning* is Communication. Just as negotiation, interpretation, and expression are the three key ingredients in Savignon's definition of communication, the national *Standards for Foreign Language Learning* and various state-implemented standards (e.g., Wallinger et al.; Sienkewicz et al. 1999) identify three modes of communication: interpersonal, interpretative, and presentational. The first mode of communication is interpersonal, a conversation in which individuals negotiate meaning through the give-and-take of dialogue. Sometimes this dialogue takes place through a face-to-face interaction, but it could just as easily take place today in a chat room or MOO (Multi-User-Domain Object Oriented). A second mode is interpretative, in which we receive and interpret language that is written or spoken: an audience listening to a speech, a lecture, or a poem, or a reader perusing a text. A third mode is presentational, in which someone creates a message to be heard or read by a group of people, such as speeches, philosophical dialogues, or historical narratives. Of course, these modes overlap. Yet by highlighting each person's role in the production and reception of language, these modes underscore the commonalities and interconnections between oral and written speech rather than their differences (Hall).

Indeed, Greek and Roman texts exhibit all three modes of communication. For example, when two characters in a play of Euripides or Plautus are speaking to one another, they are involved in an interpersonal exchange that involves the negotiation of meaning. At the same time, the audience listening to the performance is attempting to interpret the actions and words of the actors on stage. Finally, the poet-playwright has created the text that is being presented on stage. The overlap between interpersonal, interpretative, and presentational modes becomes even greater in the case of an orator delivering a speech or a poet giving a poetry reading. At times, each is presenting a speech or poem, but each is also engaged with the audience in negotiating meaning. The audience is involved in understanding the oration or lyric poem, but it also affects the performance and message(s) communicated. Even when we read these texts two thousand years later, we must never forget the interaction between speaker and audience in cultures that were both oral and to varying degrees literate.

The texts of Homer, Euripides, and Plato, Plautus, Cicero, and Vergil, through formulae, drama, and dialogue, beckon us to hear them spoken and to perform them, or at least to understand them as performance. Yet how can our students begin to comprehend these different modes of interchange without some experience of them as performance, without some experience of listening and speaking these texts as well as reading them? If students are to comprehend a text that was meant to be delivered to a live audience, then they need to feel comfortable with its rhythms and sounds. Too often, beginning language students read a text word by word without recognizing phrase units or the larger structures of meaning. But listening forces them to pay attention to the greater meaning of an utterance and to the broader discourse context. Speaking helps students hear and produce those units of meaning in phrases and clauses, not just word by word. Finally, through listening and speaking, learners become more fluent and more interested in expressing and negotiating meaning with others. In short, the three communicative domains—interpersonal, interpretive, and presentational—overlap and contribute to greater language competence.

Communicative Competence and the Role of Grammar

Certainly grammar is a topic many of us teach most explicitly in a beginning language course. And certainly, adolescent and adult students ask for and can benefit from knowledge of grammatical rules and structures. But if grammar is the primary focus of a language course, then the course will be primarily *about* the language rather than using the language to interpret and express ideas, feelings, attitudes, and stories. It is important to put grammar in its place: it is a necessary tool, but not a sufficient one, to help language learners communicate effectively.[3]

So what knowledge and skills does a language learner need in order to communicate effectively with other people in a variety of contexts? Communicative competence, according to Marianne Celce-Murcia and her collaborators Zoltán Dörnyei and Sarah Thurrell, comprises five main areas of knowledge—discourse competence, sociocultural competence, linguistic competence, actional or rhetorical competence, and strategic competence.[4] To be sure, sentence-level morphology and syntax (linguistic competence) are important for comprehending meaning, but they are only one aspect of what it means to know a language. Equally important is how one sentence or paragraph is connected to another (discourse structure), how various decisions about how to express an idea make a difference in how one's intended meaning is received (actional and sociocultural competence), and how to solve problems when communication breaks down (strategic competence). Learners of Greek and Latin, in order to become fluent, accurate readers of Greek and Latin texts, need opportunities to practice all aspects of communication. If we teach grammar to the exclusion of these other communication skills, we produce students with a limited ability to comprehend and produce complex discourse fluently and accurately.

How We Learn Languages

Expressing, interpreting, and negotiating meaning is at the heart of communication. Meaning and communication is also at the heart of learning a second language. Research has shown that learners benefit when instruction focuses on communication of information, feelings, and ideas, using the language to comprehend and produce discourse in meaningful, creative, and spontaneous ways (Lightbown and Spada; Pica; VanPatten 1998a). A communicative approach means listening or reading for ideas first, to share knowledge in order to learn from another person, to present a story for the sake of telling a story, to negotiate with another what a story or text means, to listen to a message in order to understand its relevance. As a result, learners improve their vocabulary, grammatical accuracy, comprehension of extended discourse, and the ability to produce the language. At the same time, a meaning-based approach does not mean an end to a focus on form, but rather to focus on form within a variety of communicative tasks (Doughty; Lightbown and Spada). In other words, students not only become more fluent but also become more comfortable with a wider range of language skills that will help them understand a greater range of texts and discourse.

Why does meaning-based language instruction work? People remember new information (and learn languages) through the active construction of knowledge into an interlocking network or roadmap of ideas, called a schema by cognitive psychologists: "Whereas a concept can be viewed as a single unit of information, a schema may be described as an interconnected set of propositions or elements; a schema is a more holistic segment of knowledge" (Goldstein). Each schema is composed of a number of concepts, an interconnected web of nodes and associations. For example, a *symposium* specifies a set of behaviors, people, and activities pertinent to a Greek after-dinner drinking party. Within the schema *symposium*, one node in the web may be a *hetaira,* and this node has various strands or associations, such as the sound of the word, its written representation, its morphology and syntax, what a *hetaira* looks like (her age and dress), her status, and what she does at the symposium. Groups of nodes with their attendant associations are linked together to form a schema or script. Thus, the schema *symposium* also includes other nodes—such as wine and the mixing of wine and water in a *krater,* the presence of men without their wives, the order of drinking, other activities such as talking politics or singing poetry—to form a script or map of how the nodes are connected together. Learning a new word, then, involves many layers of information and associations, from specific phonological, grammatical, and semantic information to broader cultural, social, and political notions. When language learners are using the language within a coherent context, they are hanging the structure of the language on a meaningful message.

Contexts

My discussion of communicative competence and schema theory has highlighted the importance of context in communication. If someone does not understand a specific cultural reference, such as what an oracle does, how it may be interpreted, and its effect on the recipient, then one cannot fully understand Oedipus's murder of Laius or Herodotus's story of Solon and Croesus. Knowledge of typical rhetorical strategies (actional intent), moreover, may help a reader be able to predict and therefore comprehend better a general's speech before battle, a politician's campaign promises, or a mother's advice to her daughter before marriage. Third, the situational context—for example, the death of Cicero's daughter Tullia in 45 B.C.E.—may affect how one reads the letters or philosophical dialogues written during the last years of the orator's life. In this section, we explore some aspects of how contexts are crucial for learning a language and understanding texts.

The Cultural Context

Clearly, cultural schemata—the framework about how a culture thinks, works, acts, and values—shape the message of a Greek or Latin text. Yet it is sometimes easy to slip into thinking of culture as a capsule, as an interesting diversion from learning grammar, as a "fun activity" to do at the end of class or the end of the week. If I am running short on time, furthermore, it is usually culture that takes a back seat. Recent research on teaching culture confirms the notion that culture is often treated as separate from the rest of what we do in the language classroom. Recent studies on culture show that students (and teachers) tend to compartmentalize language study as distinct from the study of culture, to exaggerate differences between cultures, and to generalize from these differences to all peoples of a culture (Robinson-Stuart and Nocon). In addition, students in beginning-level classes tend not to see the connection between foreign language study and issues of gender, race, and class in the target culture (Kubota, Austin, and Saito-Abbott).

The *Standards* recognize the centrality of culture as a crucial context for communication, and goal 2 puts culture on an equal footing with communication. As Ross Steele has written, "every word, every expression we use has a cultural dimension. . . . Speakers of a language share not only the vocabulary and structure of a language; they share perceptions of reality represented by that vocabulary and structure" (1). As experienced language teachers know, vocabulary items and grammatical structures rarely have a simple one-to-one correspondence from one language to another. For language learners to succeed in communicating, they need to understand the values, attitudes, customs, and rituals of a culture that are expressed in what they hear and read, speak and write. Language learners need to learn not only *information* about the culture but also the deeper *process* of how a culture works—for example, how values about honor and status affected ancient politics, economic exchange, and friendship.[5] By envisioning the study of cultures as one that examines the target culture's *products* and *practices* in order to gain insights into *perspectives*, the *Standards* point to an integrated approach to culture. Instead of looking at isolated works of art, individual stories about the gods, single events from ancient history, the *Standards* ask us to explore the connections between these isolated products or practices to show how they contribute to the broader tapestry of Athenian and Roman life. Without a coherent and consistent cultural context, students of the ancient world cannot succeed in the task of reading, understanding, and interpreting Greek and Latin texts.

Interdisciplinary Learning and Intercultural Competence: Creating Connections and Making Comparisons

Goal 3, Connect with other disciplines and acquire information, and goal 4, Comparisons, point to the need for language learners to see how their study of the target language and culture makes a difference in how they understand the world around them. Instead of being focused on a language and culture that may not seem relevant to their own language and culture, goals 3 and 4 encourage language learners to view their studies as applicable to how we live and function in our world: they help students develop higher order thinking skills, cultivate empathy for others, and think across disciplines and across cultures. Indeed, fulfilling these two standards makes it easier to argue that Greek and Latin are core subjects that contribute to the entire school curriculum and influence our lives and culture today.

One of the attractions of our field is the multi- and interdisciplinary nature of Greek and Roman studies. The ancient world has produced artists, architects, historians, lawyers, mathematicians, philosophers, poets, and scientists who first explored questions about friendship, ethics, gender, hierarchies, power, life and death, and our relationship to the natural and spiritual world. Their discussions offer springboards for how we think and feel and understand our world today. Goal 3 underscores the need to connect with other disciplines, to show how Greek and Latin, and Greek and Roman culture have made a difference in our world. For example, connections with science can be made by asking students to describe the steps of an experiment of Archimedes (past tense) and the reasons for the results (cause-and-effect relationships). A unit on Greek or Roman food can make connections between Greek or Latin terms for plants and animals and related words in English (scientific terminology), discuss the impact that climate and topography and technology have on the type of farming in various parts of the world (meteorology, geography, and technology), and recognize the role of slaves in supporting agriculture, whether on ancient *latifundia* or on plantations in the southern United States (social studies). Students can make connections with art by using vase-painting or sculptures as springboards for stories, drama, or song. In short, goal 3 makes explicit that we should use Latin and Greek to understand the subject content of other disciplines.[6]

Goal 4, Comparisons, is a second way to deepen the context for language learning and for demonstrating the intercultural connections between the ancient and modern worlds. It is easy to become so busy teaching the target language and culture that comparative work is often left out of the classroom. Goal 4, however, articulates the need to be explicit about making comparisons. Learning another language and culture raises provocative questions about how language and culture shape the way we think and act, how each culture has a different worldview that may not at first glance seem "rational" but has its own inherent logic. By making comparisons, language learners can view their own language and culture from a new vantage point. In the process, they increase their own awareness of their identity, of their language, of their culture. They become critical of their roles in society and become capable of producing a transformation of the self and of one's relation to others. This awareness is what Paolo Freire terms "critical consciousness," and what Socrates alludes to when he says that the unexamined life is not worth living. By making comparisons and increasing awareness, students develop intercultural competence—that is, the ability to view other cultures from both within and without the culture, from both an insider's and an outsider's perspective.

Sometimes these comparisons can be made purely at an intellectual level, as in a Venn diagram of the similarities and differences between the political system of Athens and the United States, but frequently an affective element or an experiential activity can help sharpen the issues and deepen students' awareness. For example, a unit on friendship in Rome might begin by asking students to list words for love, affection, and friendship in Latin and in English. Who is considered a friend and in what circumstances? What qualities bind us to friends? Then students could view the opening five minutes of Mario Puzo's *The Godfather* in order to see how Don Corleone, similarly to the Romans, defines friendship. After viewing the film, students then revise their original lists and begin to see the importance of *fides*, *officium*, and *beneficium*, the notion of gift-exchange, face-to-face interaction, and patronage and community in Roman culture, in contrast to American emphasis on affection, monetary exchange, impersonal interaction, and rugged individualism in defining friendship (Gruber-Miller). By adding an affective or experiential component to the intellectual process, learners process the similarities and differences more deeply, create personal connections to the material, and see these intercultural perspectives from an insider's and an outsider's perspective. In essence, they create a critical awareness of other cultures and their own. Finally, including these multiple perpectives helps reach learners of varying learning styles in more ways.

Communities

In the first two sections, we have seen that the focus on meaning is a prerequisite for communication and that communication (and language learning) cannot take place without contextualizing it. The third ingredient for discourse is community. At a minimum, communication involves at least two people: a speaker and a listener, or a writer and a reader. In the Greek and Roman world, dramatists, orators, poets, and writers all presented their "texts" to the community through performance, recitations, or "publication." And the public responded, applauding, arguing, considering, and interpreting. In a similar fashion, language learners, by listening and responding to each other in the classroom, form communities that can guide them in interpreting what they hear and read. After modeling communities in the classroom—learning to respond to each other, interpret each other's language and ideas, and receive feedback—students are more prepared to "participate in wider communities of language and culture," goal 5. In short, communication—the conveyance of meaning—is not a one-way process but can only take place within a set of contexts (situational, discourse, cultural, interdisciplinary, and intercultural) that will facilitate how the community (audience or readers, ancient or modern) interacts with the message produced.

Language Learning Styles

One of the assumptions of the *Standards* is that foreign language is "for all students" (National Standards in Foreign Language Education Project, 7; Gascoyne et al., 3). To make this a reality in the classroom, we need to pay attention to individual learner characteristics. Do all language learners learn the same way? Intuitively, we know this is not the case, but we often teach using the same types of activities over and over again without considering the diversity of learning styles that our students have. For example, some of us may tend to use a visual mode, presenting the language in written form most of the time. But what effect does this have on those who learn by listening and speaking or acting it out? Or we may prefer to do most class activities as a whole class instead of breaking the class into groups. Or we may prefer to present language deductively instead of letting students discover it for themselves. The question to ask is, are we choosing these types of activities because they were most successful for us when we were learning, or do we recognize that how we learn best may not correspond to how our students learn best?

In my classroom, there are artists, scientists, actors, sociologists, writers, and economists. They all have different ways of learning languages. Some prefer to learn by acting things out or using their hands to make things. Others prefer to learn by listening, others by seeing. Some prefer to learn by interacting with their peers, others by listening to the instructor, and still others by reading the text. Some work well in large groups, others in small groups, and still others on their own. Some are good at noticing detail while others are better at understanding the "big picture." It is my job as teacher to activate as many different parts of their cognitive, social, and affective domains as possible to help them learn Greek and Latin efficiently.

I have found that an eclectic approach works well at helping students reach their potential. Learners will discover the ways that they learn language best, but I as their teacher must provide the opportunities for them to find those ways. Since students learn in more than one way, they need opportunities to learn both analytically and experientially, both deductively and inductively (Allen et al.; Stern).[7] As teachers, we need to engage all the senses of our students, not just through traditional options such as reading and writing translations but through listening and speaking, story-telling, drama, and music. Since language is interactive and involves community, students need to be engaged with each other through pair work, peer tutoring, and small groups as well as whole class activities. Since Greek and Latin are languages that express emotions and feelings and values, we need to teach our students words for expressing beliefs, suspicion, sympathy, and affection. And we can offer them activities that help build community within the classroom through cooperative games, values surveys, interviews, and problem solving (Richard-Amato, chs. 9–11, 13). We should explore with our classes not only how our values and beliefs have been shaped by the Greeks and Romans but also how and why some of our values differ. We must encourage students to become conscious of how they learn successfully, and trust that they will discover it with our help. There is no one way to learn languages best, and no certainty in predicting what will work for any one individual (Chaput 1998: 16).

What results from this attention to the learner is a sense of community. The instructor is not the only audience of a skit, dialogue, or minidrama; students in the class respond to the messages created by other students. Instead of only practicing grammar, students begin to convey messages to each other—messages in which meaning comes first and grammar becomes a tool for expressing one's thought clearly and effectively. Once students begin to share ideas, tell stories, enact dramas, or write letters to each other in the target language, they learn from each other.

When learners interact with each other, they receive feedback, whether implicit or explicit, that helps them modify their understanding of Greek or Latin and re-structure the emerging linguistic system (Gass and Selinker; McLaughlin). When they work in pairs or small groups, they have more opportunities for interaction, and research has suggested that students learn just as much through interaction with their peers as with their instructor (Pica et al.). When learners work together to interpret texts, they become a community of readers that can help construct the meaning of a passage or a text. Finally, when they display artwork illustrating mythology or ancient culture in school halls, stage Greek and Roman plays for family and friends, and send Latin messages to students at other schools through e-mail or a MOO such as VRoma, "they participate in wider communities of language and culture" (goal 5). In short, language is not only a cognitive enterprise but also a social one.

The Teacher's Role in Creating Community

Frequent metaphors for the language teacher come from the performing arts: actor, director, choreographer, conductor. Yet as Patricia Chaput writes, "these roles tell us . . . more about our assumptions about teaching language. Consider, for example, *who* is in the spotlight, *who* is on stage, and *who* is doing the creative work. These roles all put the instructor in that position" (1998: 11). But if languages are acquired by using them, by interacting with other people and with texts, then it is the students who are the performers. We as teachers cannot pour language into the heads of our students; we can only facilitate their acquisition of Greek and Latin. It is the language learner who must process the language that is heard and read, and create mental structures that make sense of it all (Tarone and Yule). After all, acquiring a language is a gradual process. Even after learners seem to have mastered a word or a structure, they will still make slips in progress while they integrate new knowledge within their developing understanding of Greek and Latin (Bardovi-Harlig; McLaughlin). Therefore, we as teachers need to be patient with students' attempts to master the intricacies of Greek and Latin and to balance our expectation of accuracy with our desire for fluency. A better metaphor for our role as teacher, Chaput argues, is that of coach. "Coaches use all kinds of techniques to impart knowledge and skill, but it is clearly the players who play the game. . . . There are many ways to teach language, suitable for different personalities and styles. The instructor's role is to put the students on center stage—to facilitate their acquisition of language, through organizing, motivating, and instructing, but ultimately remaining off center stage" (1998: 11).

One way to make sure that learning is accomplished is through backward planning (Chaput 1996). Rather than starting at the beginning of a book and wondering how far the class might progress, it might be better to start at the end of the course and articulate specific goals for the course or for the entire language sequence. We might begin by allocating time for all aspects of communicative competence to be taught: listening and speaking to become more familiar with the rhythms of Greek and Latin and the types of exchange that are present in ancient texts (see chapter 8, this volume), providing prereading exercises so that readers are ready for the form and content of a new text, exploring discourse patterns and cohesive elements, providing strategy training for reading more efficiently, and integrating relevant cultural notions (chapters 6 and 7). We might consider how to create more connections between topics and make comparisons between the ancient world and our own (chapter 5). We might become more conscious of sequencing activities and returning to old topics so that language skills and cultural knowledge are frequently reinforced and enhanced (chapters 7 and 9). We might work on teasing out the various components of communicative tasks so that learners, with the help of their peers or teacher, can discover how to accomplish these same tasks later on their own (chapters 4 and 9). We might decide to include more time for students to work in pairs or small groups so that they can spend more time using the language productively and teaching each other (chapters 4, 5, and 9). We might explore how to tap into the various learning styles and preferences of our students and create multisensory activities (chapters 2 and 3). In order to reduce anxiety, increase motivation, and reach students of varying learning styles, we might want to introduce some affective elements into the classroom, such as games, word puzzles, role-playing, music, or theater. Finally, we might choose different homework assignments, keeping in mind that some exercises are better done at home and some can be done most profitably in class.

When I first began to reflect on what I was trying to accomplish in beginning Greek and Latin, I started experimenting with small changes. I began putting students in pairs or small groups so that they would have more opportunities for using the language. I added bits of oral work into my beginning Greek and Latin classes: simple question-and-answer, role-playing, and drama. I gradually planned more communicative activities and started preparing students for more open-ended tasks through sequencing activities and strategy training. Experiments do not always work the first time. There have been moments when I left the classroom and wondered why a particular activity did not work. But upon more reflection, I realized that perhaps I had not prepared students for the activity, or that I had not always thought through all the steps needed in making the activity work, or that my students simply were not at the right stage in the learning process for such an assignment. I am still in the process of rethinking how I teach, but I am convinced that an emphasis on communication, context, and community is the way to make learning Greek and Latin more effective for more of our students. As you read through the essays in this volume and explore the resources in the annotated bibliography, you will begin to think of ways to transform your classroom into a setting where all learners can learn more efficiently, where language is used to communicate ideas, feelings, and values. εὐτυχῶς, *bona fortuna*, good luck with your journey!

Notes

1. Chafee describes foreign language instruction that is dictated by the textbook as the "coverage model." In other words, the teacher is responsible for covering the content in the

textbook, and the student is responsible for learning that material. Standards-based instruction, however, is not tied to a textbook but provides opportunities for students to exchange, interpret, and present information in multiple contexts to different audiences. Allen reports that the majority of teachers in her study still believe in the coverage model.

2. In 1994, Congress passed the Goals 2000: Educate America Act and the complementary Improving America's Schools Act. *The Standards for Foreign Language Learning* and *Standards for Classical Language Learning* contribute to this nationwide educational reform to set voluntary goals and standards within core disciplines. The *Standards for Foreign Language Learning* (National Standards in Foreign Language Education Project), published in 1996, are the result of a task force of foreign language educators to develop foreign language standards. The American Classical League and the American Philological Association and various regional classics organizations assembled a task force to adapt the standards to the learning of classical languages in the *Standards for Classical Language Learning* (Gascoyne et al.). The *Standards* do not mandate a methodology, do not prescribe a certain textbook, and do not tell how to teach. Rather, they establish five broad goals—Communication, Culture, Connections, Comparison, and Communities—as a framework for language programs, and set content standards to describe the knowledge and abilities students should acquire. While the *Standards for Foreign Language Learning* were developed initially for K–12, most educators recognize that they apply to the college level as well: all but two of the collaborating organizations have subsequently adapted them as guidelines for K–16 (Phillips 6). See Abbott, Davis, and Gascoyne for more information about the *Standards for Classical Language Learning*. See Phillips and Draper for a workbook to help teachers reflect on the standards and create activities that incorporate the five Cs into the classroom.

3. Research has shown that attempts to acquire competence solely by the drilling of specific grammatical forms has four possible negative results:

1. The form is never learned.
2. The form is learned but overgeneralized to the wrong contexts.
3. The use of the form declines quickly after intensive practicing ends.
4. One learned form may disappear when another related form is learned.

When a group that practices the form intensively is compared with other learners who do not undergo intensive practicing, the results are the same. Both groups of learners arrive at the same point (Doughty 130).

4. At the heart of communicative competence, according to Celce-Murcia, Dörnyei, and Thurrell, is *discourse competence*, which deals with "the selection, sequencing, arrangement of words, structures, sentences, and utterances to achieve a unified spoken or written text" (13). It is discourse competence where the bottom-up, lexico-grammatical building blocks intersect with the top-down components, sociocultural context and communicative intent. *Linguistic competence* includes knowledge of vocabulary, understanding of the relationship of phonology and the writing system, and rules of morphology and syntax at the sentence level. *Actional or rhetorical competence* is competence in "conveying and understanding communicative intent, that is, matching actional intent [what one intends to happen] with linguistic form" (17). It involves functional aspects of language, such as greeting and making introductions, asking for and giving information, expressing opinions and feelings, suggesting, persuading, and giving orders, complaining and criticizing, apologizing and forgiving. *Sociocultural competence* depends on knowledge of variables such as social context, stylistic appropriateness, nonverbal behavior, and cultural background to know how to express and interpret messages appropriately within the overall social and cultural context.

Finally, *strategic competence* is crucial for successful communication. Strategies may be ways of compensating for imperfect knowledge, such as parsing words, using a dictionary, scanning for information, reviewing the discourse context, or using background knowledge to predict the meaning of a passage. But strategies may include linguistic and extralinguistic choices made by an author to create a mood, persuade an audience, or establish sympathy with the speaker, such as hyperbole, direct address, use of emotionally resonant terms, or the juxtaposition of key words. Celce-Murcia and Olshtain offer a more thorough guidebook for language teachers interested in an approach that emphasizes discourse and context from the viewpoint of applied linguistics.

5. Robert Hanvey and Milton Bennett point out that intercultural awareness is a process from denial or minimization of difference to acceptance and integration of difference: understanding between cultures occurs when language learners begin to go beyond superficial recognition of similarities and differences and begin to see these differences as intellectually understandable, as motivated within a cultural framework, and finally understandable because they approach these differences from a viewpoint within the target culture. See Storme and Derakhshani for a summary of recent research, a model of culture teaching, and suggestions for evaluation of cultural proficiency.

6. For ideas on making connections with other disciplines, see chapters 5, 7, and 9, this volume; Gascoyne et al.; Met (153–7); and Sienkewicz et al. 2003–4.

7. So often, teachers of Greek and Latin think that the reading approach is always inductive while the grammar-translation is always deductive. And many of the practitioners of the two approaches have in fact emphasized this distinction, either implicitly in the way that a particular textbook is arranged, or explicitly through statements in the book's preface or teacher's manual. For example, Frederic Wheelock's daughters quote their father as saying "Inexorably accurate translation from Latin provides a training in observation, analysis, judgment, evaluation" (LaFleur x). On the other hand, the teacher's manual (Phinney and Bell) to the 3rd North American edition of the *Cambridge Latin Course* (1988) asserts: "Ideally, the students themselves will derive general principles of grammar and groupings of vocabulary from the specific instances they remember from their readings" (8). The contributors of this volume hope to get away from such an either/or mentality and strive to offer our students different ways to acquire language, as long as the focus remains on integrating this information within a meaningful context. Once again, attention to morphological endings without constantly linking them to larger patterns of meaning within a discourse is a return to a strictly analytical approach rather than an approach that integrates analysis within meaningful contexts.

Works Cited

Abbott, Martha G. 1998. "Trends in Language Education: Latin in the Mainstream." In Richard A. LaFleur, ed., *Latin for the Twenty-first Century: From Concept to Classroom*. Glenview, IL: Scott Foresman–Addison Wesley, 36–43.

Abbott, Martha G., Sally Davis, and Richard C. Gascoyne. 1998. "National Standards and Curriculum Guidelines." In Richard A. LaFleur, ed., *Latin for the Twenty-first Century: From Concept to Classroom*. Glenview, IL: Scott Foresman–Addison Wesley, 44–58.

Abernathy, Faye, Jill Crooker, Margaret Curran, and David Perry. 1990. *The Development of Oral Skills in Latin with Visuals. A Supplementary Guide to the Syllabus Latin for Communication*. Draft copy. Albany: New York State Education Department.

Allen, Linda Quinn. 2002. "Teachers' Pedagogical Beliefs and the Standards for Foreign Language Learning." *Foreign Language Annals* 35: 518–29.

Allen, Patrick, Merrill Swain, Birgit Harley, and Jim Cummins. 1990. "Aspects of Classroom Treatment: Toward a More Comprehensive View of Second Language Education." In B. Harley, P. Allen, J. Cummins, and M. Swain, eds., *The Development of Second Language Proficiency*. Cambridge, UK: Cambridge University Press, 57–81.

Bardovi-Harlig, Kathleen. 1997. "The Place of Second Language Acquisition Theory in Language Teacher Preparation." In K. Bardovi-Harlig and B. Hartford, eds., *Beyond Methods: Components of Second Language Teacher Education*. New York: McGraw-Hill, 18–41.

Bennett, Milton J. 1993. "Toward Ethnorelativism: A Developmental Model of Intercultural Sensitivity." In R. M. Paige, ed., *Education for the Intercultural Experience*. Yarmouth, ME: Intercultural Press, 21–71.

Bonefas, Suzanne, and Barbara F. McManus, eds., *VRoma: A Virtual Community for Teaching and Learning Classics*. Available at www.vroma.org.

Celce-Murcia, Marianne, Zoltán Dörnyei, and Sarah Thurrell. 1995. "Communicative Competence: A Pedagogically Motivated Model with Content Specifications." *Issues in Applied Linguistics* 6: 5–35.

Celce-Murcia, Marianne, and Elaine Olshtain. 2000. *Discourse and Context in Language Teaching: A Guide for Language Teachers*. Cambridge, UK: Cambridge University Press.

Chafee, J. 1992. "Teaching Critical Thinking across the Curriculum." In C. A. Barnes, ed., *Critical Thinking: Educational Imperative*. San Francisco: Jossey-Bass, 25–35.

Chaput, Patricia. 1996. "Difficult Choices: Planning and Prioritizing in a Language Program." *ADFL Bulletin* 28: 29–34.

———. 1998. "Fifteen Common Errors in Language Teaching Assumptions and Strategies." *ACTR Letter* 24: 1, 9–12, 15–9, 27.

Doughty, Catherine. 1998. "Acquiring Competence in a Second Language: Form and Function." In Heidi Byrnes, ed., *Learning Foreign and Second Languages: Perspectives in Research and Scholarship*. New York: Modern Language Association, 128–56.

Gascoyne, Richard, et al. 1997. *Standards for Classical Language Learning*. Oxford, OH: American Classical League.

Gass, Susan, and Larry Selinker. 2001. *Second Language Acquisition: An Introductory Course*. 2nd ed. Hillsdale, NJ: Erlbaum.

Gruber-Miller, John C. In press. "Exploring Relationships: *Amicitia* and *Familia* in Cicero's *de Amicitia*." *Classical World*.

Hall, Joan Kelly. 1999. "The Communication Standards." In J. K. Phillips and R. M. Terry, eds., *Foreign Language Standards: Linking Research, Theories, and Practices*. Lincolnwood, IL: National Textbook, 15–56.

Hanvey, Robert. 1979. "Cross-Cultural Awareness." In E. C. Smith and L. F. Luce, eds., *Toward Internationalism: Readings in Cross-Cultural Communication*. Rowley, MA: Newbury House, 46–56.

Kubota, Ryuko, Theresa Austin, and Yoshiko Saito-Abbott. 2003. "Diversity and Inclusion of Sociopolitical Issues in the Foreign Language Classrooms: An Exploratory Survey." *Foreign Language Annals* 36: 12–24.

LaFleur, Richard A., ed. 2000. *Wheelock's Latin*. 6th ed. New York: HarperCollins.

Lightbown, Patsy, and Nina Spada. 1999. *How Languages Are Learned*. Rev. ed. Oxford: Oxford University Press.

McLaughlin, Barry. 1990. "Restructuring." *Applied Linguistics* 11: 113–28.

Met, Myriam. 1998. "Making Connections." In J. K. Phillips and R. M. Terry, eds., *Foreign Language Standards: Linking Research, Theories, and Practices*. Lincolnwood, IL: National Textbook, 137–64.

National Standards in Foreign Language Education Project. 1996. *Standards for Foreign Language Learning in the Twenty-first Century*. Yonkers, NY: National Standards in Foreign Language Education Project. Available at www.actfl.org.

Phillips, June K. 1999. "Introduction. Standards for World Languages—On a Firm Foundation." In June K. Phillips and Robert M. Terry, eds., *Foreign Language Standards: Linking Research, Theories, and Practices*. Lincolnwood, IL: National Textbook, 1–14.

Phillips, June K., and Jamie Draper. 1999. *The Five Cs: The Standards for Foreign Language Learning WorkText*. Boston: Heinle and Heinle.

Phinney, Ed, and Patricia Bell, eds. 1988–91. *The Cambridge Latin Course*. Units 1–4. North American 3rd ed. New York: Cambridge University Press.

Pica, Teresa. 1987. "Interlanguage Adjustments as an Outcome of NS-NNS Negotiated Interaction." *Language Learning* 38: 45–73.

Pica, Teresa, Felicia Lincoln-Porter, Diana Paninos, and Julian Linnell. 1996. "Language Learner's Interaction: How Does It Address the Input, Output, and Feedback Needs of L2 Learners?" *TESOL Quarterly* 30: 59–84.

Richard-Amato, Patricia. 1996. *Making It Happen: Interaction in the Second Language Classroom, from Theory to Practice*. 2nd ed. New York: Longman.

Robinson-Stuart, Gail, and Honorine Nocon. 1996. "Second Culture Acquisition: Ethnography in the Foreign Language Classroom." *Modern Language Journal* 80: 431–49.

Savignon, Sandra. 1997. *Communicative Competence: Theory and Classroom Practice*. 2nd ed. New York: McGraw-Hill.

Sienkewicz, Thomas J., Danetta Genung, Carol Ihlendorf, and Sue Robertson. 1999. "Latin Teaching Standards: Process, Philosophy, and Application." *Classical Journal* 95: 55–63.

Sienkewicz, Thomas J., Edward V. George, James V. Lowe, Sue Ann Moore, and Sarah Wright. 2003–4. "Linking Latin in the Curriculum Beyond the Latin Classroom: Several Collaborative Models." *Classical Journal* 99: 177–91.

Steele, Ross. 1990. "Culture in the Foreign Language Classroom." *ERIC/CLL News Bulletin* 14: 1, 4–5, 12.

Stern, H. H. 1990. "Analysis and Experience as Variables in Second Language Pedagogy." In B. Harley, P. Allen, J. Cummins, and M. Swain, eds. *The Development of Second Language Proficiency*. Cambridge, UK: Cambridge University Press, 93–109.

Storme, Julie A., and Mana Derekhshani. 2002. "Defining, Teaching, and Evaluating Cultural Proficiency in the Foreign Language Classroom." *Foreign Language Annals* 35: 657–68.

Tarone, E., and G. Yule. 1989. *Focus on the Language Learner*. Oxford: Oxford University Press.

VanPatten, Bill. 1998a. "Cognitive Characteristics of Adult Second Language Learners." In Heidi Byrnes, ed., *Learning Foreign and Second Languages: Perspectives in Research and Scholarship*. New York: Modern Language Association, 105–27.

———. 1998b. "Perceptions of and Perspectives on the Term 'Communicative.'" *Hispania* 81: 925–32.

Wallinger, Linda, et al. 1997. *Framework for Foreign Language Education in Virginia*. Richmond: Foreign Language Association of Virginia.

Wills, Jeffrey. 1998. "Speaking Latin in Schools and Colleges." *Classical World* 92: 27–34.

PART II

Focus on the Learner

CHAPTER 2

Cognitive Style and Learning Strategies in Latin Instruction

Andrea Deagon

Cognitive Style in the Classroom

Classroom teachers know that all students learn differently, showing not only different levels of intelligence but also different specific talents and different tendencies to error and confusion. These inherent variations in talents, attitudes, and approaches to learning are a factor of a student's cognitive style. *Cognitive style*, also referred to as *learning style* in educational contexts, is the individual's propensity to perceive and learn in particular ways. Cognitive style is largely a factor of personality, and personality tests such as the Myers-Briggs Type Indicator (MBTI) have proved to be accurate measures of individuals' abilities and preferences in learning. For example, studies indicate that subjects classified by the MBTI as "intuitives" prefer rule-oriented learning with only enough examples to get the rules, while those identified as "sensing" prefer pattern drills and numerous examples.[1] The many other tests of personality and cognitive style developed by researchers in the past thirty years (e.g., the Gregorc Style Indicator) continue to measure and refine this connection between personality and learning.

The fact that personality plays such a crucial role in students' ability and inclination to learn is of clear importance in education. Consider the case of two students in a recent introductory Latin class. One of them, Paul, approached the material deliberately, with some anxiety: he disliked class drills that required individual answers, and would rarely speak up in exercises calling for class responses.[2] Despite his reticence, he enjoyed group work and would often work more quickly and effectively in joint projects than on his own. His assignments were usually accurate, though when he did make errors they were often structural (e.g., repeatedly misforming the imperfect tense). Sometimes he turned his assignments in late because he was unwilling or unable to rush to complete them. He was usually one of the last to complete quizzes and tests, and his performance improved when he took time to recheck his answers. Paul felt he needed to learn and apply *rules*, and to understand the details of a grammatical concept or a reading passage before he moved on. He responded well to pattern exercises and felt like he had accomplished something when they became clear. He disliked making errors and found it hard to accept that some level of inaccuracy and guesswork was necessary. He was not naturally attuned to fine differences in words (such as case endings), but when he understood that they were important, he made a largely successful effort to reattune himself.

In contrast, Bryan was oriented toward the reading passages and cultural notes of the textbook, and often his translations and discussions of reading passages indicated that he understood them on a personal level, if some of their cultural or grammatical subtleties escaped him. He tested quickly, rarely rechecking his work, and turned in assignments that often had careless errors. He always spoke up in class, asking questions and giving drill responses quickly, though often his initial answer would not be fully formed. Bryan was not especially interested in rules and details; he wanted to do the readings, talk about them, and move on. Since he was naturally attuned to fine details, he could often deduce rules from context and exercise examples, and did not feel a need to fully understand grammatical explanations. He learned from errors, both in class and in his homework, and was not embarrassed about being wrong.

Both Paul and Bryan were successful students, earning Bs in the course. But their cognitive styles, and thus their skills and aptitudes, were very different. Consequently the assignments and class exercises that they found most comfortable, interesting, and conducive to learning were different as well. Paul—to use terms I will shortly define—is a field-dependent operation learner, with some language anxiety, and low tolerance for ambiguity and risk-taking. Bryan, in contrast, is a field-independent comprehension learner, with high tolerance of ambiguity, little anxiety, and a positive view of risk-taking. In order for both students to work to their potential, and overcome their natural limitations, both they and I needed to be aware of their learning styles. Furthermore, the class needed to be structured in a way that allowed both students to work to their ability.

Research in modern language pedagogy has focused in part on *learning-centered* methods, which discuss the best ways to present language to learners as a whole (grammar-translation, audio-lingual, natural method, etc.). Other research has been more concerned with *learner-centered* methods, investigating the individual talents and limitations students bring to their learning process (Ellis 194–5). Studies of cognitive style fit into this category. Some central issues of cognitive style research are: In such a complex field as the organization of the mind, are there standard categories into which individuals' learning styles can be divided and studied? Is there a correlation between cognitive style and success in different topics or in different types of programs? Can students' cognitive styles be influenced by the adoption of different strategies for effective learning? How can the teacher present materials to benefit the variety of individual preferences and problems of her students? In short, how can we fulfill the goal of the *Standards for Classical Language Learning* to make it possible "for all students" (Gascoyne et al. 3) to be successful in learning Latin?

In this chapter, I will present (1) an overview of research into cognitive style and its implication for classroom learning, especially as it relates to Latin instruction; (2) some specific suggestions, focused on the basic tasks of vocabulary learning and intermediate reading, about how teachers can structure materials and instruction to benefit students of all learning styles; and (3) a discussion of how teaching *strategies* of language learning can encourage students to be more aware of their own learning processes, and consequently more effective and self-directed in their approach to learning Latin.

An Overview of Cognitive Styles

Since the cognition involved in language learning is so complex, it has been perceived and described by researchers in many different ways; table 2.1 summarizes key axes of distinction. There are, however, two global distinctions of learning styles that are consistently acknowledged, though different terminology may be used to describe them: first, comprehension/operation learning, and second, field (in)dependence.

Comprehension and Operation Learning

The terms "comprehension and operation learners" are those of G. Pask (128–48); other researchers have formulated other terms for describing this distinction.[3] Comprehension learners prefer to get a feel for an entire topic before approaching details; they learn well through stories, anecdotes, and different kinds of examples, and often look ahead and back; details fall into place last. They learn through *using* a language, and are often less attuned to minor errors than operation learners. In contrast, operation learners approach a topic methodically, preferring a step-by-step approach and building an overall picture of the topic from details. They tend to be more rule-oriented and more concerned about monitoring their performance for accuracy.

Field (In)dependence

Field independence is a measure of a student's analytical inclinations and attunement to fine distinctions. The "field" at issue is not simply the language to be learned but also the circumstances of learning it: classroom, peers, teacher, materials, and so on. Field-independent learners are able to distinguish details in complex fields and tend not to be confused by changing circumstances or different perspectives; field-dependent learners are more oriented to the whole field and are more likely to be influenced by external factors such as changing contexts or the opinions of others.[4]

Other Approaches to Learning

In addition to these two global and generally agreed-upon distinctions of learning style, there is the equally global but more problematic distinction between *shallow/reiterative* and *deep/elaborative* learners. Shallow/reiterative learners focus on mechanical, surface learning; for example, learning vocabulary sequentially from a word list, memorizing paradigms. Deep/elaborative learners aim for a deeper level of comprehension and ability to use the material; for example, recognizing vocabulary through reading, noticing differences in meanings as words appear in context, recognizing the meaning implicit in case endings (Schmeck 236–8). A similar distinction can be made between *active* and *passive* learners: active learners feel more personal commitment to and control over their learning processes, and show more problem-solving ability and persistence; passive learners rely on others to explain material to them, and tend to take less initiative and personal responsibility for their work (Ellis 203–5).

To the extent that the tendency toward active or passive and shallow/reiterative or deep/elaborative approaches to learning are a factor of personality, they may be considered cognitive styles. On the other hand, there are some grounds for classifying these types of learning as *phases* of the learning process. Some students may be inspired by interest to adopt a more active approach to their learning, and some may respond to training in more active, and therefore more effective, learning strategies. Likewise, many students who begin with simple memorization and reiteration may eventually proceed to a more complex understanding of the material (Schmeck 236–8, 245–51). While these learning styles do reflect a deeply ingrained mindset, they may be responsive to change.

Other Axes of Distinction

In addition to these global distinctions, the literature of learning style contains a wide range of studies of other discrete elements of personality and perception as they relate to academic achievement. There is likely to be correlation between some of these characteristics: from the list that follows, for example, risk-taking behavior, impulsiveness, and tolerance of ambiguity are likely to be found in the same student, though this is not always the case.

Among factors that have been examined with particular relation to language study are the following:

1. *Orientation toward risk-taking.* Some students are willing to be adventurous, others are not; orientation toward risk-taking affects classroom behavior and adventurousness in language use (Ely).

2. *Predilection toward impulsive or reflective choices.* Some students are able to answer quickly in class situations, while others need time to reflect before answering; some students are willing to make mistakes and are attuned to learning from them, while others prefer to spend enough time preparing that they make very few mistakes (Claxton and Murrell 16–7).

3. *Visual/aural/tactile perceptual style.* Some students are visually oriented, learning well from the written word and especially from visual stimuli to reinforce meaning; others are more aurally oriented and are better able to learn and create language well in an aural/oral context;[5] still others respond best to material/tactile/kinesthetic stimuli (Dunn and Dunn 13–5)

4. *Tolerance of ambiguity.* Some students are able to continue to look for meaning even when they do not understand everything they hear or see; others are disconcerted by ambiguity and do not get much from exposure to overly challenging material (Birckbichler and Omaggio 342–3, 346–7).

5. *Anxiety.* Some students are given a competitive edge by a small amount of anxiety, while others experience it as debilitating or inhibiting (Gregersen; Horwitz and Young; Young).

6. *Orientation toward external or internal measures of success.* Some students are essentially grade oriented, while others want to make sure that they understand a topic to their satisfaction. Each type of student will appreciate or dislike different elements of course work.[6]

7. *Structure.* Some students work well in a highly structured classroom environment, with specific and clearly outlined tasks; other prefer less structure and more individual choice in, for example, their approach to readings or the format of group work (Hunt).

8. *Orientation to authority.* Some students learn better in classrooms where the teacher's authority and direction is emphasized, while others work better in an open classroom in which group work and learning from peers is encouraged. This element of learning style, as indeed many others, may be culturally influenced: a study of Chinese and Mexican school children learning English as a second language showed that the Chinese children learned better in a teacher-centered classroom, while the Mexican children learned better in a peer-centered classroom.[7]

Cognitive Style and the Ability to Learn

All of this research on learning style in language instruction has left us with a great deal of often contradictory information, but a few points are generally agreed upon.

First: in any measure of learning style, gradations along the scale, rather than completely opposite types, are the norm. Very rarely will a student be entirely operational or comprehensive in her or his approach to tasks. Furthermore, different subjects, teaching methods, or types of task will often evoke different approaches from the same student. Learning styles are tendencies rather than absolutes.

Second: all learning styles are or can be effective and lead to mature comprehension of a subject. There have been a great many studies aimed at correlating one factor or another with greater success in language learning. Risk-taking behavior, for example, has been positively correlated with achievement in some studies, but other studies suggest that reflection leads to better achievement in language learning. One researcher's "risk-taking" may be another's "impulsiveness."[8] Field independence has been most convincingly linked with success in language learning, but even here the correlation is not strong.[9] The difficulty with correlation studies is that the number of factors involved prevents most conclusions from being definitive. Variables such as the requirements of the class, the researcher's interpretation of what constitutes, for example, risk-taking, the details of the experiment, and so on, make correlations hard to prove, and explain the often contradictory results of such studies. Many other measures of learning style, for example, comprehension/

Table 2.1 Axes of Distinction of Cognitive Style

Cognitive Styles	Significance
Comprehension/operation learning	Comprehension learners prefer to get a feel for the whole topic before approaching details; operation learners prefer to apply rules and build an overall picture of the topic from details.
Field dependence/ field independence	Field-dependent students are less oriented toward specific details and more likely to be influenced by external factors (classroom situations; opinions of others) than field-independent students.
Shallow-reiterative vs. deep/ elaborative learners	Shallow/reiterative learners focus on mechanical, surface learning; deep/elaborative learners aim for a more complete comprehension of the material.
Active vs. passive learners	Active learners feel more control over their learning processes; passive learners learn more receptively.
Risk-averse vs. risk-taking learners	Risk-takers enjoy experimenting and guessing; risk-averse students are unwilling to answer or guess when they feel they do not fully understand the material.
Impulsive vs. reflective	Some students are inclined to impulsive choices, often learning effectively from their errors; others prefer to reflect and work until they are confident in their answers.
Visual vs. aural vs. tactile style	Different students respond better to visual/written, oral/aural, or material/tactile information.
Tolerant vs. intolerant of ambiguity	Some students are comfortable looking for meaning in material they do not fully understand; others are put off by ambiguity and prefer material they can fully control.
Responses to anxiety	Some students respond well to the anxiety of classroom situations (such as drills); others experience their anxiety as inhibiting.
Internal vs. external measures of success	Some students are more oriented toward simply getting the grade; others are more focused on their relationship to the topic studied.
Preference for structured vs. unstructured study	Some students respond well to structured settings (e.g. specific class time allotted for activities requiring specific answers); others prefer more flexibility and choice of activities in the classroom situation.
Authority oriented vs. peer oriented	Some students learn better in classrooms where the teacher overtly provides all information and direction; others are more peer oriented and prefer group work and communication with peers.

These axes of distinction detail some important variations in students' cognitive styles. Most students fall somewhere along the axis rather than clearly at one extreme or the other.

operation learning or visual/aural orientation, cannot be linked to more or less success. In short, it appears that learners of any cognitive orientation are capable of success in language learning.

Third: all cognitive styles have their pathologies as well. The approach a learner naturally uses sometimes proves ineffective and leads to typical kinds of errors. Pask, in his discussion of comprehension and operation learning, defines the characteristic error of comprehension learners as "globetrotting," which involves jumping to unjustified conclusions and overgeneralizing. "Improvidence," the pathology of operation learning, is the failure to grasp the "big picture," to allow major points to be obscured by details (Pask; Schmeck 236). Students, therefore, will tend to particular kinds of errors as well as to particular kinds of effective learning strategies.

Fourth: Good students are able to adapt. An academically talented comprehension learner can achieve well in an operationally designed course, and vice versa. Other students, less supported by intelligence, motivation, or academic preparation, may become mired in the characteristic errors of their cognitive style.

Fifth: The teacher's cognitive style can play a part in how students learn and how they are evaluated. For example, teachers who believe that quick responses are the only measure of how well the material has been learned tend not to be sympathetic to the needs of students who require time to reflect. Teachers who value detail will be less inclined to sympathize with the experimental errors of the comprehension learner. Studies have indicated that teachers tend to rate students who share their learning style as better than students who do not (Claxton and Murrell 10). In order to be fair, teachers will need to be aware of their own cognitive orientations as well as of the needs of their students (Cooper).

Cognitive Style and Latin Instruction

Traditional Latin instruction, emphasizing a strong orientation to grammar and meticulous attention to detail, favors a particular kind of student: one who learns well sequentially, is field independent (i.e. sensitized to subtle differences such as case endings), puts high value on memory work and rules, prefers abstractions to concrete realities, and prefers to study alone. Students who measure high in the "introverted," "sensing," "thinking," and "judging" scales of the MBTI, "abstract sequentials" in the Gregorc scale,[10] and who are operation learners are well suited to study according to the grammar-translation method. But such students are a minority of those we are likely to get in our classrooms today: as few as 10 percent (Moody 392–3). Many talented students are extroverted and like learning through peer-group experience, prefer to work globally and later define fine points of meaning, enjoy aural communication and risk-taking (in the form of classroom drills), and learn from mistakes (as opposed to reflecting enough to avoid making them); other bright students may be field dependent and not automatically inclined to recognize such important factors as case-endings as crucial. For these students, something about their Latin class will seem unpleasant, burdensome, and wrong.

The brightest students with these learning styles will be able to adapt to the needs of a traditional course, but others will become bored and not want to continue, or become alienated from a language they may have initially been interested in learning, describing it as "too hard" or "useless." This situation must be remedied if Latin is to be taught effectively, and, bluntly, if it is going to continue to be a viable language in today's schools and universities.

Learner-Centered Approaches to Latin Teaching

Variety

In order to be comfortable and effective in the Latin classroom, all students need (1) to be presented with material in a form that they can readily and naturally understand at least some of the time; and (2) to be challenged by tasks that are at variance with their natural approach to the learning, and that combat their characteristic errors. We must therefore restructure teaching methods and materials so that they are more flexible and diverse. For example, students who learn well from concrete examples or from visual input should have text illustrations to reinforce vocabulary or suggest the topics of reading passages, and classwork that focuses on identifying or describing things or items in the real world. Students attuned to aural language need reading aloud and oral answers to help them learn and to maintain their interest and sense of rightness in the learning process. Field-dependent students, who tend to be peer-oriented, benefit from group-learning exercises. Operation learners should have clearly stated rules and some analytical exercises in applying them, but other learners, not as attuned to rules and analysis, need patterned responses to build their sensitivity to important elements of grammar.

Providing a variety of approaches to language facilitates the student's natural tendency to find his or her way into the material according to his or her learning style. A textbook designed to meet the needs of different students (as are many modern language textbooks) will contain visuals, reading passages, grammar explanations, and many kinds of exercises so that students of all styles will find something helpful. Operation learners may prefer to learn the rules, do the exercises, and then approach the reading, while comprehension learners may puzzle awhile over the reading and visuals, look at the grammar rules and vocabulary, do a few exercises, and return to the reading. Classwork can be designed to include, for example, visual and aural input, rule explanation and pattern drill, inductive and deductive approaches to relating grammar and reading.

A more varied approach to language instruction has the additional advantage of combating the characteristic errors each student is prone to. What comes naturally for some students challenges others and forces them into different learning strategies. The form-finding and distinguishing exercises that are comfortable for most field-independent learners are difficult but necessary for field-dependent learners, who might be overlooking important details. Exercises in reading for information or writing descriptions or stories would be pleasing to comprehension learners and students oriented toward risk-taking but are a necessary trial for operation learners, who might otherwise get bogged down in details.

And finally, variety is intrinsically more pleasant for all students. Gregorc (1984: 54) comments that even "despite strong preferences [in instructional methods], most individuals . . . indicated a desire for a variety of approaches in order to avoid boredom." A student whose interest is maintained is more inclined to move to active and deep-elaborative approaches to learning.

Until Latin textbooks are structured to accommodate learner-centered instruction, the teacher must be primarily responsible for making sure the class has a variety of approaches to material that the text may present in a rather monotone fashion. In order to help all students learn effectively, she or he must be aware first of the typical mindsets of students of various cognitive styles, including the characteristic errors to which they are prone. Then, the teacher must be willing to develop and maintain creative and varied approaches to new material.

Presentation for Different Cognitive Styles: Vocabulary

Most students' initial approach to vocabulary learning is shallow-reiterative: they learn to define *facio* as "do or make" on the vocabulary quiz. But this is a small part of really knowing what the word means and being able to read it. Students must learn to think in terms of each word's *Latin* semantic field, as opposed to its English equivalents. They must also be able to recognize tense, person, mood, and so on, and realize the meaning of the word in context. This is a complex task that requires, in addition to memorization, the ability to distinguish between fine points, tolerance of ambiguity, and the ability to integrate the memorized material with the demands of different contexts.

This level of deeper processing can be approached in different ways. Good students of any cognitive style will eventually be able to "read" the word, though some may lean to making a clear choice between meanings and others may be content with a more intuitive understanding of the passage containing the word. (The second approach is favored in modern languages, in which students are encouraged to think and read in the target language, while Latin instruction generally favors the precision of translation.) Some students will not realize appropriate meanings—operation learners through rigidity ("I thought it meant 'do'"), comprehension learners through failure to recognize the importance of tense and person markers; students of both types need the task made overt in order to learn strategies for overcoming their limitations.

Both the initial presentation of words for memorization and the exercises oriented toward word use in context can be presented in ways that feel natural or challenging to students of all learning styles. The approaches outlined here are more representative than exhaustive, but they do present a variety of approaches that will benefit students of different cognitive styles.

- *Inductive versus deductive approaches to lists and readings.* Textbooks almost invariably present both reading and vocabulary sections in every unit. In general, comprehension learners will prefer to start with the readings and flip back to the vocabulary when necessary, while operation learners will prefer to learn the vocabulary before approaching the readings. By varying the order of class presentation, the teacher can alternately please and challenge learners of both types. Some chapters may present readings first, so that new words must be guessed at from context. (Books that provide visuals or background information make vocabulary guessing easier and less disconcerting for students with a low tolerance for ambiguity.) Other chapters can be read after study of the vocabulary, with attention to finding the new words in the reading later.

- *Repetition aloud.* In addition to having students simply repeat vocabulary items, the teacher may add a memory exercise by having students repeat several words at a time, with each student leaving out an old word and adding a new one; this includes the dimension of group cooperation for peer-oriented students. The teacher may say the words aloud with the book closed, have the students repeat them and write them down, then compare with the actual spelling of the word, to integrate aural/visual skills for students of all orientations.

- *Visual connectedness.* Words can be presented visually for more visual learners: for example, illustrations of material things (*canis, puer*) or simple concepts (*ambulare, currere*). Illustrations may be present in the textbook, or the teacher may present them from her own resources, or assign students to prepare visual representations, which can be used in their own and in subsequent classes. Situational illustrations allow connection of several concepts: for example, a picture of a man working in the field allows the basic ideas of *vir, ager, caelum, arbor, laborat*, and so on, to be associated with visual images—and with each other—in a logically connected semantic field. In addition to helping visual learners, this sort of conceptualization is helpful for field-dependent and comprehension learners who look for the whole picture in preference to categorizations such as "nouns: *vir, ager;* verbs: *laboro.*"

- *Presentation of words through objects/actions.* Class exercises in which students either point out or act out the meanings of words are good for field-dependent, visual, and tactile learners and for risk-takers who want to guess and respond to the physical world, for example, *hic est liber, hic est ianua; nunc sedet, nunc surgit;* commands such as *ambula, surge, scribe in tabulam,* and so on. These exercises are generally straightforward, so are good for students who are "concrete" as opposed to "abstract" thinkers; they can be perceived as both teacher-oriented and peer-oriented (see Strasheim for further examples).

- *Games.* Students connect Latin words with pictures or English definitions, such as vocabulary bingo. These are enjoyable to most students, especially peer-oriented risk-takers; analytic types may find games frivolous but benefit from having to think quickly and make guesses.

- *Mnemonics: cognates.* Although the goal of vocabulary learning is for the Latin word to automatically carry an appropriate meaning in the student's mind, this state is usually not immediately achieved. Students often benefit from using mnemonic tricks as an initial approach to learning the word. Students may remember Latin words from English cognates, for example, *ager* from agriculture, *canis* from canine, *curro* from (a bit more of a stretch) current, racecourse, or cursor. Guessing from cognates can become a highly effective reading strategy (Holmes and Ramos), so some conscious attention to the relationship between English cognates and Latin words will help give the student practice and flexibility in using cognates to read. Cognates allow comprehension learners to form a global appreciation of Latin-English relations that may help them with specifics later; operation learners may form a more analytical appreciation of a word's semantic range.

- *Mnemonics: imaging.* Some students respond well to processing words elaboratively, that is, by relating them to elements of their own lives or to material reality. Such students benefit from being encouraged to visualize actions, material things, and situations, while saying or reading words, thus consciously developing the automatic recognition of meaning from Latin words. A related imaging technique is the *keyword method*, which research has shown to be very effective in boosting vocabulary recall (Kasper). In this technique, students form an image association of a Latin word and an English word that sounds similar: for example, *ianua* may be paired with January in the image of closing a door against winter cold.

- *Reading for new words.* Students read a passage specifically looking for new words or for words on a particular subject, such as food, travel, time expressions; they are asked to take note of changes in form and use. Easy for field-independent students and comprehension learners who work well with whole texts; challenges field-dependent students who tend to overlook details.

- *Word choices.* Students choose a word from two or three to complete a sentence or phrase, or match a picture; this may be presented as a homework exercise or a class drill. Good for operation learners and field-independent students, who tend to be more aware of specific meanings. The exercise can be presented so that more than one answer is correct, and students respond with their preferences; the social issues involved with personal preferences make the exercise more appealing to field-dependent learners, who tend to be more peer-oriented and are inclined to give language social meaning even when unsure of specifics of form.

- *Word distinctions.* Students choose from similar words to complete a sentence, for example, *puellae in* _____ *stant.* (a) *viro* (b) *via* (c) *vita* (d) *valde.* Easy for operation and field-independent learners, who will have learned forms well; harder for comprehension learners, who may have overrelied on contextual clues to read passages, and for field-dependent students who are not attuned to fine distinctions.

- *Eliminating unnecessary words.* Students eliminate an out-of-place word in a sentence, for example, *puellae in via arbore stant et amicos vocant.*[11] Different students will approach this exercise globally, forming quick opinions about out-of-place elements, or analytically, translating word for word and making careful choices. Class drill and group presentation will force different processes, as students are stressed by time constraints, or observe the strategies of other students in a group.

- *Semantic mapping.* Students brainstorm for all the words they can think of relating to a semantic field (e.g., *exercitus*), then categorize these words: for example, *dux, centurio, miles* (personnel); *equus, arma, gladius* (equipment), *oppugnare, proelium,* (actions/events) and so on; the exercise may include peripheral vocabulary and ideas associated with what the *exercitus* is and does (*oppidum,* where the battle happens; *tristis,* feelings associated with warfare, etc.) (Hague). As a cooperative effort, this is good for group-oriented and field-dependent students; the listing of many elements suits comprehension learners while the categorization suits operation learners. A further step in semantic mapping, clarifying distinctions between words and ranges of meanings of individual words (e.g., between *dux, imperator, centurio*) is also good for operation learners and analytic types, and encourages students who are inclined to rely on context and guessing to use these skills for an analytic purpose.

In all of these exercises, some students will find the required process easy and natural, while others will be forced to work against their natural inclinations; as usual, varying the exercises used in any one class or study unit satisfies the needs of different students. In addition, while I have suggested what sorts of students benefit from each exercise, other variables may come into play: for example, whether an exercise is presented in class or as homework, or with or without a strict time limit; whether it is a group or individual exercise; what value is put on correctness as opposed to creative exploration. It is important for the teacher to ensure that different exercises encourage and reward students of each cognitive orientation. Table 2.2 offers a sampling of activities to challenge students with different learning styles. For further vocabulary activities, see Gruber-Miller, Gairns and Redman, Holden, and Nation.

Diagnosing Learning Style

First, awareness of learning styles allows teachers to recognize characteristic errors of different types of learners and help students toward deeper processing of the language. Consider, for example, a bright student who learns quickly, but makes impulsive choices. When she reads she is tolerant of ambiguity, able to remember passages as she reads them, but prone to making impulsive errors, such as always

Table 2.2 Classroom Exercises for Vocabulary Learning and Use

Activity	Benefits
Repeating words aloud after the teacher; reading words aloud from the vocabulary list in the book	Helps aurally oriented students; operational learners who like the structure of the word list
Learning words through visual clues (*hic est liber, hic est ianua; nunc sedet, nunc surgit*)	Helps visual learners, field-dependent learners, risk-takers who want to guess and respond to the visual world
Reading text to find new vocabulary; noticing changes in form and use	Easy for field-independent students and comprehension learners who work well with whole texts; challenges field-dependent students who overlook details
Class drills in which students choose (from 2 or 3) a word to complete a sentence or phrase, or match a picture	Easy for comprehension learners and students who enjoy experimenting with new knowledge; challenging to operational learners who may want to feel they have learned words more thoroughly before using them
Students use new words in a simple sentence; group exercise or homework	Requires both creativity and knowledge of specific grammar, so all types will find different challenges; peer-oriented students and risk-takers will prefer the group exercise; those who prefer to reflect and prepare without risking error will prefer the homework
Games such as vocabulary bingo in which students connect the Latin word with a picture or English definition	Enjoyable to most students; analytic types may find it frivolous but benefit from having to think quickly

Level: Elementary. Not all of the exercises here can or should be used with every new vocabulary lesson, but by varying the approach to vocabulary learning and use, each student will find some exercises that are especially comfortable and some that are challenging.

   Also note that the *content* of the exercise is one issue: field-independent or operational learners, for example, will prefer analytical exercises in applying rules and analyzing data, while comprehension learners will be more oriented toward text and reading. The *presentation* of exercises is another issue: similar activities can be presented as class drills, homework exercises, or group activities, appealing to different types of student.

taking an -a ending on a noun as a feminine singular nominative, rather than the neuter plural accusative it may be. It may not be that the passage is especially difficult, or that she is unaware of the right endings—she may know them well enough to give correct form on a grammar test—but her impulsive reading leads to increasing misunderstanding, which she probably tries to remedy by more guessing. She is not experiencing a failure of intelligence, but a strategy that has served her well in the past—making quick choices and guessing from context—has begun to cause her problems. It is a good strategy, but she needs a teacher who recognizes her difficulty and is able to help her work past it.

Another student, one who proceeds logically and with discrimination, may still encounter problems: unknown words are disconcerting and need to be looked up, ambivalent endings must be puzzled over until they make sense; reading becomes a slow process, and he may forget contextual information that would help him in the long run. Where idioms and ungrammatical or unfamiliar structures appear, the student is reluctant or unable to guess at their meaning. He has and uses knowledge and analytical ability, but his innate strategies work only to a point.

A naive analysis of these students would probably say that the first one needs to work on her grammar and the second one needs to learn to read more quickly, and of course these analyses are correct as far as they go. But to really help these students, the teacher needs to be aware of their differing learning styles and able to prescribe exercises to develop their strengths and overcome their weaknesses. For both students, the traditional approach of translating a passage word for word, then explicating the grammar, is frustrating: for the first one, because she becomes confused and the passage stops making sense, and for the second, because reading takes so long that meaning falls by the wayside and unresolved problems dominate his attention.[12]

Second, understanding a student's learning style—and the talents and errors associated with it—allow the teacher to prescribe exercises to combat each student's weak points. For example, the student who focuses too much on detail might benefit from prereading exercises that would focus on reading for specific information, (e.g., "Find the passage that means . . ." "Find the major characters in this passage and how they are related to one another"), because such tasks encourage a global approach and using limited information to reach conclusions—for this student, an underdeveloped skill. The student who jumps to conclusions might benefit from a grammar-oriented prereading exercise, such as one in which passive and deponent verbs are distinguished from one another, or where examples of participles, genitives, or some other grammatical element are marked and reviewed with emphasis on their importance to meaning in the passage. Table 2.3 outlines some approaches to reading that encourage students of different learning styles toward a more complete appreciation of the text.

Third, diagnosing student needs is often an unconscious process for teachers, but there are tools that enable the teacher to diagnose her or his students according to their classroom performance. For example, a diagnostic inventory designed by Alice C. Omaggio has the teacher rank the student's characteristic behavior along a 1–5 scale on such issues as "tend[s] to answer questions impulsively, giving quick but often inaccurate answers"; "write[s] lengthy compositions riddled with errors"; and "get[s] easily distracted by irrelevant words and structures" (Omaggio 12). Although this diagnostic inventory does not label a student's cognitive style, it does paint a picture of the student's strengths and weaknesses and allows the teacher to determine what exercises or attitudes would help this student learn most effectively.

Finally, another approach to diagnosing and working with student learning styles is to involve the student in the process, making her aware of her own strengths and preferences, where she might expect to encounter problems, and how to deal with differences of style between herself and her teachers. Many campus tutor-

Table 2.3 Classroom Exercises for Reading

Activity	Benefits
Prereading for grammar, e.g., verb tenses, new vocabulary, new grammar, case usage, etc.	Field-independent and operational learners excel; field-dependent students benefit from the attention to detail.
Prereading for information (skim/scan the text), e.g., identifying characters and relationships, locations, specific content questions; time limit applied for some class work	Comprehension learners excel; prereading challenges operation learners who prefer sequential work; time limit encourages guessing for those reluctant to guess.
Class reading of text with new or blanked-out words; students use context to deduce possible meanings	Comprehension and field-dependent students excel; class reading helps operation learners and students who dislike ambiguity, so are slowed or stumped by vocabulary problems.
Discussion of texts without translating; students are encouraged to raise questions about content or grammar	Comprehension learners excel; operation learners may translate the text anyway, but benefit from the focus on text as primarily conveying meaning.
Group work in prereading exercises above or in translation	Depending on the exercise, different types of students will excel; all students may observe others' strategies.
Reading for strategy awareness: instructor focuses student attention on reading habits: content awareness, sensitivity to grammar and details; what is easy and what is discouraging; response to unknown words; rereading; etc.	This activity is helpful for students of all types; it is most helpful for motivated students who act to correct their "faults"; it also helps for struggling students who may find the best way to approach material that they were discouraged by before.[a]

Level: Intermediate. Not all of the exercises here can or should be used with every text; variation allows different levels of challenge for all students.

Also differences in ability and commitment to language learning are distinct from cognitive style; good students will probably do well even in exercises counter to their preferred approaches, while less committed or talented students may have problems even in exercises that cater to their natural talents.

[a]Barnett (1989) has a short questionnaire to help students and teachers detect what particular reading strategies they use when they read a foreign language that can be adapted to Latin. For additional reading activities, see chapters 6 and 7, this volume; Barnett (1989), Gruber-Miller, and Phillips.

ing, learning enhancement, and student development centers provide testing and analysis of cognitive style for students who are considered at risk, since making students aware of their cognitive style is of proven effectiveness in helping their overall performance (Claxton and Murrell 61–2). While some testing instruments are complex and require detailed analysis, others, such as the Gregorc Style Delineator, can be administered in about twenty minutes in or out of class to provide the student with basic insights about her preferred learning methods.

Of the testing instruments available, some are abbreviated, learning-oriented versions of the MBTI, and are therefore able to make use of the substantial research coordinating the MBTI with learning preferences and performance. The TLC Learning Style Inventory, for example, has students agree or disagree with statements such as "Most of what I know, I learned on my own" and "I like to study for tests with other students"; the answers rank the students along three of the four Myers/Briggs axes (Silver, Eikenberry, and Hanson). Even more simple is the test published in a recent college introductory manual (Gardner and Jewler 53–64), where the student chooses between twenty opposite preferences, for example: "making decisions after finding out what others think / making decisions without consulting others" and "helping others explore their feelings / helping others make logical decisions." The answers place the student in the MBTI scales; discussion follows of preferred learning methods, how to enhance learning methods that are less natural, and how to work with teachers and students whose learning styles are different.

Other instruments are more oriented toward specifics of study habits and classroom preferences; for example, the Canfield Learning Styles Inventory (Canfield), which asks students how they respond to various types of assignment, assessments, and value as instructional tools; or the Grasha-Riechmann Student Learning Styles Questionnaire (Grasha), which has students answer questions that place them along the gradations "competitive /collaborative," "participant/avoidant," and "dependent/independent," with learning techniques associated with each category. The abundant recent work in the classification of learning styles and strategies means that there is no "coherent, well accepted system for describing these strategies" (Oxford; see also Hsiao and Oxford). In a classroom setting, however, the teacher's continuing observation of and interaction with the student is ultimately more valuable than any one testing instrument (see Cohen).

Whatever diagnostic method is used, it appears that students who are aware of their cognitive styles and learning preferences can make use of the learning techniques that help them process information most effectively (e.g., elaborative approaches to vocabulary vs. analytical ones); they also benefit from understanding what faults they are likely to slip into and what they can do to avoid them. The same awareness that enables the teacher to give her class effective guidance also enables the students consciously to use their natural strengths and benefit from work that is less immediately pleasing. By gaining a little self-knowledge, they are able to become more effective participants in their own learning process.

Learning Strategies

The second section of this chapter dealt with some of the ways in which a teacher can present material in ways more sensitive to the needs of different learners. This section explores the notion of learning strategies: methods by which students can be taught to monitor and direct their own learning process.

Every student naturally uses strategies in order to determine meanings in language. A *strategy* is, essentially, any method a student uses in attempting to come to terms with new skills and knowledge. This includes processes such as guessing word meanings from cognates, rereading difficult passages, looking for small distinctions between words, and trying to remember the context of a reading exercise. Strategies are closely related to cognitive style; in fact, some researchers define learning style as a propensity to use some strategies in preference to others (Schmeck 233–4).

Some strategies, of course, are more effective than others. The student whose strategy is to become discouraged and stop reading is clearly not going to be as successful as the student who persists through whatever method. Where the natural attempts of each student to find the best way to learn break down into characteristic errors, teachers may help the student compensate by instructing him in how to use different strategies; that is, by overtly teaching a method for confronting problems and giving the student responsibility for using it.

Researchers speak of two different types of learning strategies: cognitive, and metacognitive. *Metacognitive* strategies are those that "involve planning and directing learning at a general level" (Cook 127). Planning one's own approach to a chapter and choosing study methods that are effective in dealing with one's own specific problems, for example, are metacognitive strategies. In many strategy-oriented instructional programs, the student is taught self-monitoring; that is, to be conscious of her own way of approaching tasks, so that she can become more precisely aware of when she encounters difficulty, how the difficulty might have arisen, and what steps she can take to solve it.[13] Since metacognitive behaviors "involve an awareness of the self as learner" (Galloway and Labarca 145) they are consequently vital to the student's sense of empowerment over her learning—but they must be supported by more specific cognitive strategies.

Cognitive strategies "involve specific conscious ways of tackling learning" (Cook 127). Cognitive strategies may be understood in broad terms, referring to general processes. For example, J. Rubin identifies six general cognitive strategies: (1) clarification/verification (confirming rules and knowledge about the target language); (2) guessing/inferencing (using hunches from many sources to infer meaning); (3) deductive reasoning (looking for and applying general rules); (4) practice (repetition, rehearsal, etc.); (5) memorization (organizing the "storage and retrieval process"); and (6) monitoring (noticing errors and processes; this may be considered a metacognitive process or a combination of cognitive and metacognitive processes) (Rubin 23–5).

Cognitive strategies may also be seen more specifically, including such activities as note-taking, translation, elaboration, visual imagining, and so on (Prokop 17), cognate guessing, risk-taking, brainstorming, learning to understand the gist of a passage, and so on (Campbell and Ortiz 165–7). Effective strategies arise naturally from all cognitive styles. From Rubin's general list, for example, verification and practice might be more appealing to operation learners, while guessing/inferencing is more natural for comprehension learners.

To metacognitive and cognitive strategies may be added *social-affective* strategies for learning: the ways students find to motivate and reward themselves, relieve anxiety, and generate energy, especially as they relate to the social milieu of the classroom (Galloway and Labarca 147).

When the teacher instructs students in specific strategies, students will learn some that seem natural to them, or be confirmed in the effectiveness of their natural ways of approaching new material; they will also learn how to proceed when their standard paths are not producing good results. For example, Campbell and Ortiz, as part of an anxiety-lessening workshop, present a list of strategies that helps students identify some goals and processes they may not have been aware of before (e.g., differentiating formal and informal expressions, using circumlocution to express ideas, developing a feeling for the gist when the entirety is incomprehensible); while at the same time instructing them on some effective ways to accomplish the more general goal of attaining language fluency. By teaching students that risk-taking, context guessing, brainstorming, paraphrasing, solving problems in groups, and so on, are proven effective means of achieving language proficiency, Campbell and Ortiz (157–68) are able to focus their students' attention on *techniques* and away from anxiety and feelings of helplessness—and away from the sense of the language as something inflexible and unattainable.

Strategy use is most effective when the processes are overt: when students are aware that they are choosing and using strategies. Other important factors are that students should understand thoroughly how to use a strategy, and experience some benefits from using it (MacIntyre). Students who use a particular strategy give a variety of reasons for doing so: it helps them learn more quickly or effectively, focus attention better, or plan a task; it helps organize ideas or accomplish specific tasks; it makes learning easier or more fun or more natural. Conversely, students describe strategies they abandon as ineffective, confusing, boring, or incompatible with their preferred way of learning (Chamot 312–9). While good teaching of strategies makes a difference in how effectively students can use them, it is natural for some students to abandon some strategies and prefer others; this is part of the individual processes by which they seek mastery of the language.

When teachers teach through strategies, they are on the road to creating more autonomous learners. Strategy instruction encourages the student to become aware of the processes through which he learns language, and to guide his own learning. The teacher becomes a facilitator in the student's learning process, first explaining and illustrating what to learn, then providing coaching and feedback, and finally monitoring the student's independent use of the strategies that are most effective for each individual (O'Malley and Chamot 116–9).

Likewise, students who both develop an understanding of their own cognitive styles and learn to use strategies effectively can gain a feeling of empowerment over their learning processes, even with difficult material. Finding that one's approach to problem solving is shared by other effective learners is an encouragement and a confirmation of the rightness of one's ways of thought. Strategies also allow the student to achieve a little distance from issues that may cloud the language learning process: issues such as anxiety or feelings of inadequacy, or the perception that the material is distant, hard, or unapproachable by ordinary means. Recognizing the variety of possible approaches, and where one is naturally adept, is encouraging. Strategy instruction also allows students to focus on discrete ideas—what tasks are they accomplishing effectively, and what needs work? What are the right tools for them to use to learn what they are committed to learn this semester?[14] The task of learning Latin, rather than looming as a huge, externally imposed, frequently confusing task, takes on a milder aspect. By focusing on the tools as well as the task, the task becomes more attainable.

Conclusion

The single-style approach to Latin still so commonly in use has the negative effect of discouraging students with noncompatible learning styles from pursuing an initial interest in the language. This is a problem for the profession, which, like many traditional academic fields, must do what it can to maintain the interest of students in today's universities, where business, computer, and communications programs compete for enrollment.

There are further problems with the traditional approach. It tends to encourage operation learning pathologies, such as memorization of endings without connecting the endings to meaning, or failure to integrate learned vocabulary with reading (as witnessed by the common phenomenon of English written over words in reading passages), and literal translations that make no sense. Students who are forced into working in a mode at odds with their natural tendencies are especially vulnerable to the pathologies of that mode.[15] Traditional Latin instruction also does not develop some generally nonoperational learning strategies, such as tolerance of ambiguity and ability to guess, that are crucial in learning to read. The operational focus does more than alienate those with incompatible learning styles, it hinders anyone from fully developing the skills that would help her to become fluent in the language, with the result that fluency in reading and speaking Latin are becoming increasingly rare.

In order to help students of all cognitive styles come to some appreciation of the classical languages, we must restructure our teaching materials and teaching styles to help students find comfortable and meaningful paths to their own manner of comprehension. We will have to move away from a model of language teaching as information transfer, and adopt an approach that teaches the processes by which language may be understood. Each text, and each teacher, may set different tasks to a class as a means of teaching Latin, but all teaching has the ultimate goal of moving students from their initial, surface learning to a real comprehension of the material. By developing an awareness of different learning styles, and by presenting information in a variety of ways, teachers can help students learn to move beyond the shallow/re-iterative stage in ways that correspond with their natural inclinations in perceiving. By meeting student needs, we have a chance to foster a new generation of learners with an interest in the classical world and a stake in the survival of the classics.

Notes

1. Moody 390–1, 397–9. The MBTI measures personality along four scales: introversion/extraversion, sensing/intuition, thinking/feeling, and judging/perceiving, for a total of sixteen personality "types," with, of course, gradations along each scale. Each scale suggests a range of differences in cognitive style, so that the entire profile of any individual's approach to learning is quite complex (Myers and McCaulley). There are a number of other such personality measures used in education. While the MBTI is the most sensitive instrument, one of the easiest to use is the Gregorc Style Delineator (GSD), designed specifically to measure learning preferences. From a brief series of personality-based questions, this test determines four types of learners along two scales: abstract (preferring symbols and ideas) / concrete (preferring experience and examples), and sequential (preferring orderly, step-by-step learning) / random (preferring holistic approaches and progress through intuitive leaps) (Gregorc 1984, 1985). For a discussion of these and other personality-based approaches to learning style, see Claxton and Murrell 13–21.

2. Students' names have been changed.

3. For example, "intuitives/analysts" (Allinson and Hayes), "lumpers" and "splitters," (Claxton and Murrell 21–37), "experiential/studial learners" (Ellis 202–3), or "holist/serialist learners" (Prokop 9). There are correlations with Gregorc's "random" and "sequential" styles and with the MBTI sensing/feeling and judging/perceiving scales (Claxton and Murrell 21–37; Schmeck 235–8).

4. On field (in)dependence in general, see Claxton and Murrell 8–13; in language learning, Cook 137–8; Prokop 6–12; Skehan 111–5. See now also Ehrman and Leaver for a reorganization of cognitive styles such as random/sequential, abstract/concrete, and field-(in)dependent/field-sensitive styles.

5. See, e.g., the Cognitive Style Inventory Profile in Flippo and Terrell 315–7.

6. This is one example of a social interaction model of cognitive style; orientation to authority is another; other studies have discussed other attitudes that are specifically relevant in classroom and other interactions in the university setting. See Claxton and Murrell 37–46; Skehan 50–72, 129–35.

7. A study by L. Wong-Fillmore, discussed in Skehan 132–4.

8. For a positive correlation of risk with achievement: McGroarty and Oxford 66.

9. Elaine Fuller Carter tested the proposition that field-dependent students would do better in a communication-oriented language course, while field-independent students would do better in a more traditional grammar-based course; she found that field-independent students performed slightly better in both types of courses. For a different view of the role of field (in)dependence, see Abraham; Skehan 111–5.

10. See note 1.

11. Omaggio presents the "word distinctions" and "eliminating unnecessary words" exercises as part of a program designed to test students for characteristic errors and assign exercises specifically to remedy them (17–29).

12. For practical techniques designed to circumvent characteristic errors, see Birckbichler and Omaggio 336–45.

13. Encouraging students' metacognitive awareness has proved effective in helping students overcome their characteristic problems in second language acquisition; see, e.g., Barnett 1988: 150–62; Carrell 122–34; McGroarty and Oxford; Oxford and Crookall 404–19. Making students aware of their cognitive styles and the learning processes they tend to employ is a commonly used technique for helping academically disadvantaged students monitor

their learning processes; my own university uses the GSD. For an overview of such general applications, see Claxton and Murrell 57–64.

14. Awareness of their own preferred strategies is also likely to be helpful to students as they make use of the hypermedia tools for learning Latin that are increasingly incorporated into language instruction. Without this awareness, some students (field dependents in particular) may be unable to choose the most effective resources for their own needs. Further, in designing and assigning hypermedia materials, it is vital for educators to be aware of students' cognitive styles both for individual exercises and in a program's overall design (Daniels and Moore).

15. In other words, students realize that they must find some way to accomplish tasks that do not come naturally, but some do not have the ability to find a productive strategy on their own. Therefore, even a field-dependent comprehension learner might fall into patterns of rigid memorization and inflexible definition that might typically be expected from a student more oriented toward operation learning.

Works Cited

Abraham, Roberta G. 1985. "Field Independence-Dependence and the Teaching of Grammar." *TESOL Quarterly* 20: 689–701.

Allinson, C. W., and J. Hayes. 1996. "The Cognitive Style Index: A Measure of Intuition-Analysis for Organizational Research." *Journal of Management Studies* 33: 119–35.

Barnett, Marva A. 1988. "Reading through Context: How Real and Perceived Strategy Use Affects L2 Comprehension." *Modern Language Journal* 72: 150–62.

———. 1989. *More than Meets the Eye: Foreign Language Reading—Theory and Practice.* Englewood Cliffs, N.J.: Prentice-Hall.

Birckbichler, Diane W., and Alice C. Omaggio. 1978. "Diagnosing and Responding to Individual Learner Needs." *Modern Language Journal* 62: 336–47.

Campbell, Christine M., and Jose Ortiz. 1991. "Helping Students Overcome Foreign Language Anxiety: A Foreign Language Anxiety Workshop." In Elaine K. Horwitz and Dolly J. Young, eds., *Language Anxiety: From Theory and Research to Classroom Implications.* Englewood Cliffs, N.J.: Prentice-Hall, 153–68.

Canfield, Albert A. 1976. *Learning Styles Inventory.* Ann Arbor, MI: Humanics Media.

Carrell, Patricia L. 1989. "Metacognitive Awareness and Second Language Reading." *Modern Language Journal* 73: 122–34.

Carter, Elaine Fuller. 1988. "The Relationship of Field Dependent/Independent Cognitive Style to Spanish Language Achievement and Proficiency: A Preliminary Report." *Modern Language Journal* 72: 21–30.

Chamot, Anna Uhl. 1993. "Student Responses to Learning Strategy Instruction in the Foreign Language Classroom." *Foreign Language Annals* 26: 308–21.

Claxton, Charles S., and Patricia H. Murrell. 1987. *Learning Styles: Implications for Improving Educational Practices.* Washington, DC: ASHE-ERIC Higher Education Report no. 4.

Cohen, Andrew D. 2001. "Preparing Teachers for Styles- and Strategies-Based Instruction." Paper presented at the International Conference on Language Teacher Education, Minneapolis, May 17–19.

Cook, Vivian. 2001. *Second Language Learning and Language Teaching.* 3rd ed. London: Edward Arnold.

Cooper, Thomas. 2001. "Foreign Language Teaching Style and Personality." *Foreign Language Annals* 34: 301–17.

Daniels, Harold Lee, and David M. Moore. 2000. "Interaction of Cognitive Style and Learner Control in a Hypermedia Environment." *International Journal of Instructional Media* 27: 369–84.

Dunn, Rita, and Kenneth Dunn. 1978. *Teaching Students through Their Individual Learning Styles: A Practical Approach.* Reston, VA: Reston.

Ehrman, Madeleine E., and Betty Lou Leaver. 2003. "Cognitive Styles in the Service of Language Learning." *System* 31: 393–415.

Ellis, Rod. 1992. *Second Language Acquisition and Language Pedagogy.* Clevedon, UK: Multilingual Matters.

Ely, Christopher M. 1988. "Personality: Its Impact on Attitudes toward Classroom Activities." *Foreign Language Annals* 21: 25–32.

Flippo, Rona F., and William R. Terrell. 1984. "Personalized Instruction: An Exploration of Its Effects on Developmental Reading Students' Attitudes and Self-Confidence." *Reading World* 23: 315–25.

Gairns, Ruth, and Stuart Redman. 1986. *Working with Words: A Guide to Teaching and Learning Vocabulary.* Cambridge, UK: Cambridge University Press.

Galloway, Vicki, and Angela Labarca. 1990. "From Student to Learner: Style, Process and Strategy." In Diane W. Birckbichler, ed., *New Perspectives and New Directions in Foreign Language Education.* Lincolnwood, IL: National Textbook, 111–58.

Gardner, John N., and A. Jerome Jewler. 1992. *Your College Experience: Strategies for Success.* Belmont, CA: Wadsworth.

Gascoyne, Richard, et al. 1997. *Standards for Classical Language Learning.* Oxford, OH: American Classical League.

Grasha, Anthony F. 1975. *Grasha-Riechmann Student Learning Styles Questionnaire.* Cincinnati: Faculty Resources Center, University of Cincinnati.

Gregersen, Tammy S. 2003. "To Err Is Human: A Reminder to Teachers of Language-Anxious Students." *Foreign Language Annals* 36: 25–32.

Gregorc, Anthony F. 1984. "Style as Symptom: A Phenomenological Perspective." *Theory into Practice* 23: 51–5.

———. 1985. *Gregorc Style Delineator.* Columbia, CT: Gregorc.

Gruber-Miller, John. 1998. "Toward Fluency and Accuracy: A Reading Approach to College Latin." In Richard A. LaFleur, ed., *Latin for the Twenty-first Century: From Concept to Classroom.* Glenview, IL: Scott Foresman–Addison Wesley, 162–75.

Hague, Sally A. 1987. "Vocabulary Instruction: What L2 Can Learn From L1." *Foreign Language Annals* 20: 217–25.

Holden, William R. 1999. "Learning to Learn: Fifteen Vocabulary Acquisition Activities. Tips and Hints." *Modern English Teacher* 8: 42–7.

Holmes, John, and Rosinda Guerra Ramos. 1993. "False Friends and Reckless Guessers: Observing Cognate Recognition Strategies." In Thomas Huckin, Margot Haynes, and James Coady, eds., *Second Language Reading and Vocabulary Learning.* Norwood, NJ: Ablex, 86–108.

Horwitz, Elaine K., and Dolly J. Young. 1991. *Language Anxiety: From Theory and Research to Classroom Implications.* Englewood Cliffs, NJ: Prentice Hall.

Hsiao, Tsung-Yuan, and Rebecca Oxford. 2002. "Comparing Theories of Language Learning Strategy: A Confirmatory Factor Analysis." *Modern Language Journal* 86: 368–83.

Hunt, David E. 1979. "Learning Style and Student Needs: An Introduction to Conceptual Level." In National Association of Secondary School Principals, *Student Learning Styles: Diagnosing and Prescribing Programs.* Reston, VA: NASSP, 27–38.

Kasper, Loretta F. 1993. "The Keyword Method and Foreign Language Vocabulary Learning: A Rationale for Its Use." *Foreign Language Annals* 26: 244–51.

MacIntyre, Peter D. 1994. "Toward a Psychological Model of Strategy Use." *Foreign Language Annals* 27: 185–95.

McGroarty, Mary, and Rebecca Oxford. 1990. "Language Learning Strategies: An Introduction and Two Related Studies." In Amado M. Padilla, Halford H. Fairchild, and Concepción M. Valadez, eds., *Foreign Language Education: Issues and Strategies*. Newbury Park, CA: Sage, 56–74.

Moody, Raymond. 1988. "Personality Preferences and Foreign Language Learning." *Modern Language Journal* 72: 389–401.

Myers, Isabel B., and Mary H. McCaulley. 1987. *Manual for the Myers-Briggs Type Indicator: A Guide to the Development and Use of the MBTI*. Palo Alto, CA: Consulting Psychologists Press.

Nation, I. S. P. 1990. *Teaching and Learning Vocabulary*. New York: Newbury House.

Omaggio, Alice C. 1981. *Helping Learners Succeed: Activities for the Foreign Language Classroom*. Language in Education: Theory and Practice 36. Washington, DC: Center for Applied Linguistics.

O'Malley, J. Michael, and Anna Uhl Chamot. 1993. "Learner Characteristics in Second-Language Acquisition." In Alice Omaggio Hadley, ed., *Research in Language Learning: Principles, Processes, and Prospects*. Lincolnwood, IL: National Textbook, 96–123.

Oxford, Rebecca. 1994. "Language Learning Strategies: An Update." *ERIC Digest*. EDO-FL-95-02.

Oxford, Rebecca, and David Crookall. 1988. "Research on Language Learning Strategies: Methods, Findings and Instructional Issues." *Modern Language Journal* 72: 404–19.

Pask, G. 1976. "Styles and Strategies of Learning." *British Journal of Educational Psychology* 45: 128–48.

Phillips, June K. 1984. "Practical Implications of Recent Research in Reading." *Foreign Language Annals* 17: 285–96.

Prokop, Manfred. 1989. *Learner Strategies for Second Language Users*. Mellon Studies in Education, vol. 2. Lewiston, Australia: Edwin Mellon Press.

Rubin, Joan. 1987. "Learner Strategies: Theoretical Assumptions, Research History and Typology." In Anita Wenden and Joan Rubin, eds., *Learner Strategies in Language Learning*. Englewood Cliffs, NJ: Prentice-Hall International, 15–30.

Schmeck, Ronald R. 1983. "Learning Styles of College Students." In Ronna F. Dillon and Ronald R. Schmeck, eds., *Individual Differences in Cognition*. Vol. 1. New York: Academic Press, 233–57.

Silver, Harvey F., Kathryn Eikenberry, and Robert Hanson. 1978. *Learning Style Inventory*. Moorestown, NJ: Hanson Silver.

Skehan, Peter. 1989. *Individual Differences in Second-Language Learning*. London: Edward Arnold.

Strasheim, Lorraine A. 1987. *Total Physical Response*. Amherst, MA: Classical Association of New England.

Young, Dolly Jesuita. 1991. "Creating a Low-Anxiety Classroom Environment: What Does Language Anxiety Research Suggest?" *Modern Language Journal* 75: 426–37.

CHAPTER 3

Latin for Students with Severe Foreign Language Learning Difficulties

Barbara Hill

"I never thought I could understand a foreign language until I found Latin. Whenever I tried to learn a language, I never knew what the teacher was saying. I couldn't even figure out when one word she said ended and the next one began. I didn't get the words on the page either. I would try to study outside of class, but I never knew what to do so I would just come back to class the next day to try to get help, but then I would feel even worse because everyone else seemed to know the answers. First, I would try to keep my eyes down to avoid being called on, but a few days later I would skip class. When I came back, I was totally lost and I knew I had to drop. But Latin is different. I have to work at it, but I can figure it out. I think I've found my language."

When words such as these are spoken, chances are good that the speaker is a student who either possesses LDs (variously defined as "learning disabilities," "learning difficulties," or "learning differences") or can be identified as a "high-risk" foreign language learner. Chances are also good that the Latin teacher who hears them has invested much thought and energy into creating the kind of classroom situation, communication structure, course materials, and evaluation processes that allow students at risk of failure in foreign language (FL) classes to succeed along with their more adept peers. Establishing and maintaining such a classroom is a continually challenging endeavor, but experience shows that it is nevertheless possible.

The fact that little difference exists between the FL learning profile of students who have been formally diagnosed as learning disabled and those who, although never diagnosed as LD, are deemed high risk for FL learning has been established by special educators Richard Sparks and Leonore Ganschow, researchers into language learning difficulties. The criteria used by Sparks and Ganschow and their team to designate "high-risk" students are scores on an extensive battery of standardized tests, the receipt of a D or F grade in the first quarter of FL study, and the judgment of their teachers that they are poor FL learners (Sparks, Ganschow, Javorsky, et al. 1992a). We should therefore consider these two student groups, LD and non-LD high risk, as one population that is "at risk" of failure when attempting any foreign language but, at the same time, benefits from similar teaching and learning strategies. The crucial first step in discussing the participation of these students in Latin classes is to recognize that we, teachers and students alike, while aware of substantial difficulties high-risk students may incur, should focus on the equally substantial achievements that can and will occur.

High-risk students, both LD and non-LD, may admittedly possess characteristics that make FL learning frustrating and sometimes impossible. Fortunately, no single student possesses all of the potentially debilitating traits, and some possess very few. Many learn compensatory techniques in language-based classes that facilitate their acquisition of Latin, and many learn compensatory techniques in Latin that assist them in other classes. A few become so dedicated to Latin that they willingly accept the extra hours of effort that success requires and continue their study past the fulfillment of basic high school or college requirements to undergraduate majors or even into graduate studies.

In general, students with LDs experience hardships in Latin and other FL classes similar to those that affected their early attempts to learn their own language. They may be slow, methodical readers, reversing letters and struggling to comprehend unfamiliar vocabulary words. They may wage a continual battle to spell correctly. Some may even have trouble copying from models, and some may exhibit awkward or incomprehensible handwriting. Memory is frequently a problem. These students may need to see or hear an item repeated several times before they remember it.

For such students, mundane classroom activities can be challenging. Anxiety may be their companion while they strive to comprehend a teacher's statements or wait to be called on in front of their peers, for they, in particular, are likely to believe their instructors speak too quickly and live in fear of the teacher who calls on specific students for rapid responses to oral questions. They may have difficulty taking notes or trouble interpreting directions, even written directions. A demonstration by their teacher is vital, but even after a demonstration of procedure, they may lag in completing assigned tasks. Sometimes needed handouts or assignments escape them entirely, lost to poor organizational skills. Timed tests may pose an additional threat because they engender stress as the students prepare for them and cause embarrassment if they take excessive time to finish.

Given these classroom difficulties, it is little surprise that students at risk of failing may experience hardship controlling their frustration, especially at earlier educational levels. These students may be anxious, inattentive, distractible, impulsive, and even hyperactive. They are, above all, distressed by their inability to function as well as their peers in a school environment, and their frustration may lead to their adopting defense mechanisms. They may claim to disdain anything related to school, refuse to participate, or cause diversionary disruptions. Is, therefore, Latin a viable option for these students? When they enroll in Latin classes, what can we educators do to make sure the classes are productive for students who struggle to learn as well as for those who learn more effortlessly? [1]

Recent History of the Enrollment of Students with LDs in Foreign Languages

In order to understand the history of the identification and accommodation of learning disabilities and the inclusion of students with LDs in FL classrooms, it is necessary to go back at least to 1968. In that year, for the first time, a comprehensive definition of learning disabilities was devised by the National Advisory Committee on Handicapped Children. The acceptance of this initial definition led to the rapid growth of testing for learning disabilities and the establishment of special education classrooms in the 1970s. It also played a part in the writing of Title 5 of the Rehabilitation Act of 1973, the initial piece of legislation protecting the civil rights of Americans with disabilities, including learning disabilities. Section 504 of this act stipulates that any institution receiving federal funding may not discriminate on the basis of disability and must furthermore make modifications to its academic requirements to ensure that disabled individuals are not denied access to or discriminated against by any program or activity offered by these institutions. While the Rehabilitation Act of 1973 guarantees the rights of the disabled to services within most educational institutions, since almost all public and private schools receive at least some funding from the government, the Americans with Disabilities Act of 1990 insists that discrimination may not occur even if an institution receives no federal monies (Moore). Thus, law guarantees students with LDs access to any and all academic courses and programs.

The decade of the 1970s saw not only an interest in defining and accommodating learning disabilities but at the same time, by coincidence, the adoption of audiolingual or natural methods of instruction in modern foreign languages. This coincidence led to an early published discussion of the topic of foreign languages, including Latin, and students with LDs. In 1971, Kenneth Dinklage, a counselor at Harvard, wrote an article titled "Inability to Learn a Foreign Language" that was to have a profound effect upon FL accommodations for students with LDs in colleges and later for LD students at the secondary level. Dinklage was influenced by the complaints of students with LDs struggling to pass foreign language classes at Harvard and the concurrent protests of Latin instructors into whose classes the beleaguered students flocked while hoping to avoid modern language classes reliant upon audiolingual methods. After hearing of the students' accounts, he recommended that students with LDs be exempt from foreign language classes and requirements.

In the years since Dinklage proffered his suggestion of FL waiver, the question of students with LDs and foreign language has been studied and debated by teachers, school administrators, learning disabilities specialists, students, parents, and health care providers alike. The debate, in fact, has become more pronounced due to several factors. Foreign language study can be very demanding, but it is generally regarded as beneficial. It provides the best way to allow students to become familiar with another culture in the same manner natives do, understand specifically how language works, and gain problem-solving skills in a unique and consistent context (Moore). At the same time, FL study, which intrinsically coordinates content and skills, enhances individual awareness of learning method and thus helps students increase their knowledge of their own language and be more ready to learn others (Frantz). Expectations have also increased that all students should study foreign language at the elementary, middle or junior high, or high school level in anticipation of their going on to college. In many secondary schools, tracking has been eliminated, and an ever larger number of LD and non-LD high-risk students have joined FL classes. An increasing number of colleges, moreover, expect proficiency in a foreign language upon matriculation or prior to college graduation. Approximately 9 percent of the freshmen enrolling in colleges in 1994 possessed learning disabilities (Henderson). In addition, an increasing number of nontraditional and transfer students from junior colleges are now entering colleges and universities, many of whom have taken little or no foreign language at the secondary level. A number of them, although never diagnosed as having learning disabilities, experience the same severe difficulties as documented students in FL classes and therefore fall into the category of "high risk" for FL learning. Finally, at both secondary and postsecondary levels, grades and grade point averages are a serious concern for students and their parents due to increasing competition for undergraduate and graduate school admission, internships, and employment.

A Definition of Foreign Language Learning Difficulties

The research of Sparks, Ganschow, and their colleagues suggests not only reasons why students with LDs experience difficulty in FL classrooms but also methods teachers and students may adopt to facilitate FL acquisition. After assessing the language learning efficiency of hundreds of secondary students of all abilities with a comprehensive battery of tests, this group concludes that FL learning ability exists on a continuum from "very good" to "very poor." Learners at the higher end of the continuum are able to memorize and manipulate all three components of a language: its phonology (sound system), syntax (grammar system), and semantics (word and phrase meanings). In contrast, learners at the opposite end of the continuum have a great deal of trouble learning and manipulating one or more of these components. Ganschow and Sparks refer to the three component parts of language as "codes" (phonological, syntactic, and semantic codes) and label the varying abilities of learners to manage the components of language "linguistic coding differences" (Downey and Snyder; Myer et al.; Sparks and Ganschow; Sparks; Sparks et al. 1991; Sparks, Ganschow, Pohlman, et al. 1992).

This research team has determined that most poor FL learners possess inadequate phonological coding or processing skills. These students may also be said to have poor auditory ability. They experience real trouble recognizing and learning the sounds of languages, including English. They cannot "listen" well, nor can they relate the sounds they hear to the appropriate letters and letter combinations in written words. A smaller number of weak learners experience trouble with the syntactic or grammatical element of language. In Latin, for example, they struggle to understand such concepts as noun case, verb tense, voice, and mood or clause subordination. The smallest number has trouble with semantics. Because of the preponderance of phonological processing difficulties, Sparks and Ganschow recommend that FL teachers examine the auditory ability of their students early in beginning courses by such means as asking them to repeat new words in the target language and noting their pronunciation or asking them to read aloud unknown foreign words or pseudowords (Sparks and Ganschow 69). This way teachers can predict which students may experience difficulties and be prepared for intervention.

After examining the effectiveness of different Spanish and Latin teaching methods, Sparks, Ganschow, and their colleagues recommend a Multi-sensory

Structured Language (MSL) approach that combines the auditory, visual and kines-thetic elements of language. Learners consistently "hear," "see," "say," and "do" (write or act out) items in the target language. The specific MSL approach this research team advocates is the Orton-Gillingham (O-G) method. This approach starts with explicit, systematic, multisensory instruction in the smallest basic unit of the FL's sound system, a single letter. Step by step, the teacher introduces additional letters and later moves on to the next level, blended sounds. After that come multisyllabic words. The phonological drill incorporated into every class provides students with a method of attacking language and breaking down words into their component sounds.[2] The team has proved that students who receive O-G instruction in either Spanish or Latin improve not only their mastery of English phonology but also their aptitude for FL learning as measured by the Modern Language Aptitude Test (MLAT). The team hypothesizes that when high-risk students who are relatively poor in listening comprehension of English attain knowledge and understanding of the sound system of a FL via a phonetic approach, this knowledge serves to remedy their phonological deficiency in English (Simon 183; Sparks and Ganschow; Sparks, Ganschow, Javorsky, et al. 1992; Sparks, Ganschow, Pohlman, et al. 1992; Sparks et al. 1991; Sparks et al. 1995). A second important aspect of O-G instruc-tion is explicit training in syntactical rules and their operation (Simon 181; Sparks and Ganschow). High-risk students need to hear from their teachers and say for themselves such syntactical rules as "A plural verb needs a plural subject" or "*ad* takes an accusative object" as part of their learning effort. The rules help students understand how words in sentences fall into "chunks" and how these "chunks" function to deliver meaning.

At this point it is important to identify other variables that should not be con-sidered fundamental causes of learning problems for most students. The official definition of learning disabilities, revised in 1988 by the National Joint Confer-ence on Learning Disabilities, specifically disallows sensory impairment, mental retardation, serious emotional disturbance, cultural differences, or insufficient or inappropriate instruction as causes of LDs.[3] While these factors and affective issues too may exist along the side of true learning problems, they do not in themselves cause the difficulties.

Students at risk for FL learning should therefore be regarded as on a par with their peers in intelligence, but deficient in linguistic coding ability or, in other words, their ability to learn and manage the three component parts of a FL, especially its system of sounds and their written representations. The question then becomes whether poor linguistic coding ability precludes high-risk students from acquir-ing proficiency in a foreign language. In contrast to Dinklage's suggestion of FL waiver, Sparks, Ganschow, and numerous other educators unanimously assert that most LD students can, in proper settings and with assistance, be successful in and benefit from FL classes and requirements (Block, Brinckerhoff, and Trueba; Fisher; Ganschow, Sparks, and Schneider; Hill et al.; Moore; Schwarz; Sheppard; Simon; Sparks, Ganschow, Javorsky, et al. 1992). Several declare, moreover, that Latin can be a good option for them (Ashe; Ganschow and Sparks; Hill et al.; Raynor).

Why Latin?

There are several reasons why Latin may be attractive. Because Latin instructors do not typically place their primary emphasis on hearing and speaking the ancient language, Latin may appeal to those learners who have relatively poor auditory ability and cannot easily distinguish the sounds of spoken language. The foremost goal of most Latin classes is the ability to read or translate, and students can customarily see Latin sentences at the same time they are read aloud. This combination of sight and sound proves helpful to LD students (Ancona 35; Ganschow and Sparks 118; Hill et al. 49). The Latin alphabet is already familiar to those who know English, and its letters customarily produce a single sound when pronounced orally. Therefore, acquiring competence in pronouncing Latin and mastering its spelling is greatly facilitated (Ancona 35; Ashmore and Madden 63). Furthermore, because Latin is an inflected language, learners are required to break words down into component morphemes and analyze inflections to determine the role Latin words play in sentences. This process improves student understanding of the mechanics of language because they must use the rules of Latin morphology and syntax and cannot rely exclusively on word order to obtain meaning (Ancona 35–6; Ashmore and Madden 63–4; Hill et al. 49). The task of learning vocabulary, in addition, is made easier by the fact that Latin has a relatively small lexicon and uses few idioms (Hill et al. 49), and, in turn, English vocabulary acquisition is improved because more than 50 percent of all English words, a far greater percent of scientific and technical terms, and most terms expressing abstract concepts are derived from Latin (Ashmore and Madden 64). A trio of learning disabilities specialists also points to the fact that "low incidence classes in which all students start at the same point in the learning curve" are beneficial for students who experience severe difficulties learning FL, and beginning Latin classes typically fall into this category (Block, Brinckerhoff, and Trueba 2–3).

What High-risk Students Can Do

Most high-risk students can, in fact, perform quite efficiently in a Latin classroom and acquire reasonable proficiency. Results obtained by the Latin Program at the University of Colorado in Boulder—where high-risk students take both traditional Latin classes and, for the past fourteen years, separate, self-contained beginning and intermediate Latin classes modified to fit their particular learning needs—and, indeed, the experience of schools at all educational levels all across the country have demonstrated this truth. A number of suggestions are helpful, however, when considering how to help weaker FL students learn Latin. One overarching point is that high-risk students are more dependent than others upon their teachers' explicit explanations; they falter and lose confidence when asked to read and understand information on their own. Not only do they distrust their ability to assimilate points presented in a text, but they need to hear, see, say, and work through their teachers' explanations. Following is a list of specific suggestions for teachers' presentations of various elements of the Latin language.

Readers will note that most of the suggestions offered in this chapter pertain to the Communication goal of the *Standards for Classical Language Learning*: standards 1.1 (Students read, understand, and interpret Latin or Greek) and 1.2 (Students use orally, listen to, and write Latin or Greek as part of the language process). This focus is purposeful, since these two standards of the Communication goal cause the most severe problems for high-risk students. Infrequently do their learning difficulties preclude them from benefiting from activities and assignments designed to advance the goals of Culture (Gain knowledge and understanding of Greco-Roman culture), Connections (Connect with other disciplines and expand knowledge), Comparisons (Develop insight into one's own language and culture) and Communities (Participate in wider communities of language and culture). It is, rather, the multitudinous and sometimes complex details of the Latin language that undermine learning efforts. This chapter, therefore, seeks to provide teachers with a number of suggestions that may help them guide students toward greater achievement.

Vocabulary

High-risk students learn vocabulary best when words are organized in lists of reasonable length that include review as well as new words and are arranged by part of speech. They tend to learn far more effectively when the words are also pronounced aloud by the teacher, practiced by the learners, and augmented by inclusion of English derivatives and related Latin words. Categorizing new vocabulary words on lists of words belonging to particular noun and adjective declensions and verb conjugations greatly aids memory because students can see similarities. These lists can be color-coded, and students can collect them in vocabulary notebooks to be used to study for quizzes and tests. An example sheet from such a vocabulary notebook may look like the short sample grid devised for first declension nouns:

First Declension Nouns   *Feminine Gender*

Chapter	Nominative	Genitive	Gender	Meaning(s)	Derivative(s)

The consistent use of such vocabulary grids benefits students by providing structure for their memorization efforts, something they find difficult to provide for themselves. Moreover, writing vocabulary information on grids is a kinesthetic activity, which appeals to all students.

Morphology

With ample practice, weaker Latin learners can master paradigms by filling in blank grids on paper or on a computer screen. When the dictionary listing and the meaning of the word is provided at the top of the grid, and students derive a word's stem and identify the declension or conjugation before writing the forms, understanding and memorization come easier. Coordinating such related paradigms as first and second declension nouns with first and second declension adjectives or third declension nouns of all three genders with third declension adjectives on the same page also helps because students can see the correspondence between word groups they may initially perceive as disparate.

Syntax

Students learn sentence syntax best when it is made visible and thus explicit by underlining, parenthesizing, bracketing, or otherwise marking subjects, verbs, direct objects, prepositional phrases, and dependent clauses. Specially formatted charts that isolate the key parts of the sentence can help students visualize the differences in syntax between Latin and English. Such charts, which may be as simple as the following example, can be used during the initial weeks of a beginning class as well as in advanced reading classes. When each horizontal line is translated, the students can see how the Latin words move into English meaning as, for example:

canem pueri in via vident.

Subject	Verb	Direct Object
pueri	vident	canem

Translation: The boys see a dog in the street.

With the addition of a column for subordinating conjunctions or relative pronouns (clause markers), such grids function well to demonstrate how dependent clauses relate to main clauses. Students particularly enjoy analyzing Latin sentences and filling in empty grid boxes, especially when they can work in pairs or small groups.

Translation

Weak Latin learners translate most efficiently when they approach a Latin passage that is of reasonable length, they have an idea of the content, and vocabulary help is easily accessible. They also appreciate a variety of approaches. A teacher, for example, can read a passage aloud while students follow visually or by repeating phrases, clauses, or sentences. That teacher can also identify sentence components on an overhead transparency, the board, a computer screen, or a handout. Teachers

can give "sentence starters" or model translations or ask students to work cooperatively in pairs or small groups. The teacher's verification of an individual student's or
a group's work provides needed closure. When translating with students, teachers
should stress preview and review in English and in Latin both. Weak students are
well advised to keep written notes concerning difficult translations since they can
often successfully translate complex passages with each other's and a teacher's help,
but do not remember how the Latin sentences achieve English meaning unless
they take and study notes. If students believe they must write the English meaning
of a Latin passage, they should include Latin references and such information as
vocabulary entries or form identification in parentheses following English words
or phrases. This technique, although time-consuming, helps students remember
the correlation between the two languages.

Evaluation

Evaluation is best accomplished when quizzes and tests are announced early enough
that students can budget in study time, a consistent format is used, and a pretest
is given. A pretest is a preliminary version of the quiz or test that students can see
and fill out as part of their review and preparation. The format on the test itself
is the same, but the questions asked and the items requested are fundamentally
changed. Through pretests, students understand a test's content and the way in
which information will be tested. They therefore carry less anxiety into the testing
situation and are far less likely to misread directions.

High-risk students also profit from receiving credit for tasks they accomplish
as they learn. They can save and assemble in a packet the materials they use as they
progress, chapter by chapter, through their text. When they submit these packets
on exam day, they may receive a modicum of credit. Through this process, students
stay better organized, have in hand the materials they need to study, and know that
they can earn full credit on a certain part of their exam or course requirement. Such
take-home assignments as word paradigm grids can also be counted as a certain
percentage of a quiz or a test. Students can thus get a "head start" toward a good
performance on a quiz or exam.

Occasionally a student's effort on tests is so drastically undermined by a single
element (e.g. vocabulary, paradigms, review translation, or sight translation) that
his or her success on the entire examination is jeopardized. In cases such as this, a
teacher may wish to provide exceptional accommodations as, for example, eliminating the vocabulary or morphology section of the test for that student alone and
scoring his or her work on the basis of the other test sections, allowing the student
to consult the book's glossary while working on review passages or allowing a
student to take the sight passage home to translate at leisure.

Mainstreaming versus Separate Classes

Not only do researchers agree that Latin may be appropriate for students at risk
for failure in foreign language study but they suggest that separate, rather than

mainstreamed, classes may be the best alternative. No formal study of the question has yet been conducted, but several instructors report positive results from self-contained classes. At the secondary level, such an outcome is noted by Stephens and Sparks et al. (1995). At the postsecondary level, positive results are reported from an individualized instructional setting by Ancona and in separate, modified FL classes by Sheppard, Hill et al., and Ashe.

The University of Colorado in Boulder has offered self-contained, modified classes in Latin, Spanish, and Italian since the early 1990s under the aegis of the Modified Foreign Language Program. This program was implemented to assist that segment of the fourteen-thousand-strong student population in the College of Arts and Sciences who encounter severe problems in FL courses. It provides options and accommodations for LD and non-LD high-risk FL learners by allowing them to complete their three-semester FL requirement for graduation either in modified classes or, when necessary, by substituting appropriate classes with focus on a foreign culture. Common characteristics possessed by the modified classes in the three languages include a maximum enrollment of fifteen students, each of whom is interviewed for admission by representatives of the program and Disability Services, completion of a battery of FL aptitude tests, the expectation that students will devote substantial daily study time to the language, maintain good attendance and communication with the instructor, particularly when learning problems arise, and take advantage of tutoring assistance. Within the classes, the pace of introduction of new material is slowed, especially at the beginning of courses, so learners can firmly acquire fundamentals. In a recent survey of a modified Latin class, all of the students identified the pace of the class as "most helpful" in helping them learn. Teachers emphasize method of language acquisition, as well as content, and systematic repetition and review is built into the classes. Test accommodations, including extended time on tests and private rooms for test taking, are consistently offered. Louisiana State University offers a similar Latin sequence for its students with LDs (Ashe). Both the University of Colorado and Louisiana State report success, pointing with satisfaction to the high completion rate for the full three-semester sequence by high-risk students in contrast to their tendency to drop traditional college FL courses after only days or weeks when the pace of instruction outstrips their ability to keep up. At the University of Colorado not only do these students stay in class but after two semesters of study they demonstrated sight translation proficiency that was lower, but within the same range, as students in the traditional sections.

The Ideal Instructor

Perhaps the most important variable for high-risk FL learners is the profile of their instructor. Strichart and Mangrum present the following list of characteristics of an ideal instructor as one who:

- Understands or is willing to learn about the nature of learning disabilities
- Supports the goals of the learning disabilities program

- Is committed to meeting individual needs of students
- Is willing to meet with students beyond class time
- Has reasonable expectations
- Is patient when working with students
- Clearly presents all course requirements
- Provides course structure
- Frequently reviews material
- Presents material at a reasonable pace
- Is flexible regarding the formats of examinations and time deadlines for assignments
- Is interested in how students perform tasks (process) as well as outcome (product)
- Provides consistent feedback
- Presents information using techniques that enable the student to learn through both auditory and visual modalities.

Strichart and Mangrum's list may not, however, be exhaustive. Meeting the academic and emotional needs of weaker learners requires, in addition, self-confidence, flexibility, and perseverance. Teachers of high-risk students must be prepared to discuss learning strategies with their students and try a variety of teaching and testing techniques. In class they should be ready to define and explain and also to repeat those definitions and explanations in consistent terms when asked. Outside of class they must be able to create additional instructional materials that help make Latin explicit and provide additional practice.

No Latin text is sufficient in itself for high-risk students, and most must be modified extensively so that these learners can benefit from using them rather than see their efforts undermined. Teachers should scrutinize readings and exercises to make sure their students can accomplish them with a low error rate. High error rates lead tentative learners to speculate that Latin is impossible. If, therefore, a task assigned in a text is too difficult, a teacher has two options—omit the assignment, or make it more doable. There are several ways to modify assignments. Teachers can select the manageable parts and assign only those or, better yet, copy doable assignments on separate handouts that include directions, often an example, perhaps a coordinated list of vocabulary words and, most important, space for students to write.

Teachers should never think, however, that they themselves are responsible for all of these supplementary materials. They have two great sources of help—the internet and their students. Assigning individual students or student pairs the task of providing a supplementary vocabulary list arranged alphabetically by part of speech, for example, provides an excellent learning experience.

The long list of characteristics belonging to an ideal instructor of students with LDs brings recognition of the complexity of helping weaker learners learn Latin. The difficulty of the task, in fact, approximates the difficulty the students have learning the language. Teaching and learning are further complicated by the fact that most schools do not or cannot offer separate classes. Rather, high-risk students are customarily mainstreamed. In mainstreamed FL classes, however, the needs of high-risk students can function to inspire teachers to reach their own highest potential, for the learning requirements of these less efficient learners promotes the best teaching practices, and the strategies and materials that help poorer learners are helpful to all students (Sheppard 92). Instructors must be careful and inventive in their planning, consistent and precise in managing classroom materials and activities, and meticulous in verification of classwork, assignments, and tests. At the same time, they must be able to handle their own occasional frustration and their students' various affective issues. Ideally, they must put themselves in the position of their students and devise ways to make the Latin language explicit, understandable, and enjoyable. Arries's suggestion that FL teachers redesign their curriculum in a step-by-step process using the assistance of learning disabilities specialists has merit in school situations in which faculty enjoy access to the services of an office of disability services, and the specialists in that office have the opportunity to work intensively with individual teachers. In most schools, however, such commodious situations do not exist, and FL teachers find themselves responsible for their own curriculum design.

Primary Recommendation: A Multisensory Approach

The first and foremost recommendation by those who study FL acquisition by LD or high-risk learners is the necessity of a systematic multisensory approach integrating, on the part of teacher and students alike, the four skills: hearing, speaking, reading, and writing. All Latin instructors who report positive results with LD students advocate this approach (Ashe; Hill et al.; Raynor 44–45; Sheppard 93; Simon; Stephens). A primarily oral/aural approach can prove incomprehensible to high-risk students who ask to see Latin words in written form and want to be able to write the words themselves. This does not mean, however, that they cannot engage in oral/aural practice once specific vocabulary and grammar has been introduced. It simply means that all four skills should be engaged when an item is introduced and that the teacher must be ready to *write* on the board or overhead transparency any item causing confusion. When students hear, see, say, and work with an item in its written form, not only is that item more likely to be learned but the pace of instruction is more likely to be appropriate for students with learning problems.

Other Recommendations

In addition to a multisensory approach to learning and teaching, a number of additional practices foster Latin acquisition for students at risk of failing.[4]

Build an Atmosphere of Trust

One has only to ask a weak learner to describe a classroom situation that has made him or her uncomfortable or angry to understand how sensitive these students are and how dependent they are upon their teachers' proficient management of classroom atmosphere. These students require much patience, repetition, and review. Provide that. Recognize too, that they falter frequently, particularly when trying to answer oral questions. Forgive them. If necessary, back up, and review before proceeding. Try again. Allow enough wait time. In general, allow open responses to questions rather than singling out individual students for individual responses. Encourage students to tell you as much as they can about their interaction with Latin either by means of journal entries or written comments. Let them have a voice in establishing requirements, quiz, or test dates or content and deadlines.

Make It Real

Students fare better when a meaningful context helps Latin make sense. Reading-based textbooks (*Cambridge Latin Course*, *Ecce Romani*, *Oxford Latin Course*) can prove helpful in providing this context as students follow Roman families living in authentic settings and coping with historical events. The Roman characters and the realistic plots allow for a consistency of vocabulary and setting that cannot be easily achieved in texts reliant upon sample sentences. The dramatic visuals and dialogues contained in these texts maintain interest and provide fodder for discussion and oral Latin communication.

Approach Topics in a Variety of Ways

Using a reading-based text as suggested in the foregoing paragraph should not, however, mandate complete devotion to the reading method, especially with students who are easily overwhelmed by a large volume of words and do not trust themselves to derive rules from examples. As Sally Davis says in her wonderfully pragmatic book *Latin in American Schools* (62), a combination of the grammar/translation and the reading approaches is the ideal solution. Such a combination greatly facilitates learning for all students.

Categorize

The various elements of the Latin language are much less intimidating to struggling students when their teachers show them how to categorize. They can then see similarities in such areas as noun and adjective declensions, verb conjugations, ablative or other case uses, or dependent clauses. They can also better identify differences in such syntactical items as nominative subjects of sentences or ablative absolutes. The list of Latin items able to be categorized is almost limitless.

Be Explicit

Tell and show students exactly what they need to know and how to learn it. Think of instances where you can teach a step-by-step process (e.g. forming Latin nouns and verbs, translating ablative absolutes) and list those steps. Students are reassured when process leads directly to content. Groups of students organized by the teacher and instructed to perform a specific mission can accomplish excellent work on exercises, composition assignments, and translation passages, but they can not be expected to teach each other new concepts. Groups of at-risk students are in special need of explicit instruction before they begin to work, monitoring during their group work, and correction of their finished products.

Organize!

Keep yourself and your students organized and accountable. Advance organization provides the structure weak learners need to help them understand Latin, since they cannot provide this structure for themselves in the way more proficient learners can. Advance organization also yields additional class time, and time is a necessity for inefficient learners. Teachers can assist students in gaining this crucial time by planning classes, assignments, and examinations in such a way that the various activities or sections function together to create a meaningful context. It helps students when teachers limit new vocabulary or include a substantial amount of vocabulary assistance on certain assignments so they can concentrate on syntax and meaning. Students learn new vocabulary better by using it in paradigm drills and in substitution exercises. Andrea Webb Deagon gives excellent suggestions concerning sequencing of exercises. Carefully constructed homework assignments are important too. High-risk students will never grasp the information and concepts they need to know during class time alone. They need quiet, extra practice, review, and, if possible, tutoring assistance.

Keep Explanations Simple; Keep Them Short

Students burn out quickly when explanations delivered orally occupy too much time. They want and need to set to work quickly on any new item.

Give Students Space to Work

On handouts, spread out material to be learned. On tests, spread out questions and allow plenty of space for answers. Be careful also to keep blackboards and transparencies neat and well organized. High-risk students have to train their focus purposefully on appropriate items. In situations where material is jammed closely together, students have trouble discriminating among words and sentences, which seem to compete for their attention. The students at Louisiana State, for example, asked their instructor to magnify the pages of their textbook so they could better manage learning the material.

Enjoy Your Classes and Bring Humor to Them

Students are our allies; without them we would no longer be able to do what we do best—teach Latin. Their primary flaw is that they don't know Latin—yet.

Conclusion

Despite our best efforts, "breakdowns" in the language learning process are inevitable both for individual students with LDs and other high-risk learners and the classes in which they participate. In many ways, however, these breakdowns can provide the key to successful learning when they become the occasion for collaboration between teacher and student or student and student. We instructors notice such breakdowns, marking them in a student's quizzical gaze, his or her "tuning out" the class activity or turning to alternative pursuits. Sometimes exercise, quiz, or test results tell the story. When such things occur, it is important to stop and find out where the students' learning process is going amiss.

Asking students to answer questions on index cards can be especially productive in ascertaining aspects of student learning. Appropriate questions are:

1. What did you understand? What did you not understand?

2. What helped you learn this information? What did not help?

Collecting the cards and letting the class as a whole know the results helps students not only recognize that they are not alone in experiencing difficulties but also helps them discover beneficial study strategies. Another way to assist students in finding good strategies is by asking individuals in groups to delineate explicitly the steps they followed to solve a certain problem or accomplish a certain assignment and then let the other members of the group know what they did.

Teachers, moreover, should seek assistance when instructing students with LDs. In some cases, reduced class size is possible. A tutor or an aide can also be invaluable, and such help can sometimes be made available in schools through compliance with provisions of the Americans With Disabilities Act. Private tutoring is cited by many students as the reason for their success in difficult classes.

Finally, some students will simply not be able to learn Latin. Their linguistic coding ability may be so poor that they can comprehend neither the phonological, syntactic, or semantic elements of the Latin language, or their life circumstances may put them in such a state that they refuse to try to learn. Fortunately, these students are a distinct minority. For most, Latin remains a viable option, and the greatest reward for student and teacher alike occurs at those times when both look back with satisfaction at how much they have achieved with each other's help.

Notes

I would like to express my sincere appreciation to my colleagues at the University of Colorado Boulder for their help not only in writing this chapter but also for their expertise, assistance, and support in the Latin classes I have taught or supervised since 1990 for students with foreign language learning difficulties.

1. A sensitive discussion of the problems LD students frequently encounter in foreign language classes and some possible remedies is provided by Schwarz and Simon. Simon adds valuable insight because she is dyslexic, is a trained speech-language pathologist and ESL specialist, and, moreover, devoted seven years to the study of French.

2. A good discussion of the Orton-Gillingham approach and the reasons for its effectiveness is given in Sparks et al. 1991. The method's effectiveness in a Latin class is reported in Sparks et al. 1995.

3. "Learning disabilities" is a general term that refers to a heterogeneous group of disorders manifested by significant difficulties in the acquisition and use of listening, speaking, reading, writing, reasoning, or mathematical abilities. These disorders are intrinsic to the individual, presumed to be due to central nervous system dysfunction, and may occur across the life span. Problems in self-regulatory behaviors, social perception, and social interaction may exist with learning disabilities but do not by themselves constitute a learning disability. Although learning disabilities may occur concomitantly with other handicapping conditions (for example, sensory impairment, mental retardation, serious emotional disturbance) or with extrinsic influences (such as cultural differences or insufficient or inappropriate instruction), they are not the result of those conditions or influences.

4. I could never claim that all the ideas in the following section are my own. I owe a deep debt of gratitude to those teachers who, over the years of my professional career, have helped give form and substance to my ideas about teaching and learning. Among the finest are Joy King and Glenn Knudsvig. I owe much to collaboration with colleagues currently involved in the specific study of Latin for students with severe language learning difficulties: Lynn Snyder, Doris Downey, Althea Ashe, Rickie Crown, Sherwin Little, and Kay Fluharty.

Works Cited

Ancona, Ronnie. 1982. "Latin and a Dyslexic Student: An Experience in Teaching." *Classical World* 76: 33–6.

Arries, Jonathan F. 1999. "Learning Disabilities and Foreign Languages: A Curriculum Approach to the Design of Inclusive Courses." *Modern Language Journal* 83: 98–110.

Ashe, Althea C. 1998. "Latin for Special Needs Students: Meeting the Challenge of Students with Learning Disabilities." In Richard A. LaFleur, ed., *Latin for the Twenty-first Century*. Glenview, IL: Scott Foresman–Addison Wesley, 237–50.

Ashmore, Rhea, and John T. Madden. 1990. "Literacy Via Latin." *Journal of College Reading and Learning* 23: 63–70.

Block, Lydia, Loring Brinckerhoff, and Cathy Trueba. 1995. "Options and Accommodations in Mathematics and Foreign Language for College Students with Learning Disabilities." *Higher Education and the Handicapped (HEATH)* 14: 1–5.

Davis, Sally. 1991. *Latin in American Schools*. Atlanta, GA: Scholars Press.

Deagon, Andrea Webb. 1991. "Learning Process and Exercise Sequencing in Latin Instruction." *Classical Journal* 87: 59–70.

Dinklage, Kenneth T. 1971. "Inability to Learn a Foreign Language." In G. Blaine and C. McArthur, eds., *Emotional Problems of the Student.* New York: Appleton-Century-Crofts, 185–206.

Downey, Doris M., and Lynn E. Snyder. 2000. "College Students and LLD: The Phonological Core as Risk for Failure in Foreign Language Classes." *Topics in Language Disorders* 21(1): 82–92.

Fisher, Elissa L. 1986. "Learning Disability Specialist Looks at Foreign Language Instruction." *Hill Top Spectrum* 4: 1–3.

Frantz, Alan. 1996, "Seventeen Values of Foreign Language Study." *ADFL Bulletin* 28: 44–9.

Ganschow, Leonore, and Richard Sparks. 1987. "The Foreign Language Requirement." *Learning Disabilities Focus* 2: 116–23.

Ganschow, Leonore, Richard Sparks, and Elke Schneider. 1995. "Learning a Foreign Language: Challenges for Students with Language Learning Difficulties." *Dyslexia (Journal of the British Dyslexia Association)* 1: 75–95.

Grigorenko, Elena L. 2002. "Foreign language acquisition and language-based learning disabilities." In Peter Robinson, ed., *Individual Differences and Instructed Language Learning.* Philadelphia: John Benjamins, 95–112.

Henderson, C. 1995. "College Freshmen with Disabilities: A Triennial Statistical Profile." Washington, D.C.: HEATH Resource Center, American Council on Education.

Hill, Barbara, Doris M. Downey, Marie Sheppard, and Valerie Williamson. 1995. "Accommodating the Needs of Students with Severe Language Learning Difficulties in Modified Foreign Language Classes." In G. Crouse, ed., *Broadening the Frontiers of Foreign Language Education.* Lincolnwood, IL: National Textbook, 46–56.

Moore, Francis X., III. 1995. "Section 504 and the Americans with Disabilities Act: Accommodating the Learning Disabled Student in the Foreign Language Curriculum." *ADFL Bulletin* 26: 59–62.

Myer, Bettye J., Leonore Ganschow, Richard Sparks, and Sylvia Kenneweg. 1989. "Cracking the Code: Helping Students with Specific Learning Disabilities." In D. McAlpine, ed., *Defining the Essentials for the Foreign Language Classroom.* Lincolnwood, IL: National Textbook, 112–20.

Raynor, Phyllis. 1991. "Foreign Language Acquisition and the Learning Disabled Student." *International Schools Journal* (Autumn): 41–6.

Schwarz, Robin L. 1997. "Learning Disabilities and Foreign Language Learning: A Painful Collision." Available at: www.ldonline.org/ld_indepth/foreign_lang/painful_collision.html.

Sheppard, Marie. 1993. "Proficiency as an Inclusive Orientation: Meeting the Challenge of Diversity." In June K. Phillips, ed., *Reflecting on Proficiency from the Classroom Perspective.* Northeast Conference Reports. Lincolnwood, IL: National Textbook, 87–114.

Simon, Charlann S. 2000. "Dyslexia and Learning a Foreign Language: A Personal Experience." *Annals of Dyslexia* 50: 155–87

Sparks, Richard L., 1995. "Examining the Linguistic Coding Differences Hypothesis to Explain Individual Differences in Foreign Language Learning." *Annals of Dyslexia* 45: 187–214.

Sparks, Richard L., and Leonore Ganschow. 1993. "The Impact of Native Language Learning Problems on Foreign Language Learning: Case Study Illustrations of the Linguistic Coding Deficit Hypothesis." *Modern Language Journal* 77: 58–74.

Sparks, Richard L., Leonore Ganschow, Kay Fluharty, and Sherwin Little. 1995. "An Exploratory Study of the Effects of Latin on the Native Language Skills and Foreign Language Aptitude of Students with and without Learning Disabilities." *Classical Journal* 91: 165–84.

Sparks, Richard L., Leonore Ganschow, James Javorsky, Jane Pohlman, and John Patton. 1992. "Test Comparisons among Students Identified as High-Risk, Low-Risk and Learning Disabled in High School Foreign Language Courses." *Modern Language Journal* 76: 142–59.

Sparks, Richard L., Leonore Ganschow, Silvia Kenneweg, and Karen Miller. 1991. "Use of an Orton-Gillingham Approach to Teach a Foreign Language to Dyslexic/Learning Disabled Students: Explicit Teaching of Phonology in a Second Language." *Annals of Dyslexia* 41: 96–117.

Sparks, Richard L., Leonore Ganschow, Jane Pohlman, Sue Skinner, and Marjorie Artzer. 1992. "The Effects of Multisensory Structured Language Instruction on Native Language and Foreign Language Aptitude Skills of At-Risk High School Foreign Language Learners." *Annals of Dyslexia* 42: 25–53.

Stephens, Stephani. 1990. "Latin and the Learning Disabled Student." *Classical Outlook* 67: 111–3.

Strichart, Stephen S., and Charles T. Mangrum II. 1986. "College for the Learning Disabled Student: A New Opportunity." *Journal of Reading, Writing and Learning Disabilities* 2: 251–66.

CHAPTER 4

Peer Teaching and Cooperative Learning in the First Year of Latin

Kathryn Argetsinger

My goal in this chapter is to propose two different alternatives to the traditional structure of the first-year college Latin classroom.[1] I will be concerned not with deciding which materials or methodologies work best in the first year, but rather with suggesting ways in which we, as teachers, can set up our classrooms to maximize learning for all of our students. Thus, whether you prefer a grammar-translation, reading-based, linguistically based, or some other approach, the classroom designs discussed here may enable you to deliver your chosen material more effectively.

The Traditional Latin Classroom and Its Woes

In the typical first-year Latin class, students are assigned a certain amount of material from their textbooks each night, generally translations from Latin to English or occasionally from English to Latin, which they are asked to prepare for the next day. The class period itself usually includes some lecture by the teacher on new grammar points, and perhaps some drill on the new items. The largest part of the class time, however, is spent as follows: the teacher calls on individual students to translate the sentences or passages they have prepared; if a student translates correctly, the teacher may or may not ask for some grammatical explanation of the sentence; if a student translates incorrectly, the teacher may offer corrections or may encourage the student to discover his own mistakes. Occasionally, in addition to the prepared work, there might be time for sight-reading. The procedure, however, is the same in either case: individual students are called upon to translate.

What could be wrong with such a class? For some students, in fact, this type of class works very well. But its essential flaw is that for most of any given class period, most of the students are not doing anything. A secondary, and not unrelated, problem is that while the traditional class does work well for some students, it tends to fail for many others.

In a traditional class of twenty students, each student might have two or possibly three chances to translate a sentence in the whole hour. In a class of forty, the number of opportunities to participate actively would be cut in half again. It is a commonplace of educational theory that active engagement with the material to be mastered is a fundamental prerequisite for learning. To learn, "students must do more than just listen: they must read, write, discuss, or be engaged in solving problems. Most important . . . students must engage in such higher-order thinking tasks as analysis, synthesis, and evaluation" (Bonwell and Eison iii). But, according to the same authors, "research consistently has shown that traditional lecture methods, in which professors talk and students listen, dominate college and university classrooms" (iii).[2] Traditional Latin classes do have the advantage that individual students, rather than the professor alone, do much of the talking; nevertheless, throughout most of each class period, any given student's primary task is simply to pay attention while others talk. There is no doubt that students are able to learn a great deal through this kind of listening, and they certainly need to do some of it. But it is equally true that students could benefit from far more opportunities than they are given in a traditional class to actively work with the language they are trying to acquire. Instead, "during class, potential practice opportunities are often missed because one person recites while the others sit idle" (Oxford 1990: 43; Christison).

A related problem for some students, even very good ones, is that when they are forced to "sit idle," or to listen to other students struggling with material they already understand, they become bored. A feeling of boredom with a class is easily transferred to a feeling of boredom about the subject matter, so that many first-semester students conclude that Latin is a boring subject (which is probably what they have already been told by other people anyhow). This sense of boredom may contribute at least as much to the attrition rate in Latin programs as the sense of confusion or inability to master the material that some other students feel.

Nevertheless, it is indeed those students who are having the most difficulty with the material being covered in the first-year Latin class who are the least well served by its traditional structure. Since these are the students who will have the most trouble following the work of the other students as they recite, they will be the least likely to be able to maintain their focus and "pay attention" throughout the time that they are not being called upon. Moreover, even the moments when they are called upon to perform may be less than productive: "The . . . language classroom can create high anxiety, because learners are frequently forced to perform in a state of ignorance and dependence in front of their peers and teacher" (Oxford 1990: 142). Though Oxford is thinking here of modern language classes, there is no denying that the same feelings are often produced in classical language classes. A student is called on in front of the whole class; he or she doesn't know the answer or can't translate the sentence and freezes. Such experiences, especially if repeated during every class period, are not conducive to learning, nor to creating positive feelings about the subject matter. As Oxford explains, "a certain amount of anxiety sometimes helps learners to reach their peak performance levels, but too much anxiety blocks language learning" (142). Indeed, a basic hypothesis of one of the most widely accepted theoretical models of second language acquisition asserts that comprehensible input (the prerequisite for language acquisition) can have its effect "only when affective conditions are optimal. . . . When learners are 'put on the defensive' . . . the affective filter is high and comprehensible input can't 'get in'" (Hadley 62).[3] Moreover, anxious, confused students are among the least likely to ask questions, one of the most important learning strategies available to any student (Oxford 1990: 145). In the somewhat formal atmosphere of a traditional Latin class, such students are in fact much more likely to try to hide their sense of incompetence as best they can.

Anxiety, inability to follow the work of other students, and hesitancy to ask questions, then, quickly reinforce each other, so that a rift is soon created between those students who will succeed in the traditional Latin class and those who will not.[4] If the "losing" students are unable to break out of their pattern, to ask questions, gain clarification, and eventually gain confidence in their ability to master the material, their chances of continuing beyond the first semester of Latin (or sometimes even of completing the first semester) will be very slight.

If, then, we hope to engage the energies of our students in the process of mastering Latin, and if we hope to retain them beyond the first semester of study, our classes, optimally, should be designed to provide each student with as many opportunities as possible for active, successful, and productive work with her new language. In addition, the optimum class design should provide ample opportunities for students to consciously think through any difficulties they are having with the language and, with the help of others, to develop new strategies to deal with those difficulties. If students who are unable to understand a Latin passage on their own come to class, and then listen while someone else translates the passage correctly, they may leave the class feeling more muddled than ever. Hearing the correct translation may not have taught them anything about how they might approach the next passage with better results. This can be true even if the correct translation is accompanied by grammatical analysis. What any student needs is not the chance to hear the right answers, whether accurate translations or grammatical analyses, but rather the opportunity to discover those answers, and the strategies that will produce them, for themselves.

These, then, are the underlying goals of the classroom designs presented here: to provide maximum practice opportunities for students in a low-anxiety and noncompetitive atmosphere;[5] to provide opportunities for students to actively engage with new material and to consciously develop new strategies for mastering that material; and to provide opportunities for structured interaction with peers and near-peers that can result in more positive attitudes to as well as more secure mastery of the material. In short, near-peer and co-peer teaching can provide opportunities for creating wider communities of language learning, goal 5 of the *Standards of Classical Language Learning*.

Near-Peer and Co-Peer Teaching: Potential Solutions

The term "peer teaching" has been used to cover a variety of situations in which students help each other to learn. Whitman (iii–iv) identifies five types of peer teaching that are becoming increasingly common in higher education. Three types—namely, the use of undergraduate teaching assistants, undergraduate tutors, and undergraduate counselors—are classified as "near-peer" teaching situations. In other words, the assistants or tutors in these situations are students who are somewhat more advanced or more experienced than the students whom they are assisting. The last two types identified by Whitman, namely partnerships and work groups, are described as "co-peer" teaching situations. These partnerships or groups are made up of students who are enrolled in the same class; work in such partnerships or groups can take place either in or outside of class. This type of co-peer teaching situation is often referred to as collaborative or cooperative learning.[6]

Near-peer teaching schemes have been found to have cognitive as well as social benefits for both learners and tutors (Whitman iii). As for co-peer teaching, structured cooperative learning is, according to Fathman and Kessler, "among the most extensively evaluated alternatives to traditional instruction today," while "research results consistently demonstrate the benefits of cooperative [as opposed to competitive] learning" (131, with references to the various studies). Again, according to Oxford,

> cooperative learning consistently shows the following significant effects: higher self-esteem; increased confidence and enjoyment; greater and more rapid achievement; more respect for the teacher, the school, and the subject; use of higher-level cognitive strategies; decreased prejudice; and increased altruism and mutual concern. In the area of language learning, cooperative strategies have accrued the same benefits, as well as the following additional advantages: better student and teacher satisfaction, stronger language learning motivation, more language practice opportunities, more feedback about language errors, and greater use of different language functions. (1990: 146)

On the other hand, even some of the strongest supporters of such schemes are willing to admit some of the possible problems to which they may give rise. Rodgers, who has used cooperative schemes extensively in second-language classes, discusses concerns that errors may go uncorrected, that students will not know enough to help each other, and that classrooms may become chaotic (11). These are problems I have encountered in my own classes as well. On the whole, however, my experience with co-peer teaching techniques has been overwhelmingly positive. I have found that introducing even a few cooperative exercises into a class can transform its atmosphere entirely; students become more relaxed, friendly, and enthusiastic about the material. I have found that problems with error correction or mutual ignorance can be minimized through careful structuring of cooperative exercises. And, as I have become increasingly comfortable with using near-peer and co-peer teaching more extensively, I have been increasingly impressed with the ways in which these techniques do indeed offer solutions to the problems of the traditional Latin classroom outlined above.

In what follows, then, I want first of all to describe the specifics of a "near-peer" teaching scheme employing undergraduate teaching assistants that I have used with considerable success in my elementary Latin classes at the University of Rochester for several years. Second, I would like to give some examples of "co-peer" learning exercises that are appropriate for the first-year classroom and when used in conjunction with more traditional approaches, offer students variety, increased opportunities for engagement with the material, and an atmosphere conducive to taking chances and asking questions.

Undergraduate Teaching Assistants in the First-Year Latin Class: One Scheme

For several years at the University of Rochester, three upper-level Latin students have been invited to assist in teaching first-semester Latin.[7] The students are not paid for this, but they do receive course credit, and are usually eager to participate. We have used this number of assistants in first-semester classes with enrollments varying from twenty to forty students. The procedure we use is as follows.

The whole group of first-year students meets together twice a week. This time can be used by the professor to lecture (present new material), administer quizzes or tests, run drills, or try some of the cooperative learning exercises described hereafter. The other two weekly meetings are small-group meetings. The class is split into four groups, each assigned to its own room or office. Each small group always meets in the same place and at the same time, so that there is no confusion among the students about where they are supposed to be. The teaching assistants and the professor, however, continually rotate among the groups, so that each of them sees each small group once every other week. Small-group time is used for going over the readings or other exercises that the students have been asked to prepare from their textbooks. Since most of the upper level students have recently been through the same text, they are quite familiar with the material.

Selection and Responsibilities of the Undergraduate Teaching Assistants

The criteria I use in selecting the teaching assistants are their ability in Latin, as demonstrated in our upper level Latin courses, and their interest in working as teaching assistants. I do not try to select students with a certain type of personality or those who look like they might have an aptitude for teaching. Experience has shown me that different first-year students will respond in completely different ways to different assistants, and that as long as the teaching assistants are highly motivated toward helping the first-year students, each will find his or her own way of working well with the small groups.

The teaching assistants must be willing to commit themselves to attending the large-group sessions of the class, to making sure they are in the right place at the right time for each of their small-group sessions, and to making time available to assist students outside of class. In addition, they attend a weekly planning session with the professor during which we decide just what material we will cover at each small-group session. We generally also go through that material ourselves to be sure that all the teaching assistants understand it completely.

At the beginning of the semester, I always stress to the teaching assistants that their job is not to do translations for the first-year students or to "give them the answers," but rather to help them find ways to figure out the Latin for themselves. Neither, however, is it their job to take my place as the teacher. Unlike some graduate assistants, the undergraduate assistants are never involved in grading their near-peers; they are not to set standards or to make judgments, but rather to help the new students reach the standards I have set in whatever way they can. Moreover, one of the ways the assistants can be most helpful is in quickly identifying students who are having serious problems and referring them to me. On the other hand, the assistants *are* asked to keep a daily attendance and preparation record for their small-group sessions. The first-year students know that this information will be used when I determine the final grades.

Advantages for the First-Year Students

Above all, the first-year students receive far more personal attention in this scheme than is usually possible in a beginning course. Half of their time is spent in a group of four to ten students rather than in a group of about thirty. In addition, they have four people worrying about their progress and offering to help them instead of just one. They have the phone numbers of the assistants, whom they are encouraged to call at any (reasonable) time. Thus they feel there is always someone available outside of class to help with problems, and many feel more comfortable going to the peer teachers than to the professor. On the other hand, the scheme also provides each student with frequent chances to work with the professor in a small, informal setting. I feel that I get to know each student well, and that I can easily ask them to come in for further help with particular problems if need be.

The rotation of the teachers among the various groups is, then, central to the success of the scheme. As long as there is careful planning and each group covers the same amount of material, the rotation does not seem to cause undue confusion. Nor do I think that the beginners are cheated by spending nearly as much time working with their "near-peers" as with me. On the contrary, the fact that four different people with different personalities and different approaches are all attempting to get the same material across to them appears to have real benefits. Different students tend gradually to gravitate for help toward the teacher whom they find most compatible, and such matches could not be achieved by random assignment (see chapter 2). In addition, studies have demonstrated that learners often benefit from the ability of near-peers to teach at the right level. The assistants, who have themselves only recently mastered the material they are teaching, may be at a stage of "conscious competence" regarding the material, as opposed to the "unconscious competence" possessed by the professor; this can sometimes make them better able to explain the material or to demonstrate the process of gaining competence (Whitman 9).

The considerable amount of time spent in small groups results in much more active involvement in the class on the part of the beginning students. At every small-group meeting, students are asked to actively participate four times more frequently than would be possible in the large group. That much is an objective fact. Subjectively, I also feel that the quality of the participation is better in the small groups. The atmosphere of the small groups is informal. There is more give-and-take than is typical in the large group setting, and much more freedom to take chances and ask questions. (The atmosphere, in fact, is more reminiscent of a typical upper level Latin class than of a typical elementary class.) There is more time to spend with each student working out individual problems or strategies. Discussion of the content of the readings often arises spontaneously in the small groups, a thing that rarely, if ever, occurs in a group of forty. The students are less bored! In addition, members of each small group get to know each other well and are encouraged to form study groups or to otherwise help each other outside of class.

Advantages for the Upper Level Assistants

The upper level teaching assistants soon discover that the best way to learn something thoroughly is to be responsible for teaching it. They are amazed at all the new discoveries there are to make about material they thought they already knew.[8] The teaching assistants must now learn to organize the material in a new way, and must strive to verbalize knowledge that before they had only needed to demonstrate. In addition to the gains made in their understanding of Latin grammar, the assistants begin to gain an appreciation of some of the problems involved in the teaching of second languages, and classical languages in particular. This experience can be especially important for those considering teaching careers. Whatever their career goals, however, the upper level students report that the opportunity to teach is an invaluable part of their undergraduate experience.

Advantages for the Latin Program Overall

Perhaps the biggest advantage to having undergraduate teaching assistants involved in the first-year Latin program is that they are able to serve as important role models for the first-year students. They are living proof that students really can learn Latin, and even enjoy it enough to go on to an advanced level. The first-year students can see that a small, engaged group of classics majors does exist at the university, and that they are in effect being invited to join that group. In other words, near-peer teaching fosters the building of wider communities of language learning, goal 5 of the *Standards of Classical Language Learning*. In addition, the chance to be chosen as one of the assistants can be a motivational factor for some students who are debating whether or not to continue their study of Latin. Perhaps I should also point out that all of these advantages are realized at no extra cost to the department or the university. In fact, the use of undergraduate teaching assistants makes it possible to deliver a highly personalized program to quite a large number of beginning students without the need to run multiple sections of first-year Latin.

Co-Peer Learning in the First-Year Latin Class

"Cooperative learning is designed to engage learners actively in the learning process. Through inquiry and interaction with peers in small groups, learners work together towards a common goal" (Fathman and Kessler 127).

The decision to incorporate cooperative learning exercises into a first-year class is perhaps an act of greater courage than the decision to use upper level teaching assistants. For while the teaching assistants can help us deliver material in a smaller, more personalized setting, the basic structure of the classroom (one person who knows more helping a group of others who know less) has not been changed. With co-peer work, however, comes a complete reorientation and, inevitably, much concern on the part of the teacher about losing control over what the students are learning.

Unlike schemes involving teaching assistants, on the other hand, co-peer learning can be initiated at any time, for as little or as much time as the teacher wishes, and without any organizational difficulties of the type presented by near-peer schemes. My first experience with co-peer learning came quite by chance when I came down with a bad case of laryngitis. Finding myself completely unable to speak to my first-year Latin class, I whispered to the students to divide into groups and go through the assignment themselves—and I was amazed at the results.

Initially, then, co-peer learning can be just that simple. Even with no planning, advantages of group work can be that students are actively involved throughout the group work time, performance anxiety (arising from having to respond in front of the whole class) is reduced, social bonds and thus a positive attitude to the class are created, and, since the teacher's role is to circulate and respond to any questions or problems that may arise, all students feel able to ask questions and to point out any difficulties they are having with the material. In addition, various approaches to the material may be openly discussed and debated among students as they spontaneously challenge each other to explain their work.

On the other hand, if a teacher decides that he or she wants to use group work on a regular basis, there are several problems that are likely to arise unless the teacher plans somewhat more carefully.[9] First of all, if all the members of a group are having trouble with the material, they may not be able to accomplish very much, and there may be no way for the teacher to monitor the quality of the work being done. Again, if only one person in the group understands the material well or is well prepared, that student may come to dominate the group, handing out answers to the rest. This type of group offers few advantages over the traditional classroom, with the major disadvantage that an untrained student is now playing the role of the teacher. Finally, the students may decide that group work provides a good opportunity to chat about anything but Latin, and the result may be a chaotic classroom with little being accomplished. In any of these situations the teacher may quickly become disillusioned with a group work approach and rush to take control back at the front of the classroom.

It is possible, however, to minimize such problems through careful structuring of the group work activities. Kessler defines a cooperative learning activity as a "group learning activity organized so that learning is dependent on the socially structured exchange of information between learners in groups and in which each learner is held accountable for his or her own learning and is motivated to increase the learning of others" (Kessler 8). Several important points about organizing successful cooperative work are embedded in this definition. First of all, group work must be structured in a way that requires an *exchange* of information between group members and ensures that all group members will participate equally, or nearly equally, in this exchange. Second, each learner is held *accountable* for the work done during the group time. Thus, a requirement that each student hand in something (or perhaps take a quiz) at the end of each group work session is perfectly legitimate and will keep the groups focused. Finally, the goal of each student in the group should be not only to master the material of the lesson themselves but to ensure that *each member* of the group has mastered the material. Thus some writers advocate basing grades on the performance, or degree of improvement, of all the members of the group rather than grading individually.[10] I should admit, however, that I do not feel comfortable using this approach to grading at the college level. Thus, while I do explain to the students that mastery of the material by every group member should be their goal, I focus more on structuring cooperation into the tasks themselves rather than into the grading system.

In addition to these general principles, it may be helpful to keep the following more specific guidelines in mind when planning cooperative exercises.

1. *Group size* should be limited to 3 or 4 students. Otherwise equal participation becomes difficult.

2. *Formation of groups*, at the college level, is perhaps best left up to the students initially. Allowing students to choose their own working partners may help reinforce nascent friendships or study groups. At some point, however, it can be a good idea to juggle people around, or to ask everyone to work with people they have not worked with before. This prevents a group that is not working well together from becoming frozen, and offers the students a chance to work with different partners. In particular, there are special advantages for students both in working with others at or near their own ability level and in working with students of very different abilities. Thus you may wish to rearrange groups periodically in a way that ensures both types of experience for each student.

3. *Give the students explicit instructions* for each type of exercise, and clarify the goals of each exercise. Students should know exactly what they are supposed to be doing during group work time, and what procedure they should be following.

4. *Require that something be handed in* or presented to the class (perhaps written on the board) at the end of the group work time. This helps to keep the students on task.

5. *Circulate* among the groups, "eavesdropping" and facilitating as necessary. Encourage the groups to call you over whenever they are stuck or unable to resolve discrepancies. If you have never tried any cooperative learning exercises before, you may be concerned that there seems to be no role for you, the teacher, during group work time. Be assured that the circulating teacher is kept very busy; in the cooperative classroom, however, the teacher's grammar explanations come most frequently not as error correc-

tions or as half-heeded lectures but in response to concrete questions that the groups of students must frame for themselves.

Examples of Cooperative Exercises for the First-Year Latin Class

Not only do cooperative exercises provide ways of building community within the classroom but also they offer ways for meeting the Communication goal of the *Standards of Classical Language Learning*. Although all the goals could be accomplished through peer-group work, the activities presented hereafter focus on the two standards of the Communication goal: standard 1.1, Students read, understand, and interpret Latin or Greek; and standard 1.2, Students . . . write Latin and Greek as part of the language learning process. In the course of using these activities, students demonstrate a knowledge of vocabulary, basic inflectional systems, and syntax appropriate to their reading level, and they read and understand passages of Latin.

Translation of Prepared Passages or Sentences

Since the largest amount of time in most first-year classes is devoted to reading Latin, or translating from Latin to English, and since the ability to read Latin is the goal most of us set for our students, it is especially important to structure this type of work carefully. Thus I discuss my own approach to this task in the most detail. I have tried various cooperative approaches to reading Latin, but the approach described here has consistently worked best, both with first-year students and with more advanced students who are tackling the texts of Latin authors.

Have the students prepare a portion of their homework assignment by copying out the Latin and labeling the cases of every word that has a case. Have them circle and connect words that agree with each other, and have them bracket and label any constructions they have studied. As new constructions are presented in the course of the year, the labeling system can be gradually expanded. For example, subordinate clauses might be bracketed and labeled, relative pronouns might be circled and an arrow drawn to the antecedent, indirect statement might be indicated by two lines after the leading verb, and so on. There are many different ways you might choose to have your students mark items of morphology or syntax; it is not important what system you use as long as you give the students a systematic guide to follow so that markings will be consistent from student to student.

When the students come to class, make sure they have *not* written out English translations; they should always work from the labeled Latin. Also make sure they have not marked in their books. They will need clean books to refer back to at the end of the exercise. The chart describes the classroom procedure to be followed after the students arrive in class with their marked papers. This procedure should be handed out and clearly explained to the students.

Classroom Procedure

Break into groups of about three students.

1. Choose one person to summarize the meaning or gist of the passage. Does everyone agree? If not, you will need to try to resolve differences *after* the rest of the steps are completed.

2. Compare case identifications. Can everyone agree on the case of every word? Be prepared to defend your own choices. When case-endings are truly ambiguous, this may involve some translation. Correct your own paper as necessary. Request help from teacher if the group is unable to reach a consensus.

3. Compare syntactical markings. Can everyone agree on the structure of the sentence? Again, request help if no consensus can be reached. Correct your own paper.

4. Take turns translating from the marked papers while other group members listen and coach. When the end of the assignment is reached, go through it again, but have each group member do different sentences from the first time. The teacher will be circulating and checking for accuracy.

5. Choose one person to summarize the meaning of the passage. Does everyone agree now?

6. Go back to the unmarked textbook and take turns translating again. N.B.: *This may be done as a whole-group exercise.*

7. Hand in marked papers.

In this procedure, the first and fifth items are intended as reminders to students that whatever they are reading actually *means* something. We have all had students who come to class with meaningless translations. In the traditional classroom, it is all too easy for students to feel that the teacher is the only one who can understand the meaning, and that if they just make a rather random try at translation, the teacher can help them take it from there. Or students may hesitate to take risks, and may only want to go exactly as far as they can without making mistakes, leaving the rest up to the teacher. These behaviors can be reduced in the peer situation if it is made clear to the students that part of their job is to figure out together what the passage or sentence means. If, by the time they reach the fifth step, the passage or sentence still doesn't make sense, they need to determine where the problem lies and to ask for help.

The second step of the procedure (case comparisons) is the heart of the process, because discrepancies in the way students have labeled cases will call forth grammatical discussion on several levels. First of all, the students will discover that to resolve case discrepancies they must be certain they know which declension they are working with as well as the correct forms of the declension. (I am certain we all tell students *ad nauseam* that they must know these things, but in the group situation they really do learn it for themselves.) Next, the students may find that they have labeled some ambiguous forms differently; they will therefore need to talk through their reasons for making the choices they made. Students whose tendency is to guess randomly at cases will begin to learn from others to be sensitive to the environment in which the word is found, to consider the structure of the sentence as a whole, and finally to correct inaccurate hypotheses as the full meaning of the sentence is revealed. Thus the attempt to resolve discrepancies in case identifications leads naturally to discussion of construction identifications and of the proper translation of a particular sentence.

In the fourth step of the procedure (translation), the now correctly labeled papers provide a means for each student to practice translating accurately and confidently. Though there may not often be time for the groups to get through the assignment more than once, each student will still have many more opportunities to translate than is possible in a whole-group setting. It is vital that students take turns translating rather than letting one person dominate this part of the group work. You might want to try assigning one person in each group the task of making sure that translations are divided up fairly.

The essential ingredient in this group approach to reading Latin is the writing-out and labeling of the Latin.[11] This is what gives the group work a concrete starting point, ensures that each student will be engaged in the conversation, and helps to produce a methodical approach and accurate results, even without any supervision from the teacher. Less structured group translation can produce some of the same problems as the traditional classroom: students who couldn't translate the passage or who translated it incorrectly on their own may listen to another student translating it correctly but may not know what to ask and may not learn anything about improving their own reading strategies.

English to Latin

Many first-year classes emphasize English-to-Latin work in addition to translation from the Latin. If your textbook supplies you with a good selection of English-to-Latin sentences, you can try assigning different sentences to different students. In class, have the students read a partner's Latin sentences without looking at the English. Can they make sense of what their classmates have written? Why or why not? Have them talk through the problems with their partners.

Even more interesting, at least occasionally, is to have the students use a dictionary and whatever sentence structures they have studied so far to compose short Latin passages on an assigned topic. (Try to choose a topic they have at least some vocabulary for.) Again, in class, compositions may be shared with a partner. The goal here is not perfect grammatical accuracy, but rather the chance to use Latin to communicate with another person. Students will often put far more effort into this type of work than they will into rote English to Latin exercises that are meant to have only one right answer.

For either of these procedures, English-to-Latin work should be handed in with the corrections or comments of the partner marked in a different color. Partners will take their job of assessment more seriously if they know they are themselves being assessed for that work as well.

Vocabulary or Morphology Drill: Simple Method

As a homework assignment, have students make up flashcards of new vocabulary items or of individual forms from a new paradigm. In class, divide into groups of three or four. The first student drills the second, using the cards made by the second student, while the others watch and, in the first round, coach or offer hints as necessary. Missed items are placed in a separate pile. Next the second student drills the third student, and so on around the circle. Coming back to the beginning, students drill each other only on the items from the "missed" pile. Students then takes home their own cards to study with their most difficult items on the top.

This type of drill works best if you can find time to repeat it the next day, so that long-term as well as short-term memory is being drilled. It should also be followed up by a quiz so that the students know they are working toward a specific goal. Admittedly, in college classrooms, there may not be time to do this sort of drilling very thoroughly; certainly we have traditionally expected our students to do most of their memorizing on their own. But if you can find time for this sort of work even occasionally, you can then encourage students to form study groups and to continue to work together in this way outside of class.

Morphology Drill: Creative Method

Most first-year textbooks have ample sections that are intended to drill morphology or new grammar points, and most teachers devise extra exercises of their own, perhaps including short pattern drills or dialogues to be done orally. The basic problem with trying to do most of these exercises cooperatively is that they are predicated on the notion of an expert who will be checking for accuracy. For example, if a book assigns a list of verb forms to be translated, it is easy enough for one student to say to another "Diximus," but when the second student replies "We say," the first student may not know whether or not this is the right answer, and to have to look it up and check it defeats the purpose of this sort of rapid drill.

The following procedure is intended both to get around this problem and also to make drill time more creative and interesting. After presenting a new grammar section, ask each student, as a homework assignment, to design his or her own drill on the material. Here are the questions they should ask themselves and the points they should keep in mind as they design the drill:

1. What are the main points of the section or chapter?

2. What is new about the material?

3. What should students be able to do or to recognize in order to demonstrate mastery of this material?

4. What would be the best type of exercise to help students achieve such mastery?

Students should come into class with their drill written out, and, if necessary, with an answer key for themselves. They will be the experts for their own drills as they try them out on the other students in their group. At the end of the group session, the drills should be handed in, perhaps along with short comments on how effective the group found each drill. Probably the biggest advantage to this procedure is that it gets the students to think analytically about the material presented in the chapter, and to focus consciously on developing learning strategies for themselves and for their peers.

Sight Reading

The traditional method of putting one person on the spot does have its advantages. Besides being an exciting challenge for some students, it gives everyone a chance to observe how the teacher guides a student through a passage. If you can get the student-on-the-spot to think out loud about what he or she is doing, it is even better. Not everyone, however, likes to be on the spot, and a "jigsaw" approach also offers some advantages and some variety if used occasionally.[12]

1. Break the passage to be read into several sections. The number of sections will depend upon the number of students in your class. As an example, let's say there are twenty students in your class, so you break the passage into five sections.

2. Number off the students from one to five, and have all the students whose numbers are the same meet together and work through the section corresponding to their number. The work of these groups is not completed until every student is certain he or she understands the section.

3. Now have groups of students with the numbers one through five meet together. With each group member contributing his or her own section, the whole passage is quickly done.

4. Reconvene the class as a whole group to sum up the passage and discuss main points of grammar, style, or content.

If your goal for a particular sight-reading session is simply to move through a great deal of material as rapidly as possible, you can vary this procedure by assigning individual sentences to individual students. After a brief allotment of time for individuals to work on their sentences and to consult you about any difficulties, you can move through the passage much more quickly than is usually possible with sight reading. If, however, you are more concerned with teaching the students something about the reading process than with speed, you are probably better off sticking to the traditional student-on-the-spot approach, varied occasionally with the jigsaw method.

The exercises presented here are intended as examples of some of the ways students can work together in a first-year Latin class. My hope is that they will get other teachers thinking about the types of exercises they might design for their own classes. Obviously, different types of exercises will work best in different classes, depending on the particular textbook and the particular methodology in use. But, whatever the textbook, if students are not being encouraged to work together in, and possibly also outside of, class, a great potential resource is being lost. There are few places students can go for better information, help, and encouragement than to fellow students in the same class.

A Postscript about Standards

One concern about moving away from a teacher-centered classroom has to do with standards. How can we be sure that students working with near-peer teaching assistants or with other students in their own class are learning what they need to learn? Does a classroom based on such methodologies result in lower expectations or achievement? On the contrary, if I did not feel certain that near-peer and co-peer teaching techniques help more students to reach a higher level of achievement, I would see no reason to recommend them. Nor do such approaches mean "cheating" the strongest students, that is, those who would probably do excellent work in a traditional classroom. These students are much less bored in a classroom that gives them so many more opportunities for active participation, and they have the pleasure (and valuable learning experience) of explaining to their peers concepts that they have been able to grasp quickly.

There is no reason to lower standards or expectations when moving to alternative classroom designs. (You may even find that you can raise them.) The only change should be in the degree of certainty on the part of your students that they have many resources available, and that many different people—professor, peers, and near-peers—are willing to work with them to help them attain the expected level of mastery.

Competition and high achievement do not, then, always have to go hand in hand. When our students know that our first goal as teachers is to help them to learn, and when our classrooms are designed to openly encourage students to work together, and with us, to discover the approaches to the material that work best for them, they will react more, not less, positively to the traditional high standards and expectations of the college Latin classroom.

Notes

1. All the suggestions given here may be taken to apply equally to the first-year Greek classroom. Many of the problems I identify in the beginning Latin classroom, however, are

a direct result of the number of students typically found in such a class. Since, at many universities, elementary Greek classes are considerably smaller than Latin classes, there may not be as pressing a need to find solutions on the Greek side of the curriculum. Nevertheless, the cooperative learning exercises discussed at the end of the chapter are as effective with small as with larger classes.

In addition, while this chapter focuses on peer teaching and cooperative learning within the classroom, these strategies can also be used to create collaborative learning environments through the use of technology, known as telecollaboration. See Bonvallet and de Luce; Gruber-Miller and Benton; McManus; and Godwin-Jones.

2. Their helpful booklet on active learning contains a number of useful suggestions for moving college classrooms away from the traditional lecture approach.

3. Krashen's Monitor Model; see Hadley (61–4) for a brief discussion. Further discussion and critique of the model may be found in Barasch and James.

4. As Chastain notes, "one problem that has always presented major obstacles to second-language teachers is the fact that there seems to be no normal curve in most second-language classes. For one group of students language study is apparently fairly easy; for the remainder of the class the same subject is impossible. The large middle group usually found in other classes is often almost nonexistent" (201). My own experience has been that the peer-teaching and cooperative learning techniques described herein do actually serve to produce a much larger "middle group" of students who, with the right kind of help, can learn a second language quite effectively.

5. For an excellent discussion of the competitive ethic in our educational system, and its pitfalls, see Coelho (31–2). While competition does not promote superior performance, according to Coelho and the research she cites, it can often have socially and psychologically damaging effects. The philosophical ramifications of a cooperative approach to learning are also placed in context by Williams, with bibliography.

6. Though the terms "collaborative learning" and "cooperative learning" are sometimes used rather loosely, it should be noted that the term "cooperative learning" in particular has come to be used quite specifically to refer to work groups whose activities are carefully structured according to principles developed by particular researchers or teams of researchers, namely David and Roger Johnson, Spencer Kagan, and Robert Slavin. Their work should be consulted for an overview of the subject as well as for detailed descriptions of cooperative classroom methodology. In some cases, the college teacher will have to make adjustments for the fact that the work is primarily addressed to teachers of younger children. As Oxford 1997: 443 asserts, "Cooperative learning as compared with collaborative learning is considered more structured, more prescriptive to teachers about classroom techniques, more directive to students about how to work together in groups, and more targeted . . . to the public school population than to post-secondary or adult education." However, Johnson, Johnson, and Smith have concerned themselves with applying the techniques in the college classroom. The books of Nunan and of Kessler discuss various aspects of cooperative methodology as applied specifically to the second language classroom, while the articles by McGroarty and by Fathman and Kessler offer concise statements of the benefits of a cooperative approach in teaching second languages; the latter includes an annotated bibliography. The more recent annotated bibliography of Akcan, Lee, and Jacobs may be found online. Again the teacher of classical languages will have to make some adjustments, as these works are largely concerned with classes having oral proficiency as the primary goal.

7. Thomson presents another scheme using third-year Japanese students to act as near-peer teachers in a first-year Japanese classroom. Thomson notes positive results similar to those experienced by my Latin students: cooperative learning "increased interactive opportunities

among third-year students as well as first-year students, enhanced motivation of first-year students, raised third-year students' awareness in learning and teaching, and as a result, promoted cooperative and autonomous learning in the learners" (569).

8. Studies have, in fact, demonstrated that the cognitive processing used to study material for teaching is different from that used to study for a test (Whitman iii).

9. This is in fact why proponents of the cooperative approach strive to make a distinction between group work in general, which in its unstructured form can so often yield unsatisfactory results, and cooperative learning activities structured by teachers who have been trained to follow specific guidelines in setting them up. See Johnson, Johnson, and Holubec (8 and 25) for basic definition of truly cooperative learning, as opposed to other types of group work. Key terms in their definition include *positive interdependence, individual accountability, face-to-face interaction*, and *appropriate use of interpersonal and group skills*.

10. See Johnson, Johnson, and Holubec 156–60; Slavin 1983: 3–5. Kagan, however, espouses the opposite philosophy, saying that "team projects which have a group grade create resentments and are unfair," and advising, "Never use group grades." (Kagan website: www.kaganonline.com/KaganClub/FreeArticles/ASK06.html)

11. It is also necessary to check that all the students *have* the assignment. Unprepared students are not able to contribute effectively to the group work; thus my policy is to segregate them into a sight-reading group of their own. This prevents students from taking group work as a "free ride" and simply copying the work of others. See Slavin 1990: 16 on the problem of "free riders."

12. On "jigsawing" see Slavin 1990: 10 with reference to the work of Aronson et al.

Works Cited

Akcan, Sumru, Icy Lee, and George M. Jacobs. 2004. "Annotated Bibliography of Works on Second Language Instruction Related to Cooperative Learning Specifically or More Generally to Small Group Activities." Available at www.iasce.net/resources.shtml#.

Aronson, E., N. Blaney, C. Stephan, J. Sikes, and M. Snapp. 1978. *The Jigsaw Classroom*. Beverly Hills, CA: Sage.

Barasch, Ronald M., and C. Vaughan James. 1994. *Beyond the Monitor Model: Comments on Current Theory and Practice in Second Language Acquisition*. Boston: Heinle and Heinle.

Bonvallet, Susan, and Judith de Luce. 2001. "Roles for Technology in Collaborative Teaching." *CALICO Journal* 18: 295–303.

Bonwell, Charles C., and James A. Eison. 1991. *Active Learning: Creating Excitement in the Classroom*. ASHE-ERIC Higher Education Report no. 1. Washington, D.C.: George Washington University.

Chastain, Kenneth. 1976. *Developing Second-Language Skills: Theory to Practice*. 2nd ed. Chicago: Rand McNally.

Christison, Mary Ann. 1996. "The Effect of Participation Structure on Second-Language Acquisition and Retention of Content." In James E. Alatis, Carolyn A. Straehle, Maggie Ronkin, and Brent Gallenberger, eds., *Linguistics, Language Acquisition, and Language Variation: Current Trends and Future Prospects*. Georgetown University Round Table on Languages and Linguistics, 1996. Washington, D.C.: Georgetown University Press, 116–25.

Coelho, Elizabeth. 1992. "Cooperative Learning: Foundation for a Communicative Curriculum." In Carolyn Kessler, ed., *Cooperative Language Learning: A Teacher's Resource Book*. Englewood Cliffs, NJ: Prentice Hall Regents, 116–125.

Fathman, Ann K., and Carolyn Kessler. 1993. "Cooperative Language Learning in School Contexts." *Annual Review of Applied Linguistics* 13: 127–40.

Godwin-Jones, Bob. 2003. "Blogs and Wikis: Environments for On-Line Collaboration." *Language Learning and Technology* 7: 12–6. Available at http://llt.msu.edu/vol7num2/emerging/default.html.

Gruber-Miller, John, and Cindy Benton. 2001. "How Do You Say MOO in Latin? Assessing Student Learning and Motivation in Beginning Latin." *CALICO Journal* 18: 305–38.

Hadley, Alice Omaggio. 2001. *Teaching Language in Context.* 3rd ed. Boston: Heinle and Heinle.

Johnson, David W., Roger T. Johnson, and Edythe Holubec. 1998. *Cooperation in the Classroom.* 7th ed. Edina, MN: Interaction Book.

Johnson, David W., Roger T. Johnson, and Edythe Johnson Holubec. 2002. *Circles of Learning: Cooperation in the Classroom.* 5th ed. Edina, MN: Interaction Book.

Johnson, David W., Roger T. Johnson, and Karl A. Smith. 1998. *Active Learning: Cooperation in the College Classroom.* Edina, MN: Interaction Book Co.

Kagan, Spencer. 1992. *Cooperative Learning.* San Juan Capistrano, CA: Resources for Teachers.

Kessler, Carolyn, ed. 1992. *Cooperative Language Learning: A Teacher's Resource Book.* Englewood Cliffs, NJ: Prentice Hall Regents.

Krashen, Stephen. 1982. *Principles and Practice in Second Language Acquisition.* New York: Pergamon Press.

McGroarty, Mary. 1989. "The Benefits of Cooperative Learning Arrangements in Second Language Instruction." *Journal for the National Association for Bilingual Education* 13, 2: 127–143.

McManus, Barbara. 2001. "The VRoma Project: Community and Context for Latin Teaching and Learning." *CALICO Journal* 18: 249–68.

Nunan, David, ed. 1992. *Collaborative Language Learning and Teaching.* Cambridge, UK: Cambridge University Press.

Oxford, Rebecca L. 1990. *Language Learning Strategies: What Every Teacher Should Know.* New York: Newbury House.

———. 1997. "Cooperative Learning, Collaborative Learning and Interaction: Three Communicative Strands in the Language Classroom." *Modern Language Journal* 81: 443–56.

Rodgers, Ted. 1988. "Co-operative Language Learning: What's News?" Paper presented at a Seminar on Materials for Language Learning and Teaching (1988), Malaysia. Available through ERIC no. ED 343412.

Slavin, Robert E. 1983. *Cooperative Learning.* New York: Longman.

———. 1990. *Cooperative Learning: Theory, Research, and Practice.* Englewood Cliffs, NJ: Prentice Hall.

Thomson, Chihiro Kinoshita. 1998. "Junior Teacher Internship: Promoting Cooperative Interaction and Learner Autonomy in Foreign Language Classrooms." *Foreign Language Annals* 31: 569–83.

Whitman, Neal A. 1988. *Peer Teaching: To Teach is To Learn Twice.* ASHE-ERIC Higher Education Report no. 4. College Station, Texas: Association for the Study of Higher Education.

Williams, Mark F. 1991. "Collaborative Learning in the College Latin Classroom." *Classical Journal* 86, 3: 256–61.

CHAPTER 5

Is There a Woman in This Textbook?
Feminist Pedagogy and Elementary Latin

Laurie J. Churchill

What then is associated with these insistent fringes? Quite simply the label of Romanness. We therefore see here the mainspring of the Spectacle—the *sign*—operating in the open. The frontal lock [of hair] overwhelms one with evidence, no one can doubt that he is in Ancient Rome. And this certainty is permanent: the actors speak, act, torment themselves, debate "questions of universal import," without losing, thanks to this little flag displayed on their foreheads, any of their historical plausibility. Their general representativeness can even expand in complete safety, cross the ocean and the centuries, and merge into Yankee mugs of Hollywood extras: no matter, everyone is reassured, installed in the quiet certainty of a universe without duplicity, where Romans are Romans thanks to the most legible of signs: hair on the forehead.

> —Roland Barthes, "The Romans in Films"

Language is not a neutral medium that passes freely and easily into the private property of the speaker's intentions; it is populated—overpopulated—with the intentions of others. Expropriating it, forcing it to submit to one's own intentions and accents, is a difficult and complicated process.

> —M. M. Bakhtin, *The Dialogic Imagination*

Language is power, and . . . the silent majority, if released into language would not be content with a perpetuation of the conditions that have betrayed them. But this notion hangs on a special conception of what it means to be released into language: not simply learning the jargon of an elite, fitting unexceptionally into the status quo, but learning that language can be used as a means of changing reality.

> —Adrienne Rich 1979, "Teaching Language in
>   Open Admissions"

Is There a Woman in This Textbook?

The past twenty-five years or so have yielded the development of a range of feminist inquiry, including feminist theory and literary criticism, the interdisciplinary field of women's studies and related fields (e.g., gender studies, women in antiquity, feminist archaeology, anthropology of gender), and pedagogical practices related to these areas of inquiry. This time period has also brought about dramatic changes in the role of classics in American education (Hallett 1983; Kennedy; LaFleur; McManus; Richlin 1989; Santirocco), a trend at least in part related to increased access for women to secondary and postsecondary education. Women now comprise more than half of college and university students (Perun); moreover, our classrooms are more representative of the population as a whole than they were fifty, even twenty-five, years ago. Such changes in demographics alone warrant reconsideration of how and what we teach, especially in a discipline as rooted in male privilege as classics has been historically and still is.[1] Although changes in demographics may have had some impact on how and what we teach in the classical civilization curriculum (e.g., courses on women in antiquity), in my experience and from what I observe in Latin elementary textbooks and related materials, strategies for teaching elementary Latin have been especially slow to respond to the increased participation of women in secondary and postsecondary education. And, although many have responded to the declining enrollments in the study of Latin and Greek and the diminished role of classics in American education, not enough attention has yet been paid to reinventing elementary Latin language programs *both* in response to the increased participation of women in education *and* in accordance with the contributions of feminist scholarship and pedagogy.[2]

In this essay I explore further the rationale for developing feminist materials and methods for teaching elementary Latin and, at the same time, provide concrete strategies for transforming Latin education in accordance with feminist scholarship and pedagogy. In the first section, I discuss how Latin education has been and continues to be gendered, how we might expand the range of classroom content, and how we can develop teaching methods that are more inclusive. In the second section, I offer concrete activities for the Latin classroom and show how a feminist approach to Latin pedagogy can enhance the implementation of the goals of the *Standards for Classical Language Learning*. My commitment to this endeavor stems from my desire to blend, combine, and bridge twenty-something years of experience as a Latin teacher with my more recently acquired familiarity with feminist pedagogy and expertise in the women's studies classroom. It also stems from my conviction that feminist revision of *how* and *what* we teach in the elementary Latin classroom will revitalize—as it demystifies—Latin as a discipline. The democratization of American education in the last century in combination with feminist scholarly and pedagogical contributions of the past twenty-five years makes this moment appropriate for feminist transformation of Latin education.

Is the Latin Classroom Gender-Free?

The epigraphs at the beginning of the chapter provide points of departure for this exploration and, in particular, for considering how Latin is constructed by elementary textbooks and teaching methods and, furthermore, how Latin education may be revised according to the insights and perspectives that feminist inquiry (both scholarship and pedagogy) affords. Latin, especially the Latin in our elementary textbooks, is as much a construct of the present as it is an artifact of the past, constituted as it is—particularly for our beginning students—of the content, structure, methods, and visual aspects of elementary textbooks, resource books, readers, and other pedagogical norms of the discipline and within the Latin classroom. And, as a culturally and historically embedded construct, Latin also bears the mark of gender. In fact, approaching Latin via feminist inquiry yields strategies by which Latin education or, if I may, Latin pedagogical culture, may be revised to suit more appropriately contemporary learning communities; furthermore, this approach enriches the Latin classroom in its utilization of feminist scholarship and methods, including the contributions of both feminist pedagogy and feminist research in classics. Indeed, adopting in the elementary classroom a broader range of the uses of Latin, literary and nonliterary, by and about women as well as men, in the ancient, medieval, and Renaissance periods and beyond, expands and revitalizes a pedagogical culture rooted in and constrained by masculist and elitist interests (Ong 1959, 1960).

It is easy to regard the elementary Latin classroom as somehow sealed off or immune from feminist inquiry. And, to be sure, the combined effects of regarding Latin as a "dead" language, the uses to which it has been put historically, the emphasis on apparently gender-neutral grammar and syntax in the study of beginning Latin, and the paucity of extant literary works written by women from the Republican and imperial Roman periods *all* undoubtedly contribute to this sense of the elementary Latin classroom as a transcendent space. Indeed, some may even take comfort in a pedagogical space that appears to offer respite from contemporary ideological concerns, including those related to feminism. However, despite such yearnings for a "green world," an idyllic, prelapsarian refuge, this urge minimizes, if not ignores, the gendered aspects—and the gender biases—of the elementary Latin classroom, its materials and methods. For the content of traditional elementary Latin textbooks is determined not only by the male-authored texts toward which the Latin curriculum is aimed but also by the history of Latin education, including how Latin has been transmitted historically, in whose interest, and toward what ends.

Indeed, the exclusion of women historically from education for the most part meant their exclusion from knowledge of Latin and Greek (Ong 1959, 1960). For instance, in his article entitled "Latin Language Study as Renaissance Puberty Rite," Ong (1959) studies the bases of gender bias in the Latin curriculum and anticipates contemporary revisions of Latin pedagogical culture. He illustrates the similarities between puberty rites and the dynamics of Latin education in the Renaissance. According to social conventions at this time, learning Latin marked the departure of the male child from the private sphere of the "mother tongue" into the public world of men, to which knowledge of Latin was the key. According to Ong, "the fact that the marginal environment" (i.e., the extrafamilial, Latin-learned male community) "was primarily a linguistic one only heightened the initiatory aspects of the situation, for the learning of secret meanings and means of communication is a common feature of initiatory rites. It is through the ability to communicate that man achieves a sense of belonging" (107). Ong also identifies Renaissance pedagogical practice as the source of the nineteenth-century notion that Latin "strengthens" or "toughens" the minds of young men.

McManus (20–48, esp. 26–31) updates and expands substantially this analysis of the historical and gendered dimensions of Latin education. On the one hand, she points out that American colleges offered women training in Latin and Greek in greater numbers and earlier than women in Europe. On the other hand, "they faced the same elitist and exclusionary masculine tradition as their counterparts in England and the Continent" (27). M. Carey Thomas, founder of Bryn Mawr College, was allowed to attend graduate lectures at Johns Hopkins on the condition that she sit behind a black curtain, lest she be "an unnecessary distraction." Women were rewarded if they adhered to traditional topics of research (e.g., Lily Ross Taylor), but their status in the profession and as scholars was devalued if their research emphasized ancient women (Grace Harriet Macurdy) or Greek romances (Elizabeth Hazelton Haight).

Even though the situation of women has changed dramatically since the nineteenth and first half of the twentieth centuries, vestiges of gender bias embedded in the history of Latin education persist, however unintentionally and unconsciously, in contemporary textbooks, readers, and methods of teaching Latin. These materials and methods, despite the good intentions of authors and teachers alike, perpetuate gender bias both by assuming an all-male community of learners and by ignoring the contributions of feminist research and pedagogy. Harwood, for instance, gives evidence that many introductory textbooks assume and construct a male audience. So, although texts such as *Latin for Americans* (Ullman, Lewis and Suskin) may pay lip service to inclusiveness (e.g., by using both "him" and "her" as the third-person objective form in English), its introduction invites students to "Step right ahead! Just through that arch is the rich inheritance the Romans have left you. It's yours—and all men's—to share" (16). Harwood also finds that male characters significantly outnumber females in reading lessons; men outnumber women by a third in illustrations; practice sentences rarely use feminine pronouns; words for women and women's roles are underrepresented. She also notes that the word *femina* doesn't appear in this text at all!

While newer editions of Latin textbooks have improved in their representation of women, they still fail to meet criteria for equity of gender representation (Rifkin et al.). Alice Garrett critiques all three reading texts from a feminist point of view and finds all three have serious problems. The *Cambridge Latin Course* (Pope) has the least gender balance: In unit 1, there are thirty-three male characters and three female ones. Unit 2 is only slightly better, with twenty-eight males and eight females. She points out that because the *Oxford Latin Course* (Balme and Morwood) develops a story line centered on the life of Quintus (Horace), students are sent the message "that a man's life is at the center of our concern." Women are simply not presented in the same number as men in most Latin textbooks. The underrepresentation of women is a major concern, since research has shown that noninclusion of women and girls in materials used to teach them seriously impairs their ability to learn (Grossman and Grossman; Klein).

One can also critique gender in these textbooks from a perspective of *how* women are portrayed. Schmitz (1985) identifies the following helpful categories for assessing the representation of women in elementary foreign language textbooks:

exclusion, subordination, distortion, and degradation. *Ecce Romani* (Brush and Lawall), for example, has fairly good gender balance, according to Garrett, since no one member of the family is given prominence, but episodes within the text may portray women stereotypically, as untrustworthy and needing a man's help. Polly Hoover comments that practice sentences in Wheelock resort to traditional female and male realms of agency: "good and pretty girls are praised while boys who ought to be good are warned." Textbooks rarely show the range of roles and interactions that women experienced. In short, in Latin textbooks, "men and boys are the default category for any display of intelligence, agency, or subversion while women and girls are predominantly compliant and pretty" (Hoover 59). This is not to say that textbooks should misrepresent or minimize differences in gender roles between the ancient world and the present, but it is important to see how gender roles in textbooks are constructed by their authors so that teachers and their students can compare textbook Roman women with what we know about women's lives in ancient Rome.

Revising Classroom Materials

The most obvious place to begin the process of feminist revision of the elementary Latin classroom is the place where academic feminism begins, namely, with revising materials—the substance of traditional disciplines—to represent more fully women's history, social roles, experiences, and achievements and, likewise, to include the contributions of feminist scholarship. In literary studies, for example, feminist scholarship has significantly enriched the canon of largely male-authored texts. Such revisions result from incorporating rediscovered literary achievements of women and extending the range of texts studied (e.g., diaries, journals, letters) to include the kinds of writing most likely to have been produced by women. Such an epistemic shift may be adapted to suit the precise contexts and materials related to the study of Latin. And, since the texts toward which elementary Latin instruction is typically directed are almost exclusively male-authored, not only should we focus on how women are represented in the texts that the ancient world provides but we also need to introduce into the elementary Latin classroom texts produced in historical periods and places (Hallett 1993) from which more extensive evidence (writing and material remains) related to women survives (see hereafter).

Specific revisionist possibilities for the elementary Latin classroom are varied and numerous. First, "made Latin" that is the stuff of many students' first encounters with the language may be revised to represent women in more active roles, as the subjects of verbs as often as objects, in activities other than domestic roles, and of worth and significance beyond their physical appearance. Existing "made Latin" stories and drill sentences may be changed to eliminate gender stereotyping (Harwood), provide critical perspectives on gender in the ancient world and on the history of the Latin language and Latin education, and include materials on women in antiquity and other evidence of the uses of Latin by and about women. Second, in addition to revising the content of stories and sentences, vocabulary lists might also be supplemented with words that provide insight into a range of women's roles and activities (Harwood), and into the dynamics of gender in antiquity (see exercises hereafter). Third, materials that illustrate the broad range of the uses of Latin historically by or about women might supplement more advanced readings of adapted Latin. Here we need not be limited to what Hallett (1983) calls the "greeting card" approach (i.e., Pompeian inscriptions by or about women); for we may adapt and annotate the works of a rich variety of medieval and early modern women writers such as Egeria, Perpetua, Hrotswitha, Hildegard of Bingen, Laura Cereta, and Anna Maria von Schurmann—to name only a few.[3] In addition, we may study these women writers in historical and cultural contexts and consider the conditions under which women's writing appears and circulates. More conventionally, focusing on the portrayal of women and the dynamics of gender in texts by canonical male authors of Republican and imperial Rome (Hallett 1983, 1993) also provides abundant material for feminist revision of the elementary Latin classroom.[4] Fourth, visual materials and supplementary readings[5] gleaned from studies of women in antiquity may be incorporated to provide a more extensive range of images of and information about women and the material remains pertaining to their experiences and roles. By these varied means of expanding the range of materials, feminist transformation(s) of the Latin curriculum may revitalize the elementary Latin classroom. Not only does feminist transformation contribute primary and secondary sources from new ancient studies (Richlin 1993) and beyond, but it also enriches students' understanding of and engagement with elementary Latin by engaging methodological questions related to study of the dynamics of language, gender, and culture.[6]

Transforming Classroom Interactions

In addition to employing feminist scholarship and perspectives in revising canons and curricula (i.e., the materials with which and toward which we teach Latin), in what other ways might feminist pedagogy transform the apparently "gender-free zone" of the elementary Latin classroom? More specifically, how might feminist pedagogy transform classroom organization, the roles of students and teachers, and interactions among them? Although there is no monolithic method or set-in-stone model for this—or any—aspect of feminist pedagogy (Maher 1987), nevertheless, several general principles undergird most feminist classroom practices. These include: accommodating difference and diversity among students; fostering nonauthoritarian learning processes and empowering students in these processes; and eliminating gender bias in interactions with and among students.

In classroom interaction, as with the revision of content and materials, feminist pedagogy recognizes diversity and difference—particularly gender difference—among students and promotes teaching strategies that are appropriate to a range of learning styles. This perspective, and the research on which it is based (Chodorow; Gilligan; Hall; Hall and Sandler; Maher and Tetreault; Weiler 1988) recognizes that gender socialization affects learning and communication styles and, furthermore, that interactive, collaborative strategies engage a broader range of learners, including women, than do traditional teacher-centered or competitive strategies (Maher 1985: 33). Teacher-centered strategies, such as lecturing and teacher-directed discussion, may be complemented in a variety of ways that carefully structure student participation and cooperation. So, for instance, in the elementary Latin classroom small groups of students may be asked to work together on assignments (both in and outside of class), on developing exercises and drills on grammar and vocabulary, and on preparing presentations on reading assignments or explanations of grammatical material (see chapter 4). The object of such activities is to develop a learning community, to engage students as coinvestigators (Maher 1985: 35; Maher and Tetreault; McCormick) who interact as much with each other as with the teacher. In addition, something as simple as arranging seats in a circle can dramatically transform classroom dynamics, as students face and communicate with each other, not only with the teacher.

Decentering classroom authority in this way not only accommodates a fuller range of learning styles but also empowers students in the learning process and, likewise, fosters their responsibility for and engagement with learning processes. Feminist pedagogy shares this objective with liberation pedagogy, or "educating for critical consciousness," as developed by Paolo Freire. For both feminist and liberation pedagogy emphasize the dialectical and interactive aspects of learning, the aim of which is social change. According to these models (Maher 1987; hooks 1989, 1994), social change evolves from empowering learners, not least by engaging the knowledge, skills, abilities, personal experiences, and interests that they bring to their studies. Liberation pedagogy, in other words, is founded on the belief that political and social inequities may be diminished—if not eliminated—through educational practices that empower oppressed groups. According to this perspective, empowerment is achieved, at least in part, through educational practices that validate learners' experiences. The primary difference between liberation and feminist pedagogy is that the former does not specifically focus on women as an oppressed group or on gender oppression as a primary target for social change (Kenway and Modra; Weiler 2001).

As for classroom practice, a variety of strategies may be adopted to promote the empowerment of students, especially women students, and fostering their investment in the learning process. In the Latin classroom, journals may provide an effective means of developing students' "voices" in relation to the material and in helping them clarify and articulate their motivation and objectives for studying Latin (Hannan). In their journals, students may record assignments, notes taken in preparation for class, etymological studies based on individual areas of interest, responses to relevant campus and community events, and responses to secondary readings on Roman culture and the study of Latin and classics as a discipline. The purpose of the journal is to engage students more fully, self-consciously, and critically in learning Latin.

Feminist pedagogy also involves a commitment to gender equity in interacting with students. Not only must women students be acknowledged by validating their learning and communication styles and experiences, but teachers must also be aware of the variety of ways in which they may, however unconsciously and unintentionally, discriminate against women in their classrooms. Research indicates that in a variety of types of interactions, male students receive more positive reinforcement from and are taken more seriously by their teachers—men and women teachers alike (AAUW; Hall; Hall and Sandler; Sadker and Sadker). This research indicates that male students receive more encouragement and sustained attention from teachers. Similarly, the kinds of responses that male students receive on written work is usually more extensive and substantive. The overall effect of these patterns of interaction is that male students are taken more seriously, suggesting that they are the focus, the intended audience, of the educational process.

Unconscious patterns of interaction with students may inadvertently privilege male communication styles and encourage male more than female students, thereby producing gender bias in the classroom. Although we may be consciously committed to equal opportunity, gender equity, and eliminating gender bias in the classroom, unconscious patterns of interaction with students and unexamined teaching styles may belie unintentional gender bias. Such unconscious patterns of interaction necessitate critical examination of behaviors that may in effect "silence" and otherwise disempower women students. Sadker and Sadker and the AAUW report provide specific recommendations for measuring and eliminating gender inequities in the classroom.

Beyond the Classroom: Possibilities for Renewal

In addition to the revisions suggested earlier for the transformation of the elementary Latin classroom, activities outside the classroom must also help bring about feminist transformation of Latin education. First and foremost is the need for feminist revisions of elementary textbooks and intermediate readers. These would implement feminist teaching methods and engage women as much as men as students of Latin. Feminist companions to *all* elementary Latin textbooks need to be written, a series perhaps that might be undertaken by an individual publisher. Of course, such supplements would become unnecessary with the publication of elementary textbooks that *themselves* incorporate feminist methods and materials. In addition, "language across the disciplines" (see note 6) readers might be developed for the intermediate level. The primary sources in such readers might focus on topics such as women in antiquity, women writers of the Middle Ages and Renaissance, women religious writers, or a survey of the uses of Latin historically by and in relation to women. Secondary readings on methodological issues and scholarship related to primary sources might also be included in such readers.

The proliferation of electronic resources is both promising and daunting. This wealth of resources needs to be refined for pedagogical purposes. The internet now abounds with online discussion groups, websites, primary sources, journals, and search engines, many of which are devoted to feminist scholarship and teaching, research on women and gender in antiquity, and teaching Latin. At the same time, there is no website devoted exclusively to feminist pedagogy in the Latin classroom and feminist transformation of the Latin curriculum, nor is there a *crossdisciplinary* database of feminist research and primary sources by and about women that are specifically relevant to the elementary thorough intermediate Latin classroom (e.g., Churchill; Luschnig and Raia). The Women's Classical Caucus, for instance, might provide a search engine for linking crossdisciplinary resources geared specifically to enhancing the Latin curriculum, together with course syllabi, reviews of textbooks, and other relevant materials from back issues of the *Women's Classical Caucus Newsletter.* Electronic databases might also be used to disseminate conference papers and proceedings, workshop materials, and the like[7] in order to make feminist content and methods more immediately available for classroom use. This would ensure the availability of materials to a wider community of teachers and students, beyond the limited range of those who either belong to sponsoring organizations or have the resources to attend conferences and workshops.

Finally, local, regional, and national classics organizations can help promote feminist transformation of Latin (and classics) education by continuing to organize workshops and panels on feminist pedagogy and devoted to bridging the gaps between feminist scholarship in classics (and related fields) and the undergraduate curriculum, including elementary Latin and Greek (e.g., McClure). Here classicists might work collaboratively with the regional and national organizations of other disciplines that share similar objectives (e.g., foreign language organizations, the Modern Language Association, the National Women's Studies Association). In this regard we might foster the kinds of alliances suggested by Habinek's model of "un-Romantic Latinists," who "would seek more rather than less contact with those outside the profession, and even within the charmed circle they would value collaboration, interaction and open conflict as much as private and individual achievement" (Habinek 241).

All of this, of course, is a tall order—one that involves the efforts not only of individual teachers but also of educational communities and scholarly organizations. Indeed, the very health and survival of Latin education demands such efforts. At the same time, and as I hope this essay has shown, the possibilities for feminist transformation are expansive and exciting, providing as it does the opportunity not only to reinvent but also revitalize the methods and materials of Latin education.

There *Is* a Woman in This Textbook! Feminist Pedagogy in the Elementary Latin Classroom

Although the following exercises are based on materials in the *Oxford Latin Course,* they may be adapted easily to suit other elementary textbooks. I developed these exercises according to the following feminist pedagogical objectives.

- To accommodate difference and diversity—in methods and materials and among students

- To empower students in the learning process

- To study materials on women's history, social roles, experiences, and achievements

- To provide critical perspectives on the assumptions that undergird the Latin education, its materials and methods

- To foster nonauthoritarian learning processes (and otherwise flatten out hierarchy), for example, by incorporating collaborative learning strategies

- To challenge, revise, and otherwise destabilize gender stereotyping in methods, materials, and interactions with students

At the same time, I show how a feminist pedagogy can enhance the implementation of the *Standards for Classical Language Learning* by listing appropriate standards for each exercise. Use these principles and the accompanying exercises as *guidelines* in developing your own feminist pedagogical practice. Supplementary readings are intended for students as well as instructors.

Latin Language Journals: Self-Evaluations

1. *Purpose/Level*

The journal is designed to help students engage actively in the learning process and develop their awareness of the history of Latin education and how gender figures in this history.

The journal will help elementary through advanced level students chart their Latin-learning processes and progress. It will assist them in identifying individual learning strategies, styles, and areas of strength and weakness. The journal will also provide a useful tool for reviewing for exams and the basis of students' self-evaluations at the end of the term. Both the Latin journal and the self-evaluation are intended to engage students in the learning process and reinforce their accountability for and self-awareness in relation to these processes.

Responding in their journals to the readings on the history of Latin education and feminism and classics will help students (1) clarify their motivation for studying Latin and (2) understand both key feminist issues in classics and their implications for the study of Latin—and for them (as participants Latin class undergirded by feminist pedagogy).

2. *Materials*

Notebook

3. *Guidelines/Model*

Students will write in their journals *frequently*, perhaps on a daily basis and in any case no fewer than *four* times per week. They will *date* and *label* each entry, and bring journals to class (for discussion, note-taking, and correcting homework assignments). Journals will be collected and reviewed three times during the course of the semester—twice by the instructor and once by another class member.

Use the journal to record the following.

- Answer the following questions as fully as possible: What was/is Latin? Why study Latin?

- What do feminist perspectives contribute to the study of Latin?

- Goals and objectives for learning Latin

- Assignments

- Class notes

- Homework and corrections to homework

- New vocabulary and sentences that illustrate the use of new vocabulary

- Summary/responses (one page) to events related to the Latin language, its uses or history, or Roman culture

- Summary/responses to supplementary reading (discussed later)

- Notes from peer sessions

- Grammar rules that you have learned or figured out, and sentences that illustrate these rules

- Assessments of your process and progress with learning Latin

- Other insights related to learning Latin

At the end of the semester, students will submit a three-page *self-evaluation* (typed and double-spaced) in which they revisit the questions "What was/is Latin?" and "Why study Latin?" and assess their overall progress and performance on the basis of evidence in their journals, written work, class participation, and contributions to peer groups.

The *supplementary readings* listed here provide some historical background on the history of Latin education and on feminist transformation of classics. The readings are intended to help students clarify (and write about!) their interest in studying Latin and its culture(s), and grapple with the questions: "What was/is Latin?" "Why study Latin?" and "What do feminist perspectives contribute to the study of Latin?"

4. Supplementary Readings

Cameron; Habinek; Hallett 1983, 1993; Hannan; Harwood; Joshel 3–24; Kelly; Kennedy; Mackail; McManus; Ong 1959, 1960; Reinhold; Rich; Richlin 1989; Santirocco (1987); Snyder; "Yale Report of 1828."

5. Source

Adapted from Oxford and my syllabus for "Introduction to Women's Studies in the Humanities."

6. Reflection on Standards

1.1 Students articulate for themselves new grammar learned, demonstrate a knowledge of vocabulary and grammar in completing and revising homework, and read and understand passages of Latin appropriate to their level.

2.1 Students demonstrate an understanding of perspectives of the Romans on gender and education as revealed in the practices of the Romans.

4.2 Students compare Roman educational practices with practices today. They compare the lives of women and men with those of today.

5.2 Students show evidence of connecting the past to the present by applying their knowledge of the gendered nature of pedagogical practices in antiquity and later to their own education and their study of Latin.

Using the Oxford Latin Dictionary

1. Purpose/Level

This exercise will enrich elementary through intermediate level students' vocabulary and at the same time compensate to some degree for standard elementary Latin textbooks' marginalization of women's roles and experiences. Students will gain insight into attitudes toward women and gender roles and the uses of Latin historically by and in relation to women.

2. Materials

Oxford Latin Dictionary (OLD) (Glare)

3. Guidelines/Model

Students (individually or in peer groups) select a small section of the *OLD* (several pages) to search for and record words that pertain to women's roles and experiences, or that provide some insight into expectations of or attitudes toward women, their bodies, and female sexuality.

A quick survey of entries under the letter "l" included some of the following:

lamia

lampadifera

landica

lanifica

laudatrix (cf. laudator)

lecticariola (cf. lectarius)

lucernaria

lupa (cf. lupus)

Make photocopies of vocabulary lists for students to include in their journals. During class discuss word lists and what they suggest regarding women's roles and attitudes toward women. Use lists as a word-source to supplement vocabulary lists in the elementary-intermediate Latin textbooks (e.g., in constructing sentences that illustrate grammatical principles, in drills, etc.).

4. Supplementary Readings

Richlin 1997: 291–94.

5. Source

Adapted from Harwood.

Gender, Words, and Work

1. Purpose/Level

Same as for using the *Oxford Latin Dictionary*.

2. Materials

Journals

Required reading: Joshel 173–82.

3. Guidelines/Model

Prior to class, students will study Joshel's glossary, use it as the basis of a journal entry (one to two pages), and then generate *eight* Latin sentences based on the terms in the glossary. Use the journal entries to initiate discussion of work, status, and gender in Rome. Students will exchange and translate each other's sentences.

4. Supplementary Reading

Joshel 3–24; Kampen; Will.

5. Source

Original.

6. Reflections on Standards

1.1 Students demonstrate a knowledge of vocabulary illustrating the occupations of Roman women, and they read each other's sentences about women's work in ancient Rome.

1.2 Students write sentences illustrating Roman women in a variety of occupations and daily tasks.

2.1 Students demonstrate a knowledge of women's occupations and roles in ancient Rome.

3.1 By analyzing roots of words for women's roles, students transfer their knowledge of economics and social relations in ancient Rome to their understanding of modern economies and social relations.

4.1 Students understand basic suffixes used to denote female jobs in ancient Rome and observe the same suffixes in use in English.

4.2 Students compare the Roman attitudes toward women's roles in the ancient economy with those toward women today.

5.2 Students recognize from their study of women's roles in the Roman economy that subordination and dependence on men have been an integral feature of economies from antiquity to the present. At the same time, they compare issues of work and attitudes toward women's bodies in ancient Rome with similar issues in modern cultures.

Prose Composition

1. *Purpose/Level*

Elementary through intermediate level students will revise the gender stereotyping in the readings in their textbooks at the same time that they develop prose composition skills.

2. *Materials*

Drill sentences or passages from Latin readings in elementary through intermediate textbooks.

3. *Guidelines/Model*

Select a passage or sentences suitable for "cross-dressing." An assignment from the *Oxford Latin Course* (OLC), part 1 (Balme and Morwood), might look like the following:

After reading "Flaccus Quintum laudat" (*OLC* 20), revise the story by reversing the activities of Horatia and Quintus, and Scintilla and Flaccus. So, for instance,

Quintus domum redit et Scintillam salutat; Argum in hortum ducit et Horatiam vocat. Horatia in hortum festinat; laeta est quod Quintus adest. Flaccus ab agro redit; fessus est; in casa sedet et quiescit. Mox "Quintus" inquit "puer bonus est. in agro manet et me iuvat." Scintilla laeta est, quod Flaccus puerum laudat. cenam celeriter parat.

might become

Horatia domum redit et Scintillam salutat; Argum in hortum ducit et Quintum vocat. Quintus in hortum festinat; laetus est quod Horatia adest. Flaccus ab agro redit; fessus est; in casa sedet et quiescit. mox "Horatia" inquit "puella bona est. in agro manet et me iuvat." Scintilla laeta est, quod Flaccus puellam laudat. cenam celeriter parat.

or

Horatia domum redit et Flaccum salutat; Argum in hortum ducit et Quintum vocat. Quintus in hortum festinat; laetus est quod Horatia adest. Scintilla ab agro redit; fessa est; in casa sedet et quiescit. mox "Horatia" inquit "puella bona est. in agro manet et me iuvat." Flaccus laetus est, quod Scintilla puellam laudat. cenam celeriter parat.

An assignment from the *Oxford Latin Course*, part 2, might look as follows: Chapter 24 introduces the comparison of adjectives. Rewrite (and gender-bend!) the following sentences, by substituting the word in parentheses for the underlined word, and making other changes as necessary. For example:

nullum *virum* cognovi meliorem quam te. (mulier)
nullam mulierem cognovi meliorem quam te.

Achilles erat fortissimus *Graecorum*. (Boudica; Britannae)
Boudica erat fortissima Britannarum.

4. Source

Original; see Harwood (31) and Hoover (60) for additional ways to use composition.

5. Reflection on Standards

1.1 Students read each other's compositions revising stereotypes about gender roles.

1.2 Students "rewrite" stories from their textbook in order to revise gender stereotyping in their textbooks.

2.1 Students understand the roles of women and men in ancient Rome.

4.2 Students compare the roles of women and men in ancient Rome with the modern world through analysis and discussion of each other's compositions.

5.1 Students present and exchange information about the roles of women in ancient Rome through discussion of their compositions.

5.2 Students compare issues of stereotypical gender roles that reveal cultural differences between the ancient world and modern cultures.

Of Participles and Warrior Women: Camilla

1. *Purpose/Level*

This exercise is based on the sequence in which participles are introduced in part 2 of the *Oxford Latin Course* (Balme and Morwood) and may be adapted for use with other intermediate level textbooks. Students will review present participles (*OLC*, chapter 26), preview the ablative absolute (*OLC*, chapter 37), and practice reading the perfect passive participle (*OLC*, chapter 30) in the context of learning about Vergil's Camilla.

Prior to doing the exercise, students will read English translations of relevant selections from the *Aeneid* that provide narrative context. Secondary readings will provide social/historical context. Individual students may be asked to report on supplementary readings.

2. *Materials*

Selections from *Aeneid*, books 7 and 11 (in English translation) related to Camilla. Selected reference readings: Entries on Camilla in *Oxford Classical Dictionary* (Hornblower and Spawforth) and Salmonson.

Selected secondary source readings: Fantham et al. 128–35.

Quotations from *Aeneid* 7 and 11 related to Camilla and using participles. Instructors will provide vocabulary and notes as needed.

a. hos super advenit Volsca de gente Camilla
   agmen *agens* equitum et *florentis* aere catervas
   bellatrix . . . (*Aeneid* 7.803–5)

b. turbaque miratur matrum et prospectat *euntem*
   attonitis *inhians* animis . . . (7.813–4)

c.   . . . (gerit) ipsa pharetram
   et pastoralem *praefixa* cuspide myrtum. (7.816–7)

d.   . . . matrisque vocavit
   nomine Casmillae *mutata* parte Camillam. (11.542–3)

e. ipse sinu prae se *portans* iuga longa petebat
   solorum nemorum . . . (11.544–5)

f. dixit, et *adducto* contortum hastile lacerto
   immitit: sonuere undae, rapidum super amnem
   infelix fugit in iaculo *stridente* Camilla. (11. 561–3)

g. at medias inter caedes exsultat Amazon
   unum *exserta* latus pugnae, pharetrata Camilla. (11.648–9)

h. caeca sequebatur totumque incauta per agmen
   femineo praedae et spoliorum ardebat amore . . . (11.781–2)

i.   nihil ipsa nec aurae
nec sonitus memor aut *venientis* ab aethere teli
hasta sub *exsertam* donec *perlata* papillam
haesit virgineumque alte bibit *acta* cruorem. (11.801–4)

j.   simul his dictis linquebat habenas
ad terram non sponte *fluens.* tum frigida toto
paulatim exsolvit se corpore, lentaque colla
et *captum* leto posuit caput, arma *relinquens,*
vitaque cum gemitu fugit *indignata* sub umbras. (11.827–31)

3. Guidelines/Model

Students will read primary (in English translation), reference, and secondary texts prior to class and peruse quotations from *Aeneid* 7 and 11. In addition, they will provide principal parts and English meanings for all verbs from which the underlined participles are formed.

After discussing readings in class, each of several small groups (three or four students) will translate two or three passages from the *Aeneid*, paying close attention to the use of participles.

Groups will present their translations, comment on the use and translation of participle(s), and discuss the significance of the passage to the study of warrior women.

4. Source

Original.

Of Participles and Warrior Women: Boudica

1. Purpose/Level

Same as for Camilla.

2. Materials

Selections from Tacitus: *Agricola* 14.4–16.2 and *Annales*, Book 14.29–39 (in translation).

Selected reference readings: entries on Boudica (Boudicca, Boadicea) in *Oxford Classical Dictionary* (Hornblower and Spawforth) and Salmonson.

Selected secondary readings: Fraser 43–57 and 58–76; Dudley and Webster 143.

Selections from Tacitus (in Latin) in which "Boudicca" appears:

a. His atque talibus in vicem instincti, Boudicca generis regii femina duce (neque enim sexum in imperiis discernunt) sumpsere universi bellum . . . (*Agricola* 16.1.1)

b. Boudicca curru filias prae se vehens, ut quamque nationem acces-
serat, solitum quidem Britannis feminarum ductu bellare testabatur,
sed tunc non ut tantis maioribus ortam regnum verberibus corpus,
contrectatam filiarum pudicitiam ulcisci. (*Annales* 14.35)

c. quippe sunt qui paulo minus quam octoginta milia Britannorum
cecidisse tradant, militum quadringentis ferme interfectis nec
multo amplius vulneratis. Boudicca vitam veneno finivit. (*Annales*
14.37.12)

3. Guidelines/Model

After discussing in class primary, reference, and secondary readings, students
will peruse the Tacitus passages in which the name "Boudicca" appears. Since
the Latin is perhaps a bit advanced for comprehension at the intermediate level,
students will read the passages several times and identify participial forms. Then
they will provide principal parts and English meanings for verbs from which
all participles are formed. They will translate passages with instructor's assistance. They will discuss the relevance of these passages to the study of warrior
women.

4. Supplementary Readings and Visual Materials

Chicago; Constantimides; duBois; Dudley and Webster; Fantham et al. 128–35;
Fraser; Salmonson; Smiles; Webster; Winterbottom.

5. Source

Original (with some inspiration from Richlin 1992).

6. Reflection on Standards

1.1 Students read and understand brief passages from Vergil's *Aeneid* or Tacitus's
Annals that feature participles.

2.1 Students demonstrate a knowledge of warrior women, gained in part
from the texts they read, and relate that knowledge to an understanding
of Roman perspectives on warrior women.

3.2 Students acquire information about warrior women in Roman mythology
and history through the texts they read.

4.2 Students compare Roman models of strong women who are leaders with
modern examples.

5.2 Students recognize that Amazon women have been a part of society from
antiquity to the present.

Notes

1. Fowler, Habinek, Hallett 1983, 1993, Kennedy, McManus, Ong 1959, 1960, and Skinner provide critical perspectives on how Latin has circulated historically and on the role of gender in Latin education. While none of these authors presents a blueprint for revising Latin education according to contemporary epistemic and demographic changes, Skinner in particular recognizes the challenges of these changes: "The strategies developed for instructing a small, homogeneous and generally docile group of well-to-do male youths cannot be extended to teaching the pluralistic mix of students we face nowadays, students of two sexes and diverse races, religions, ages, degrees of educational preparation and levels of aspiration, who will be called upon to perform many different functions in society" (207).

2. Allan, Garrett, Hallett 1983, Harwood, Hoover, Ronnick, and Strange present critiques of the gender stereotyping in some of the more widely used elementary Latin textbooks and offer some suggestions for making the classroom more inclusive. They are building on the pioneering work in modern languages of Stern, Rochette-Ozzello, Wright, and Schmitz. For a summary of current research on gender and foreign language teaching, see Chavez.

3. See Snyder's (141–51) discussion and English translation of selected passages of Egeria's "Travel Memoirs." Weber's commentary may be adapted for an introductory class and perhaps used in conjunction with the *Oxford Latin Course* (Balme and Morwood) readings on the adventures of Odysseus and Aeneas. Vierow and Gold made me especially aware of these possibilities. Gold's subsequent essay (1997) provides historical and literary context(s) useful for teaching Hrotswitha's dramas, epics, and legends. Robin's translation of the letters of Laura Cereta offers an excellent starting point for considering works by early modern women to adapt for the Latin classroom. This volume is just one in an entire series entitled "The Other Voice in Early Modern Europe" published by the University of Chicago Press. Finally, for other women writing in Latin, see the Medieval Women Writers website (www.owu.edu/~o5medww/index.html) and Churchill et al.

4. As a specific example of such feminist revision, elementary readings may be developed on the topic of Roman women in myth and legend. Vergil and Livy alone present numerous possibilities: Book 1 of *Ab Urbe Condita* provides portrayals of Rhea Silvia, Laurentia, the Sabine women, Tarpeia, Tullia, and Lucretia; in the *Aeneid*, we might look beyond the more obvious female characters (e.g., Creusa, Dido, Juno, and Venus) to Helen, Andromache, Camilla, Anna, Amata, Allecto, Lavinia, and communities of women, such as the women who depart with Aeneas from Troy. Keith 1994 on the Italian women of book 7 identified passages and proposed a series of questions related to the dynamics of gender in the *Aeneid*. See now Keith 2000.

5. Secondary readings that incorporate feminist scholarship and materials on women in antiquity also provide a means of revising the elementary Latin curriculum. Such texts, however, need to be carefully selected and supplemented. In my recent experience, I recommended Tingay's *These Were the Romans* as a source of supplementary readings for beginning Latin students. Unfortunately, this book ignores relevant information on women. So, for instance, in its narration of the founding of Rome (3), neither Rhea Silvia nor Laurentia is mentioned. Chapter titles such as "Men and the Land" and "Gods and Man" conspicuously indicate the exclusion of women, and the chapter on "Growing Up" doesn't mention female experience at all. "Everyday Life," however, includes a discussion of women's clothing, cosmetics, and hairstyles. These examples illustrate clearly the extent to which gender biases of contemporary authors, critics, scholars, editors, commentators, and translators may reinforce, intensify, and distort the gender biases of ancient Roman culture(s), much as they disregard the contributions of feminist research methods and scholarship on women in antiquity.

6. This content-based approach is similar to the study of "language across the disciplines," which has been adopted in many modern foreign language programs. I suggest using gender in antiquity, women in antiquity, or the uses of Latin historically by and in relation to women as the "content"—the bases for reading and study—of elementary through intermediate Latin courses. In this way, it also provides the basis of fulfilling goal 3 of the *Standards of Classical Language Learning*: Connect with other disciplines and expand knowledge.

7. E.g., the Women's Classical Caucus Panel, "Transforming Texts on the Secondary and College Levels: How are Multicultural and Women's Topics Included," Eileen Mooney Strange and Bella Vivante, organizers, section 38 at the annual meeting of the American Philological Association, Philadelphia, PA, January 5, 2002. See also Raia et al.

Works Cited

Allan, Charlayne D. 1986. "Images of Women in Introductory Latin Texts: Problems and Alternatives." *Classical Outlook* 64: 1–4.

American Association of University Women (AAUW). 1995. *How Schools Shortchange Girls: The AAUW Report: A Study of Major Findings on Girls in Education*. Washington, D.C.: AAUW Educational Foundation.

Balme, Maurice, and James Morwood. 1996. *Oxford Latin Course*. 2nd ed. New York: Oxford University Press.

Brush, Peter C., and Gilbert Lawall. 2000. *Ecce Romani*. 3rd ed. Glenview, IL: Prentice Hall.

Cameron, Deborah. 1989. "'Released into Language': The Study of Language Outside and Inside Academic Institutions." In Ann Thompson and Helen Wilcox, eds., *Teaching Women: Feminism and English Studies*. New York: St. Martin's Press, 5–14.

Chavez, Monika. 2001. *Gender in the Language Classroom*. Boston: McGraw-Hill.

Chicago, Judy. 1979. *The Dinner Party: A Symbol of Our Heritage*. Garden City, NJ: Doubleday.

Chodorow, Nancy. 1978. *The Reproduction of Mothering: Psychoanalysis and the Sociology of Gender*. Berkeley: University of California Press.

Churchill, Laurie J., ed. *Medieval Women Writers*. The Five Colleges of Ohio Consortium. Online. Available at www.owu.edu/~o5medww/index.html.

Churchill, Laurie J., Phyllis Rugg Brown, and Jane E. Jeffrey, eds. 2002. *Women Writing in Latin: From Roman Antiquity to Early Modern Europe*. 3 vols. New York: Routledge.

Constantimides, Elizabeth. 1981. "Amazons and Other Female Warriors." *Classical Outlook* 59: 3–6.

duBois, Page. 1982. *Centaurs and Amazons: Women and the Pre-History of the Great Chain of Being*. Ann Arbor: University of Michigan Press.

Dudley, Donald, and Graham Webster. 1962. *The Rebellion of Boudica*. New York: Barnes and Noble.

Fantham, Elaine, Helene Peet Foley. Natalie Boymel Kampen, Sarah B. Pomevoy, and H. A. Shapiro, eds. 1994. *Women in the Classical World*. New York: Oxford University Press.

Fowler, R. 1983. "'On Not Knowing Greek': The Classics and the Woman of Letters." *Classical Journal* 78: 337–49.

Fraser, Antonia. 1989. *The Warrior Queens*. New York: Knopf.

Freire, Paolo. 1972. *Pedagogy of the Oppressed*. Hammondsworth, UK: Penguin.

Garrett, Alice. "Teaching Latin with a Feminist Consciousness." Classics Technology Center. Available at ablemedia.com/ctcweb/netshots/lat101garrett1.html.

Gilligan, Carol. 1982. *In a Different Voice: A Study of Women's Construction and Resolution of Moral Problems.* Cambridge, MA: Harvard University Press.

Glare, P. G. W. 1982. *Oxford Latin Dictionary.* Oxford: Oxford University Press.

Gold, Barbara. 1992. "'Hrotsvita Writes Herself': Clamor Validus Gandeshemensis." Paper presented at the annual meeting of the Classical Association of the Mid-Western States, Austin, TX, April.

———. 1997. "Hrotswitha Writes Herself: *Clamor Validus Gandeshemensis.*" In Barbara K. Gold, Paul Allen Miller, and Charles Platter, eds., *Sex and Gender in Medieval and Renaissance Texts: The Latin Tradition.* Albany: State University of New York Press, 41–70.

Grossman, H., and S. Grossman. 1994. *Gender Issues in Education.* Boston: Allyn and Bacon.

Habinek, Thomas N. 1992. "Grecian Wonders and Roman Woe." In G. Karl Galinsky, ed., *The Interpretation of Roman Poetry: Empiricism or Hermeneutics?* New York: Peter Lang, 227–42.

Hall, Roberta. 1982. *The Classroom Climate: A Chilly One for Women.* Project on the Status and Education of Women. Washington, D.C.: Association of American Colleges.

Hall, Roberta M., and Bernice R. Sandler. 1984. "Out of the Classroom: A Chilly Climate for Women?" Washington, D.C.: Association of American Colleges.

Hallett, Judith P. 1983. *Classics and Women's Studies.* Working paper no. 119. Wellesley, MA: Wellesley College Center for Research on Women.

———. 1993. "Feminist Theory, Historical Periods, Literary Canons, and the Study of Greco-Roman Antiquity." In Nancy Rabinowitz and Amy Richlin, eds., *Feminist Theory and the Classics.* New York: Routledge, 44–72.

Hannan, MaryAnne. 1995. "The Education of Women in the Classical Languages." In Jane Donawerth, Judith Hallett, and Adele Seeff, eds., *Sappho and Lady Mary Wroth: Integrating Women Writers of Classical Antiquity and the English Renaissance into the College Curriculum.* College Park: Center for Renaissance and Baroque Studies, University of Maryland, 17–9.

Harwood, Nancy. 1992. "Writing Women into Textbooks." *Feminist Teacher* 6, 3: 16–7, 31.

hooks, bell. 1989. *Talking Back: Thinking Feminist/Thinking Black.* Boston: South End Press.

———. 1994. *Teaching to Transgress: Education as the Practice of Freedom.* New York: Routledge.

Hoover, Polly. 2000. "Contextual Learning and Latin Language Textbooks." *Classical World* 94: 56–60.

Hornblower, Simon, and Antony Spawforth, eds. 1996. *The Oxford Classical Dictionary.* 3rd ed. Oxford: Oxford University Press.

Joshel, Sandra R. 1992. *Work, Identity, and Legal Status at Rome: A Study of Occupational Inscriptions.* Norman: University of Oklahoma Press.

Kampen, Natalie. 1982. "Social Status and Gender in Roman Art: The Case of the Saleswoman." In Norma Broude and Mary D. Garrard, eds., *Feminism and Art History.* New York: Harper and Row, 63–77.

Keith, A. M. 2000. *Engendering Rome: Women in Latin Epic.* Cambridge, UK: Cambridge University Press.

Kelly (Kelly-Godol), Joan. 1977. "Did Women Have a Renaissance?" In Renate Bridenthal and Claudia Koonz, eds., *Becoming Visible: Women in European History.* Boston: Houghton Mifflin, 137–64.

Kennedy, George A. 1987. "The History of Latin Education." In Matthew S. Santirocco, ed., *Latinitas: The Tradition and Teaching of Latin.* Special issue of *Helios* 14, 1: 7–16.

Kenway, Jane, and Helen Modra. 1992. "Feminist Pedagogy and Emancipatory Possibilities." In Carmen Luke and Jennifer Gore, eds., *Feminisms and Critical Pedagogy*. New York: Routledge, 138–66.

Klein, Susan Shurberg. 1992. *Sex Equity and Sexuality in Education*. Albany: State University of New York Press.

LaFleur, Richard A., ed. 1987. *The Teaching of Latin in American Schools: A Profession in Crisis*. Chico, CA: Scholars Press.

Luschnig, C. A. E., and Ann Raia, eds. *De Feminis Romanis. Latin Readings on Roman Women*. Diotima: Materials for the Study of Women and Gender in the Ancient World. Online. Available at www.stoa.org/diotima/dfr/.

Mackail, J. W. 1925. "The Place of Greek and Latin in Human Life." In *Classical Studies*. London: J. Murray, 1–16.

Maher, Frances. 1985. "Classroom Pedagogy and the New Scholarship on Women." In Margo Culley and Catherine Portugues, eds., *Gendered Subjects: The Dynamics of Feminist Teaching*. Boston: Routledge and Kegan Paul. 29–48.

———. 1987. "Toward a Richer Theory of Feminist Pedagogy: A Comparison of 'Liberation' and 'Gender' Models for Teaching and Learning." *Journal of Education* 169, 3: 91–100.

Maher, Frances A., and Mary Kay Thompson Tetreault. 2001. *The Feminist Classroom: Dynamics of Gender, Race, and Privilege*. Expanded ed. Lanham, MD: Rowman and Littlefield.

McClure, Laura. 2000. "Feminist Pedagogy and the Classics." Introduction to Special Section on Feminist Pedagogy. *Classical World* 94: 53–5.

McCormick, Theresa M. 1994. *Creating the Nonsexist Classroom: A Multicultural Approach*. New York: Teachers College Press.

McManus, Barbara. 1997. *Classics and Feminism: Gendering the Classics*. New York: Twayne.

Ong, Walter J. 1959. "Latin Language Study as a Renaissance Puberty Rite." *Studies in Philology* 56: 103–24.

———. 1960. "Latin and the Social Fabric." *Yale Review* 50, 1: 18–31.

Oxford, Rebecca. 1990. *Language Learning Strategies: What Every Teacher Should Know*. Boston: Heinle and Heinle.

Pascal, Paul, ed. 1985. *Hrotsvitha's Dulcitius and Paphnutius*. Bryn Mawr Commentaries. Indianapolis: Hackett.

Perun, Pamela J., ed. 1982. *The Undergraduate Woman: Issues in Educational Equity*. Wellesley College: Center for Research on Women. Lexington, MA: Lexington Books.

Pope, Stephanie. 2001. *Cambridge Latin Course Unit 1*. 4th ed. New York: Cambridge University Press.

Raia, Ann, Cecelia Luschnig, and Judith Lynn Sebasta. 2005. *The Worlds of Roman Women: A Latin Reader*. Newburyport, MA: focus Publishing.

Reinhold, Meyer. 1987. "The Latin Tradition in the U.S." In Matthew S. Santirocco, ed., *Latinitas: The Tradition and Teaching of Latin*. Special issue of *Helios* 14: 123–39.

Richlin, Amy. 1989. "'Is Classics Dead?' The 1988 Women's Classical Caucus Report." In Phyllis Culham and Lowell Edmunds, eds., *Classics: A Discipline and Profession in Crisis?* Lanham, MD: University Press of America, 51–65.

———. 1992. "Barbarian Queens." Paper presented at the annual meeting of the Philological Association of the Pacific Coast, San Diego, CA, November.

———. 1993. "The Ethnographer's Dilemma and the Dream of a Lost Golden Age." In Nancy Sorkin Rabinowitz and Amy Richlin, eds., *Feminist Theory and the Classics*. New York: Routledge, 272–303.

———. 1997. "Pliny's Brassiere: Roman Medicine and the Female Body." In Judith P. Hallett and Marilyn B. Skinner, eds., *Roman Sexualities*. Princeton: Princeton University Press, 197–220.

Rifkin, Benjamin, et al. 1998. "Gender Representation in Foreign Language Textbooks: A Case Study of Textbooks in Russian." *Modern Language Journal* 82: 217–36.

Robin, Diana, trans. 1997. *The Collected Letters of a Renaissance Feminist*. Chicago: University of Chicago Press.

Rochette-Ozzello, Yvonne. 1980. "Women's Studies and Foreign Language Teaching: A New Alliance." In Maurice W. Conner, ed., *New Frontiers in Foreign Language Education: Selected Papers from the 1980 Central States Conference*. Skokie, IL: National Textbook, 35–48.

Ronnick, Michele. 1995. "Writing Women Out of Textbooks: *The Oxford Latin Course*." *Women's Classical Caucus Newsletter* 23: 22–8.

Sadker, Myra, and David Sadker. 1990. "Confronting Sexism in the College Classroom." In Susan L. Gabriel and Isaiah Smithson, eds., *Gender in the Classroom: Power and Pedagogy*. Urbana: University of Illinois Press, 176–87.

Salmonson, Jessica Amanda. 1991. *Encyclopedia of Amazons: Women Warriors from Antiquity to the Modern Era*. New York: Paragon House.

Santirocco, Matthew S. 1987. "Latin as a Scholarly Discipline." In Matthew S. Santirocco, ed., *Latinitas: The Tradition and Teaching of Latin*. Special issue of *Helios* 14: 17–31.

Schmitz, Betty. 1985. *Integrating Women's Studies into the Curriculum: A Guide and Bibliography*. Old Westbury, NY: Feminist Press.

Skinner, Marilyn B. 1989. "Expecting the Barbarians: Feminism, Nostalgia, and the 'Epistemic Shift' in Classical Studies." In Phyllis Culham and Lowell Edmunds, eds., *Classics: A Discipline and Profession in Crisis?* Lanham, MD: University Press of America, 199–210.

Smiles, Sam. 1994. *The Image of Antiquity: Ancient Britain and the Romantic Imagination*. New Haven, CT: Yale University Press.

Snyder, Jane McIntosh. 1989. *The Woman and the Lyre: Women Writers in Classical Greece and Rome*. Carbondale: Southern Illinois University Press.

Stern, Rhoda H. 1976. "Review Article: Sexism in Foreign Language Textbooks." *Foreign Language Annals* 9: 294–9.

Strange, Eileen Mooney. 2000. "Weaving a Tapestry of Knowledge: A Collaborative Approach to the *Somnium Scipionis*." *Classical World* 94: 61–6.

Tingay, G. I. F., and J. Badcock. 1989. *These Were the Romans*. 2nd ed. Cheltenham, UK: Thornes and Hulton.

Ullman, B. L., Berthold Lewis, and Albert I. Suskin. 2002. *Latin for Americans: First Level, Student Edition*. 9th ed. New York: Glencoe/McGraw-Hill.

Vierow, Heidi. 1992. "Feminine and Masculine Voices in the Passion of Saints Perpetua and Felicitas." Paper presented at the conference on Feminist Theory and Classics, Cincinnati, OH, November.

Weber, Clifford, ed. 1994. *Itinerari Egeriae*. Bryn Mawr Commentaries. Indianapolis, IN: Hackett.

Webster, Graham. 1978. *The British Revolt against Rome A.D. 60*. Totowa, NJ: Rowman and Littlefield.

Weiler, Kathleen. 1988. *Women Teaching for Change: Gender, Class and Power*. South Hadley, MA: Bergin and Garvey.

———. 2001. "Rereading Paolo Freire." In Kathleen Weiler, ed., *Feminist Engagements: Reading, Resisting, and Revisioning Male Theorists in Education and Cultural Studies*. New York: Routledge, 67–88.

Wheelock, Frederic M., and Richard LaFleur. 2000. *Wheelock's Latin*. 6th ed. New York: HarperResource.

Will, Elizabeth Lyding. 1979. "Women in Pompeii." *Archaeology* 32, 5: 34–43.

Winterbottom, Michael, tr. and ed. 1978. *Gildas: The Ruin of Britain and Other Works*. Totowa, NJ: Rowman and Littlefield.

Wright, Barbara Drygulski. 1983. "Feminist Transformation of Foreign Language Instruction: Progress and Challenges." Working paper no. 117. Wellesley, MA: Wellesley College Center for Research on Women.

"The Yale Report of 1828." 1961. In Richard Hofstadter and William Smith, eds., *American Higher Education: A Documentary History*. Vol. 1. Chicago: University of Chicago, 275–91.

PART III

Focus on the Language

CHAPTER 6

Reading Latin Efficiently and the Need for Cognitive Strategies

Daniel V. McCaffrey

As you skim over this paragraph, trying to decide whether or not to read the whole chapter, you are not consciously aware of all the mental processes you are using to read it. For example, without looking back at the last sentence or running over the words in your mind, you might find it hard to recall the main verb or whether the sentence contained a relative clause. Many of the workings of language are buried so deep in our minds that psycholinguists can discover them only with clever experimental sentences and electronic equipment recording reaction times in milliseconds. "Participants in psycholinguistic experiments, for example, cannot self-report on how syntactic and semantic information come together to produce meaning because the process is normally entirely unconscious" (Ainsworth-Darnell et al. 128).

But what about Latin? In this chapter we will try to discover how the Romans read their language. Our hope is that by reading in a manner closer to that of the Romans, we may be able to read Latin more easily and fluently, and that we can then pass on our improved skills to our students.

Since there are no more truly native readers of Latin, we cannot run experiments to get direct access to the mind of Latin. We have only a few of the texts they read. These texts, however, are reflections of the minds of their authors and of the authors' understanding of how they would be read. Careful examination of the texts can reveal much about Latin mental processes because, as Philip Baldi wrote, "sentences and other linguistic units must be structured in such a way that they are analyzable and decodable by hearers. These perceptual constraints are sensitive to the communicative needs of speakers and hearers" (Baldi 13). If Latin authors wanted to be understood, they could not use the full freedom granted them by the language's formal grammar. They had to avoid certain extreme word-order practices that, though grammatically legal, would hinder their readers' understanding. So while poets might challenge their readers, they were forced to respect the limits on their readers' processing capacities. These limits were even more critical in those genres, including oratory and poetry, that were intended for listening rather than reading, because backtracking and looking ahead were limited or impossible.

This chapter, however, will concentrate on reading because it remains the chief focus of most Latin teaching. As the *Standards for Classical Language Learning* emphasizes, "reading is the first standard and the key to communicating with the ancient world" (Gascoyne et al. 7). There are dissenting voices: Daniel Carpenter has recently written that making reading our primary objective "no longer meets the needs of our students and teachers" (Carpenter 391). He calls for a new approach that would "hone students' analytical skills if a method emphasizing grammar and syntax is used" (Carpenter 395). Lee Pearcy and Jeffrey Wills have respectively advocated the writing and speaking of Latin (Pearcy; Wills). Even Standard 1.2 calls for students to "use orally, listen to and write Latin or Greek" but qualifies these skills "as part of the language learning process" (Gascoyne et al. 8). Thus they are means to the end of learning the Latin language.

The following pages will apply the discoveries of the cognitive sciences to reading Latin. I will start with research about reading in general and about second-language reading in particular. The second section will apply those findings to the situation of Latin readers. The third section will focus on one particular Latin reading situation: "How and when did a Roman decide whether a noun like *equites* was the subject or object of its clause?" The final section will suggest practical methods and exercises to help students learn the necessary strategies and internalize them into their own Latin reading. It is hoped that the reading techniques described here will prove useful and necessary for students of all ages. They will, of course, have to be adapted to the needs of the particular students and to the structure of the curriculum being implemented.

Review of Reading Research

Four Ways of Reading

While most Latin curricula seek to give students a reading knowledge of Latin, they are not explicit about the kind of reading they will teach. Psychological research has shown that there are different ways of reading that we choose according to the text we are reading and our purpose in reading it. Grellet (4) has identified four different ways of reading: skimming, scanning, extensive reading, and intensive reading.

1. When we *skim* a text, we read it over quickly, trying to get the gist of it without worrying too much about the particulars. This is probably the method of reading which we first apply to a new Latin textbook. We might skim over a few pages to get an impression of the approach, or the balance of grammatical and cultural material incorporated into the readings, and so on.

2. When we *scan* a text, we read it over quickly to obtain a particular bit of information. If we wanted to find the story of Daphne and Apollo in an unannotated text of Ovid, we might scan the text until one of the names "leapt off the page" at us.

3. When we read *extensively*, we read a relatively large amount of text efficiently and with good comprehension. This is the approach we probably take to our pleasure reading: be it an English novel, Virgil or Cicero.

4. *Intensive* reading seeks to uncover the inner workings of a text: its grammar, its formal and logical structure, its artistic and rhetorical techniques, and so on. This is the way we read a text we are preparing to teach in class.

The goal of most elementary and intermediate Latin classes is to enable students to read fluently or extensively a genuine Latin literary text of moderate difficulty. These days, it is a matter of some hope that most high school students will be able to read English fluently. More intensive reading methods may well be reserved for AP language and literature courses. Students entering college may be expected to read English fluently and will be introduced to intensive reading during their first year. It is, therefore, not reasonable to expect students to read Latin at a higher level than they do English. Students should not concentrate on analytical, close reading in Latin at least until AP classes or their first classes in a college major. It is important to be explicit about the mode of reading chosen as a primary educational goal, because different modes of reading require different emphases in instruction.

Two Kinds of Reading Processes

After a lengthy period of debate, researchers are coming to a consensus that reading involves the efficient coordination of two kinds of mental processes, characterized as bottom-up versus top-down processes (see Bernhardt for details). *Bottom-up processes* decode the marks on the page into a mental representation of the author's intended meaning. *Top-down processes* use the preexisting contents of the reader's mind to construct a new idea in response to the words sampled on the page. Carrell, Devine, and Eskey and Swaffar, Arens, and Byrnes both discuss models that integrate these processes.

The chief bottom-up processes, which extract meaning from the text, perform two tasks: the decoding of the word and phrases, and the mental representation of their meaning.

1. The first bottom-up process is *decoding*. It begins with letter and word recognition and culminates in what most Latin teachers call parsing: the reader identifies the significant morphological signals in each successive word and decides what syntactic function to give that word in the present sentence.[1]

2. The second bottom-up process, the *mental representation* of the intended meaning, transforms the morphological signals and syntactical relationships into a form the mind understands.[2] Latin teachers have developed several different techniques to represent the developing meaning of a Latin sentence.[3] In whatever form, the students will have to learn to develop a mental representation of the meaning of a Latin sentence in its original order.

The top-down process *integrates* the meaning of the sentence with the reader's prior knowledge. The integration process starts from the reader's understanding of the current status of the text, common sense, knowledge of the real world and of Roman culture, expectations of a coherent idea structure, and awareness of the conventions of the genre. The top-down process then combines this view of the world with the emerging meaning of the sentence (for an overview see Carroll, ch. 7; for a more detailed account, see Smith, ch. 1).

These reading processes are used in different ways by each of the reading methods. Researchers in second-language (L2) learning have shown that "because different factors play different roles in different types of L2 reading comprehension, reading purposes must be clearly defined, and teaching must be appropriately adapted" (Taillefer 475). While readers who are skimming texts need some decoding skill to recognize the basic structure of the text, they need a still greater facility at integrating the text with their background knowledge so as to grasp the gist of the passage. To scan a text for a particular bit of information requires mostly decoding skill to recognize the key word or words in any appropriate forms.

Extensive reading deserves special attention as the chief goal of our instruction. To read fluently is to concentrate on the integrating processes of reading. Much of the pleasure in reading comes from comparing and contrasting our previous knowledge and expectations with the world or worldview developed by the author.

In extensive reading, the bottom-up processes are so efficient that the fluent reader will be able to do most of the decoding automatically, that is, without conscious attention: "Good readers know the language: They can decode, with occasional exceptions, both the lexical units and syntactic structures they encounter in texts . . . by a kind of automatic identification that requires no conscious cognitive effort" (Eskey 94); and "readers who do not have automatic processing are doomed to fretful decoding with little effort left over for trying to understand a message" (Bernhardt 76). The latter quotation is a painfully apt description of some students' struggle with their first real Latin author. Efficient reading strategies are important in extensive reading because the pleasure of reading is quickly lost if we constantly need to reread or jump around a sentence just to sort out its grammatical structure.

Intensive reading seeks to bring to conscious attention all aspects of the author/reader interaction: the grammatical, artistic, and rhetorical techniques of the author and the personal, cultural, and ideological predispositions and responses of the reader. Intensive readers, therefore, can dispense almost entirely with processing strategies, since the amount of time spent on reading is of little consequence. They must, on the other hand, possess the highest level of skill in all the other reading processes.

This analysis has important consequences for the way we teach Latin. Since we want the students coming out of our elementary classes to be able to read fluently, we should ensure they have mastered the basics, teach them the strategies, and give them the practice that will enable them to read quickly, without having to pay conscious attention to grammar. When we want them to read analytically, we will teach them to read slowly and with conscious attention to every nuance of technique and meaning.

Reading Processes in Latin

Many of the reading processes just described can be transferred from English right into Latin. This is particularly true of the top-down processes. In fact, making the students aware of their English repertoire of reading techniques can also make some contribution to *Standards for Classical Language Learning*, 4.1: "Students recognize and use elements of the Latin and Greek language to increase knowledge of their own language" (Gascoyne et al. 13). If students are going to use their own top-down processing skills, they must first be convinced that Latin texts have real meaning. The more modern reading-first books do a particularly good job of this. While Latin readers will need a special knowledge base of Roman cultural and historical background and a special set of literary expectations, the top-down processes themselves are not very different in Latin from those used in English. The bottom-up processes, on the other hand, must be different both because of our students' learning environment in dealing with a dead language and because of the special nature of Latin.

Decoding in Latin

The chief question about the decoding process is How much grammar must students know in order to read Latin? In a living language, it is possible and even common to read without a conscious knowledge of the grammatical rules. The Romans themselves got along perfectly well without having a very formal understanding of the system of Latin grammar. It was only in the first century B.C.E. that the grammarian Varro, for example, made the crucial conceptual breakthroughs that led to the identification of the five noun declensions so familiar to us. The audiences of Plautus and Terence fully comprehended and enjoyed their plays without knowing the noun paradigms. The same principle applies to individuals as well as nations: conscious knowledge about grammar often comes years after practical mastery of the language itself. Modern students, like their Roman predecessors, learn to speak their native language as children and generally do not acquire a grammatical metalanguage until years later in school. They become truly objective about their native language only when they learn a foreign language.

Since modern students of Latin cannot be immersed in a Latin-speaking culture, they need to master the basics of grammar for all methods of reading. Only then can the grammatical decoding go on with little or no conscious effort. Vocabulary, morphology and syntax have always been the forte of Latin teaching. Particular attention must be paid to those aspects of Latin that are most different from English and are most important for the correct understanding of Latin (e.g., verb and noun morphology, the use of cases, etc.). Crucial topics on which English and Latin agree should be pointed out and used (e.g., the case of personal pronouns, the use of prepositions.). Topics of Latin grammar that are not important for the simple reading of Latin should be mentioned but not stressed (e.g., the Latin sequence of subjunctive tenses).

Latin Reading Strategies

A good grasp of the basics of grammar and of English meaning, however, does not guarantee that students can read Latin fluently. Anyone who has struggled to take them from textbook Latin to real Latin can attest to this fact. Psycholinguistics supplies an explanation: grammatical decoding must be filtered by appropriate cognitive strategies in order to allow the efficient development of a mental representation of the sentence's meaning. Barnett refers to strategies as "the problem solving techniques readers employ to get meaning from a text" (Barnett 36). Phillips says "good readers are good guessers and good problem-solvers" and "since maturing readers decode more than fluent ones, an efficient way to proceed is essential" (Phillips 292). Readers must have strategies that permit them to construct a mental picture of the meaning quickly and efficiently as a sentence develops. Such strategies generally seek to reduce uncertainty about the present state of the sentence and make predictions about the probable meaning and form of its completion (Smith 16–9). Only then can real reading comprehension take place. As Alice Omaggio Hadley puts it, "comprehensive processes and strategies need to be taught actively in second language classrooms" (Omaggio Hadley 163). Keiko Koda expands the idea: "L2 learners . . . will benefit from cognitive strategy instruction and from corresponding exercises designed to help them improve their use of linguistic knowledge during reading comprehension" (Koda 498).

Because there are no native speakers or readers of Latin, we cannot ask them about or even observe their mental processes. We can only examine the writings that have come down to us in order to find evidence of the strategies that the authors presume their readers will use. The strategies we find are likely to be quite different from those used by readers of English, because Latin grammar is different from English grammar. "The linguistic knowledge and coding capability for effective text comprehension are largely determined by the morphosyntactic structure of the target language" (Koda 497). Since these strategies will be unfamiliar to English readers, we must teach them overtly to our students. To develop a full repertoire of Latin reading strategies would require a complete reconstruction of the Latin mind, a process Colin Renfrew calls "cognitive archaeology."[4] This chapter begins the process by looking at one crucial problem: how the Romans dealt with the nominative/accusative ambiguity of some nouns.

Morphological Ambiguity in Latin

The Nature of Morphological Ambiguity

If there were a unique form for every noun in every syntactical function and if there were only one syntactical function for each noun form, decoding a Latin sentence would be a simple, mechanical matter, but learning the paradigms would become a Herculean task. Like other natural languages, Latin has made certain trade-offs to balance morphological simplicity and syntactic clarity.

Morphological ambiguity occurs in Latin when one surface form of a word (*puellae*, for example) can represent two or more grammatical cases (here, genitive singular, dative singular, or nominative plural). In fact, the fifty possible basic case/number combinations in the five nonneuter noun declensions are expressed by only thirty-five different surface forms (fewer still if you count only once those endings that occur in more than one declension). Moreover, twenty-seven of those fifty cases are expressed by twelve ambiguous surface forms. English has an even greater degree of morphological ambiguity than Latin, but its rigid word order provides many signals to allow understanding. The freedom of Latin word order makes most English resolution strategies useless, so students can benefit from overt instruction in Latin strategies.

One preliminary question is "At what point in their reading or hearing of a Latin sentence did the Romans resolve morphological ambiguities?" On an intuitive level, it seems unlikely that the Romans waited for the end of a lengthy sentence to sort out all its words and clauses. Just to remember the individual words would often be a daunting task in itself; to parse them all in the brief moment between the end of one sentence and start of the next sounds impossible.

Processing Ambiguous Forms

In order to show how ambiguity affects language processing capacity, metaphrasing will represent the continuous growth of a reader's mental image of a sentence's meaning. To metaphrase a Latin sentence, the reader starts with framework representing the expected word order of a minimal English sentence:

"Subject Verbs Object"

As the sentence is read, each successive Latin word is given its proper place in the metaphrase:

magnam	"Subject Verbs **the large** Object
urbem	"Subject Verbs **the large city**"
videt	"Subject **sees the large city**" and so on.

Using this representation, it is possible to chart the development of some ambiguous sentences. If the first word of the sentence, *omnes*, is ambiguous, it has a separate metaphrase for each case/number.

All Subjects	Verb Object
Subject	Verbs **all** Objects

If the next word, *puellae*, is also ambiguous, a large number of possible combinations ensue.

all Subjects of **the girl**	Verb Object
all Subjects	Verb Object **of the girl**
Subject **of the girl**	Verbs **all** Objects
Subject	Verbs **all** Objects **of the girl**
All Subjects	Verb Object **to the girl**
Subject	Verbs **all** Objects **to the girl**
girls	Verb **all** Objects
all girls	Verb Object

All of these interpretations are grammatically possible, but the last is clearly the most likely. Did the Romans remember each of those possibilities until it violated some grammatical rule, or did they drop unlikely ones? After just a few words, this sort of combinatorial explosion could soon overwhelm even the memory of a Seneca the Elder, so it seems reasonable to think that the typical Roman dropped from consideration any but the most likely parses. From an examination of English processing strategies, George Dillon found that the strategies that are used to determine the most likely interpretation of an ongoing sentence are "probabilistic in nature, they are based on expectations and likelihoods; they are not categorical" (Dillon xxvi). As a result, when we read or hear our native language, we have "a sense of immediate understanding, of recognizing and interpreting every word as we see or hear it . . . as a sentence unfolds over time, every new word is related to the local sentence context within only a few hundred milliseconds, both in terms of its syntactic features ("parsing") and in terms of its semantics" (von Berkum, Brown, and Hagoort 147).

The Hunt for Disambiguating Strategies

The strategies by which the Romans simplified their understanding of a sentence as they went along can be discovered by careful observation of the extant texts. In particular, we want to see how the Roman authors restrained their relative freedom in word order so that their readers would not be overwhelmed by morphological ambiguities. By looking at the order in which Roman authors arranged the words of their sentences, it is possible to infer what disambiguating strategies they expected their audience to use.

This study draws its examples from the first books of Vergil's *Aeneid*, Ovid's *Metamorphoses*, and Livy's *Ab urbe condita*. These authors were chosen because they are all commonly read, they all come from the Augustan period, and they all practice their art at the highest level. Livy was chosen because prose writers were generally more restrained in their word order than poets. Poets were included because their self-restraint in this area is all the more remarkable in the light of the traditional license granted them.

In these books, the nominative/accusative plural ambiguity of third, fourth and fifth declension nouns was singled out for examination. Such forms occur often enough to provide a good pool of examples, and they are subject to a wide variety of possible resolution strategies. Other common ambiguities like dative/ablative or genitive singular/nominative plural could be studied next. They would produce some of the same strategies used by the nominative/accusative plural ambiguity; they would not use some others; and finally, they would have some special strategies of their own. Once the need for such strategies, and the method for documenting them, is established, the example can be extended.

As successful readers, Latin teachers have and use at least one or two of these disambiguation strategies. They probably learned them by informal means: by example or by trial and error. Until now, the disambiguation strategies have been largely unsystematic and undocumented. This chapter seeks to change that.

The Eight Strategies

The eight strategies that follow occur most often in our test corpus. They will, therefore, be the most useful to our students. They are arranged here according to the part of speech of the trigger word. Individual teachers may or may not find this the best order. It may not suit the order of grammatical topics in their textbook (some books give third declension nouns before adjectives), so they may be rearranged as needed. The present order is practical, however, in that the strategies dealing with adjectives, nouns, verbs, and other parts of speech are kept together. In actual reading, the students will probably recognize possible disambiguators by their part of speech. The groups are here arranged roughly in the order of the frequency with which they are successful in the test corpus.

Adjective Strategies

1. Agreeing Adjective
   If the ambiguous noun occurs before or after an unambiguous, agreeing adjective that is not yet bound to another noun, make the noun in question the same case:

   > . . . hic fessas non uincula *naves*
   > *Aeneid* 1.168

   The ambiguous *naves* can immediately be made accusative because of *fessas*.

   > . . . *sedes* ubi fata quietas
   > *Aeneid* 1.205

   The reader must wait three words for *quietas* to resolve *sedes*.[5]

2. Possibly Agreeing Adjective
   If the ambiguous noun occurs before or after an ambiguous adjective that is not yet bound to another noun and that agrees with one of the possibilities of the noun in question, consider them to be the same case:

   > hinc atque hinc uastae *rupes*
   > *Aeneid* 1.162

   Although *vastae* could also be genitive or dative singular, those possibilities are discarded along with the accusative of *rupes*.

   > haud aliter *puppes*que tuae
   > *Aeneid* 1.399

   > pulsabantque novi montana cacumina *fluctus*
   > *Metamorphoses* 1.310

   > instructae acies
   > *Ab urbe condita* 1.1.7.1

3. Disagreeing Adjective
In the environment of an unambiguous disagreeing adjective, make the noun in question the other case:

> non hic armenta *gregesque* / horridus . . .
> *Metamorphoses* 1.513–4

Noun Strategies

4. Conjoint Noun
In apposition, conjunction or parallel construction with an unambiguous noun, resolve the noun in the same case:[6]

> *arma* virumque . . .
> *Aeneid* 1.1

Strictly speaking, this neuter plural example does not belong in this chapter. I could not resist mentioning it because of its great mnemonic value.

> illic et nebulas illic consistere *nubes*
> *Metamorphoses* 1.54

The repetition of *illic* marks the parallel construction, so *nubes* is taken as the same case as *nebulas*.

> uicimus perfidos hospites, imbelles *hostes*;
> *Ab urbe condita* 1.12.8.4

This line is an interesting, but uncommon, example of a two-step process: the resolution of *hostes* refers back to *hospites*, to which it is appositive and which in turn was previously resolved by the adjective *perfidos*.

5. Disagreeing Noun
In the presence of an unambiguous noun, either nominative or accusative, which is not subject to strategy 4, resolve the current noun to the other case:

> mox etiam *fruges* tellus . . .
> *Metamorphoses* 1.109

> . . . silvasque tenent *delphines* . . .
> *Metamorphoses* 1.302

Verb and Other Strategies

6. Disagreeing Subject
If the noun in question does not agree in person or number with the verb, consider it the accusative, probably direct object:

> . . . ut quiete et pabulo laeto reficeret *boves* . . .
> *Ab urbe condita* 1.7.4.4

> disiecitque *rates* . . .
> *Aeneid* 1.43

7. Disagreeing Object
   If the verb in a clause does not govern an accusative object because it is a linking, intransitive or passive verb, consider the ambiguous noun nominative.

   > interea ad templum non aequae Palladis ibant/crinibus *Iliades* . . .
   > Aeneid 1.479–80

   > inde ad foedus faciendum *duces* prodeunt.
   > *Ab urbe condita* 1.13.4.2

8. Preposition
   After a preposition, resolve a nominative/accusative ambiguity into an accusative.

   > inque *sinus* scindit sese
   > Aeneid 1.161

Before we turn to pedagogical methods and exercises, we must examine some additional consequences of these strategies. The adjective strategies are crucial to the efficient processing of ambiguity because they are most often successful, at least in the three authors studied. This is not surprising, since adjectives most often come near the nouns they modify. Verbs, on the other hand, are often rather distant from the nouns, since they tend to come at the end of their clauses.

The adjective strategies are also interesting because they are merely probabilistic: using them, a reader refuses to consider parses that are grammatically possible but he or she trusts the author will not use. For example, a good Latin reader should find the sentence

urbes multas vias habent.

more difficult to read than

urbes vias multas habent.

After reading *urbes multas*, they would bind the noun and the adjective together in the accusative and drop the nominative *urbes* from consideration. Then, when *vias* entered, they would have to stop, rethink and maybe even reread the sentence from the beginning in order to parse it correctly. Such technically grammatical sentences that mislead the reader about their grammatical structure are called "garden-path sentences" in English. Because they reveal so much about unconscious language processes, they have been extensively studied.[7] It is a new finding, though probably no surprise, that Livy, as prose writer, avoided this disruptive word order. It is remarkable, however, to find that even Ovid, who seems to be devoted—some would say addicted—to word play, did not avail himself of this kind of tricky language. Even he carefully avoided sentences in which a reader would be led astray when applying these strategies.[8] This avoidance is a fortiori evidence for the acceptance and importance of the strategies. That this phenomenon is not remarked upon by ancient or modern critics suggests that the process was carried on subconsciously by native readers and writers.

Strategy 6, which is based on the agreement of subject and verb, is probably the most familiar and most overused of the strategies. The reason for its popularity is obvious: this strategy can fail only if the author wrote an ungrammatical sentence or, at least, an anacoluthon. When the sentence starts "leges laudat", the reader does not have to worry that *leges* could turn out to be the subject. Exclusive or excessive dependence on this strategy, however, brings several problems. First of all, it is not the most useful strategy. The adjective strategies are much more often successful in resolving the test ambiguity in Livy than the verb strategies. So failure to use them makes the reader's job much harder than it needs to be. There is also the danger that excessive reliance on this strategy, combined with students' reluctance to let go of English word order, might lead them to resort to the infamous hunt-and-peck method. The overriding importance of the adjective strategies and their sensitivity to slight variations of word order now provide another reason, if one were needed, not to break out of the given Latin word order.

Attention must also be paid to semantics, that is to say, the meaning of words.[9] No possible grammatical combination of words should be maintained in memory if they do not make sense together or if they contradict the reader's real world or contextual knowledge.[10] It is unclear even now whether English readers "make use of semantic information . . . to avoid syntactic misanalysis" (Clifton 319). While we cannot say how often a Roman reader might have used such a strategy in reading the test corpus, we can say that passages that require them to do so are very few.[11]

Teaching Latin Reading Strategies

Let us now examine some practices that will help students develop the specific skills necessary for extensive reading. First I will suggest some ideas to help students internalize their recognition of grammar, believing with Grabe "that methods of instruction for rapid visual recognition, for extensive vocabulary development, and for syntactic pattern recognition should become major pedagogical concerns" (63). I will then develop in rather more detail some methods for presenting and drilling the ambiguity strategies.

Prereading Activities for Extensive Reading

One of the first tasks is to get the students to believe that Latin does have meaning, of the kind they can understand.[12] All too often a student hands in a translation that is absolute gibberish and seems genuinely surprised to find that it is not correct! They have to be taught that Latin does have real meaning. One important preliminary step is to ensure that the readings in the text are not just grammatical but also meaningful. The story should have some point or point of view that one can agree or disagree with; it should not be a series of disjointed drill-and-practice sentences.

Before students start a reading assignment, it is useful to engage their sense and expectation of meaning by placing the reading in context. If the assignment is part of an ongoing story or series of stories, have the students summarize the plot to date even before they open their books. Encourage them to imagine the rest of the story or develop several alternate plot directions for the ending. Then have them develop specific predictions for the next incident in the light of the immediate past and their expectations for the ending. Different versions can be recorded on the board for future reference.

Once the books are opened, look for any clues in the form or decoration of the page: the cast of characters, any illustrations, the format of the printing. Then have the students scan the page to see if any words or phrases stand out in any way. Finally read (or have the students read) the passage aloud once or twice at a reasonably fast pace without worrying about the exact details. This will be the equivalent of skimming the passage. Have the students comment on their impressions of the passage: which of their predictions seem to be confirmed by the passage? Try to identify the clues from which the students have gleaned their impressions and supplement them only as necessary. If they are missing important clues or going in false directions, try to keep your "corrections" or redirections to a minimum at this stage. It is best to incorporate the missing information or strategies in the teaching section of the lesson. After these prereading activities, the students should be ready to read the passage with their sense of meaning engaged.

Reading Processes

The learning of Latin grammar should always be connected to the goal of reading for meaning. The emphasis should be on those topics that are crucial for reading Latin, and those topics should be so well learned as to be automatic. To help students make them automatic, have them practice not just slow, analytical answers but quick, compiled responses. For example, when they have learned a new declension, bring in a set of cards with one noun form on each. Choose a card at random and have the students respond quickly with the case. On a second repetition, they should respond with the typical grammatical function of the case. A third level of compression would be to respond to the card with an appropriate representation of the meaning and function (e.g., *puerum* draws the response "Somebody verbs a boy").

Since cognitive strategies generally work best when they work unconsciously, students do not need to memorize the list of strategies. We want students to be able to use the strategies, not enumerate them. Their use involves more skill than formal knowledge. We should try to inculcate the habit of looking back in the sentence to resolve ambiguities with information already presented. If the backward look does not resolve the ambiguity, the students must learn to wait to see if each new word provides the clue. Under no circumstances should we allow or encourage them to jump out of the Latin order.

The most effective way to introduce these strategies is to allow the students to discover them for themselves. When the first ambiguous forms are covered, see if the students realize the problem for themselves. If they do not, pose the question "How can we tell one case from the other? Who can decide correctly soonest?" Decide which strategy or strategies to start with. If they have had adjectives, give preference to those strategies. Then give them, one word at a time, a series of sentences that use one of the strategies. Let the clue come sometimes before, sometimes after the ambiguity. Do not let them break out of the Latin word order. When presenting the adjective strategies, admit to the students that they are based merely on probabilities but assure them that the Latin authors will not lead them astray.

Once the idea has been introduced, model the process for them: read a sentence to the class one word at a time, verbalizing the mental processes by which you understand it. Here is a sample that uses the model of metaphrasing:

milites:

  nominative or accusative plural masculine;

  subject or object;

  soldiers Verb Object or Subject Verbs **soldiers**.

bonos:

  accusative plural masculine,

  could agree with milites, so *milites bonos* is the object;

  Subject Verbs **good soldiers**.

Caesar:

  nominative,

  the subject;

  Caesar Verbs the **good soldiers**.

laudavit:

  verb, perfect,

  agrees with *Caesar* as subject, takes an accusative object, *milites bonos*, so the sentence is complete.

  "Caesar praised the good soldiers."

To emphasize the need for automatic decoding, you might, on a later example, skip the analytical steps and jump from the Latin word to the mental representation. For practice, students could vocalize their mental processes at first as a group, then individually to the teacher, and then individually to a peer partner (if classroom conditions permit).

Once the students understand the principle and one or more of the strategies, they should practice them in exercises specifically created for this purpose. The first two suggested exercises could use sentences drawn from the class text or from any other source; the third uses sentence start fragments chosen from the same source.[13]

Exercise 1

Reveal a sentence one word at a time to the class. (Uncover it slowly on an overhead, write it on the board, or even speak it slowly aloud.) Note each ambiguous form as it occurs and have a student say whether it can be resolved immediately on the basis of the sentence start or whether they must wait for another word to trigger a resolution strategy. Add each new word until the end of the sentence, noting in turn each ambiguity and its resolution.

Exercise 2

Give the students an ambiguous form and have them supply a trigger for its resolution. The teacher may dictate the case to aim for, or the students may be allowed to choose. Similarly, the teacher or students may choose the strategy or part of speech to be used. For example,

Teacher: "Make *leges* nominative by adding an adjective."

Student may answer either *leges Romanae* or *leges Romanos* if they have learned both the agreeing and the disagreeing adjective strategies.

Exercise 3

Let the students read the whole sentence and then have them note each ambiguity, the point of its earliest resolution, and the successful strategy. This can even be done on paper.

Directions: In each of the following sentences there is an underlined ambiguous word. Circle the first word in the sentence that allows you to resolve the ambiguity. Then name the successful strategy.

a. *milites* bonos laudavit Caesar.

(Student circles *bonos* and writes "Agreeing Adjective")

Exercise 4

For a higher level class beginning to study a new author in an undoctored text, you can keep track of how long the author continues each ambiguity. Count how many words come between the ambiguous word and the word that triggers the resolution. Use a minus if the trigger precedes the ambiguity, a plus if it follows. You can also record the frequency with which the author uses each strategy. By keeping cumulative statistics, you can see which strategies will be most useful for reading your new author. It is hoped that skilled readers can even unconsciously adjust their strategies as they become familiar with a new author, "so that particular structures favored by a writer can be most efficiently processed" (Dillon xxvi). The latter point has not yet been empirically demonstrated. Experiments by Gibson and Schuetze showed "that the sentence comprehension mechanism is not using corpus frequencies in arriving at its preference in this ambiguity" (Gibson and Schuetze 263). At least we can make a conscious effort to fine-tune our strategies for each author.

Give the students a sentence start that contains an ambiguous form and a trigger that resolves it. Students show they have understood by supplying an appropriate continuation or completion of the sentence. You may leave them free or supply multiple choice.

For a sentence completion try:

a. leges orator . . . (laudavistis, laudavimus, laudavit, laudaverunt)

(The correct answer is *laudavit*.)

For a sentence continuation try:

b. leges bonos . . . (puellam, puellas, oratores, oratorem)

(The correct answer is *oratores*.)

These exercises are intended only to drill the students in the use of the disambiguating strategies. Other writers have described techniques to teach other parts of the reading process for Latin. Wells Hansen has described "drill sequences that are effective in teaching students accurate reading in Latin word order" (Hansen 173). The drills are called (1) recasting English sentences in nonstandard word order; (2) hidden-word drills using an overhead projector; and (3) multiple possibility sentence completions in hidden-word drills (176–80). B. Dexter Hoyos has published a complete handbook on reading Latin that can be used in coordination with any Latin textbook. It prescribes rules, procedures, and exercises to teach students to read and understand Latin in the original order directly without recourse to translation (Hoyos 1997). The disambiguating strategies discussed in this chapter form another small part of the total Latin reading process.

Postreading Activities for Extensive Reading

After students have read a passage, they need to keep thinking about the meaning of what they have read. Tell them to close their books, put away any notes, and write down from memory as detailed a summary as they can of what was said or done in the passage. Collect these not as a quiz but an assessment of their reading. From the summaries you can decide what grammar points or reading techniques need work in subsequent lessons.[14] Then you can move on to specific comprehension questions and finally grammatical points that arose, caused problems, or were new in the lesson. At this stage, keep the grammar in the context of the meaning. In all these activities, remember that the main intention is to make the bottom-up processes as nearly automatic as possible, so the student's top-down knowledge and sense of meaning can be involved and applied to the reading.

With the foregoing instructional strategies, it is possible to explain to students how to react to ambiguous forms. The last exercises will give them the practice they need to internalize the what they have learned. If they combine these strategies with a good grasp of the essential grammar, they will be well on their way to becoming fluent, efficient readers of Latin.

Notes

The initial insight for this chapter came from my work as a Dana Fellow for Computer-Aided Instruction in the Humanities at Carnegie-Mellon University. The preliminary research was supported by a grant from the Walter Williams Craigie Teaching Endowment. An early version of the essay was read at the September 1991 meeting of the Classical Association of the Atlantic States (CAAS). I thank those institutions for their support. I am also grateful for support, encouragement, and advice from many colleagues, to name but a few: Alan Boegehold, Francis Cairns, John Camp, Gregory Daugherty, Elizabeth Fisher, B. Dexter Hoyos, Ginny Lindsey, and John MacIssac; I especially thank my patient and supportive wife and family.

1. B. Dexter Hoyos, in his valuable 1993 article on reading Latin, used the term "decoding" in a slightly different sense, to apply to the practice of jumping around in a sentence to find the verb, etc. This practice probably prevents the students from ever escaping from the low-level processing that psycholinguists call decoding.

2. For a detailed model of the knowledge building process, see Gernsbacher.

3. The textbook *Ecce Romani* has a series of exercises that direct students to "build up the meaning" in the Latin order by adding both the dictionary meaning and syntactical function of each word to their emerging understanding of the meaning. Wells Hansen has developed a series of exercises that will help students learn to "store the information the way a Roman would, waiting for each idea to emerge in its own time" (Hansen 175). The University of Michigan group has developed a system called metaphrasing. Sweet et al. provides a "summary of metaphrasing" with thirteen rules. Some other textbooks (e.g. Knudsvig, Seligson, and Craig or Randall) make these techniques of mental representation the foundation of their instruction; others do not. Many teachers use such techniques even when their textbooks do not.

4. See Renfrew and Zubrow for a survey of largely archaeological studies. Hoyos 1993 has also begun looking into cognition and Latin, discussing principles of pattern recognition in Latin sight reading.

5. In the authors studied the ambiguities can be resolved according to the following chart:

	% by look-back	% in 1–3 words	% in 4+ words
Vergil	72	20	8
Ovid	74	21	5
Livy	60	33	6

6. This strategy points out the importance of these constructions. We need to do more research on how the Romans used and recognized them and how we can teach our students to do likewise.

7. There is also direct evidence that readers of English do not focus equally on all possible grammatical interpretations of a sentence start. Instead, they follow the path of the most likely interpretation. An English sentence such as

The horse raced past the barn tripped.

provides psycholinguists with evidence about our reaction to ambiguity. Most English readers find this a difficult sentence. Some can figure out its meaning only upon a second or third reading. The problem stems from the ambiguity of the word *raced*. If readers remembered that *raced* could be either a participle or a finite verb, they would have no more difficulty in reading and understanding this sentence than its close relative:

The car driven past the barn crashed.

Because they focus on the most likely interpretation of a sentence start, they can be led down the garden path and find themselves lost (see Milne).

8. Instances in which the apparent agreement of a noun and an adjective is later contradicted are extremely rare in books 1 of the *Aeneid* and the *Metamorphoses* and nonexistent in *Ab urbe condita* 1. The only examples that turned up are these (and not all involve a nominative/accusative noun ambiguity):

ut terrae utque *nouae* pateant Karthaginis arces

Aeneid 1.298

montibus in liquidas *pinus* descenderat undas
praeside *tuta* deo nemorum secreta subibis

Metamorphoses 1.594

In the first two instances, the reader's knowledge of the context and the real world would easily rule out *novae Karthaginis* and *liquidas pinus* as likely noun phrases. The second example is possibly misleading only if it is read rather than heard: in recitation, the quantity of the last vowel in *pinus* would reveal it to be nominative singular rather than in accusative plural. In *Met.* 1.594 Jupiter is trying impress upon Io the dangers of going into the woods alone, so the reader knows to bind *tuta* to the subject of *subibis*, not to *secreta*, because of contextual knowledge.

In the next two sentences, the case of the adjective does not change, but it does turn out to modify a noun different from the first possibility.

ipse uno graditur comitatus Achate
bina manu *lato* crispans hastilia ferro.

Aeneid 1.312

cum consorte tori *parva* rate vectus adhaesit

Metamorphoses 1.319

In both sentences *lato Achate* and *parva consorte* are unlikely noun phrases from a semantic point of view. The reader is not likely to be seriously fooled by them.

9. F. Jones has argued that semantics and real-world knowledge can keep many potential ambiguities from surfacing, but psychological research has shown that ambiguity can have an effect on readers even if it does not come to consciousness. The primacy of syntactical or semantic processing has not been established. Spivey-Knowlton and Sedivy propose a "constraint-based" model for ambiguity resolution that uses both kinds of processes in parallel. Pearlmutter and MacDonald are conducting experiments that examine the factors influencing the individual's choice of strategy. The fact remains that very few ambiguities in the test corpus require semantic resolution

10. This principle probably enables English readers to understand the words "Time flies" instantly without worrying that it is grammatically possible for *time* to be an adjective,

a verb, or a noun. No one expects a sentence beginning "Time flies" to be completed in either of these ways: "Time flies to see how long they stay in one spot" or "Time flies move from century to century as easily as house flies move from room to room," except perhaps in science fiction. As a result we are never even consciously aware of them.

11. One example is the following.

at raptarum *parentes* tum maxime sordida ueste lacrimisque et querellis ciuitates concitabant.

Ab urbe condita 1.10.1.2

Here neither *parentes* nor *civitates* can with confidence be called the subject on strictly morphological grounds. At the beginning of the sentence, one might argue that *parentes* is a very likely subject, but that is more a semantic judgment and should be kept in abeyance until more of the sentence is seen. The final decision awaits the verb at the end of the sentence and is made on the basis of meaning. The choice here is quite simple, almost obvious. And it is so in all the other such sentences where syntactical strategies fail.

12. For an analysis of the stages of reading instruction from prereading to integrating skills, see Phillips 289–95. Many of the articles on reading instruction concentrate on modern languages. Often their examples are not directly applicable to Latin teachers because of the inaccessibility of genuine cultural materials. With some effort, however, their principles and structures can be adapted to Latin.

13. Be very careful in using sentences from textbooks. Since the adjective strategies (strategies 1–3) are grammatically optional and have not been previously articulated in this way, many authors of textbook Latin do not observe them as carefully as the ancient authors did. The result is that they sometimes contain sentences such as

Duces novos milites in castra mox vocabunt. (Jenny, Scudder, and Baade 80)

This is precisely the sort of garden-path sentence the Romans carefully avoided.

14. The prereading and postreading activities here presented are adapted from a procedure described in Bernhardt 186–7.

Works Cited

Ainsworth-Darnell, Kim, Harvey G. Shulman, and Julie E. Boland. 1998. "Dissociating Brain Responses to Syntactic and Semantic Anomalies: Evidence from Event-Related Potentials." *Journal of Memory and Language* 34: 112–30.

Baldi, P. 1983. "Speech Perception and Grammatical Rules in Latin." In Harm Pinkster, ed., *Latin Linguistics and Linguistic Theory. Proceedings of the First International Colloquium on Latin Linguistics*. Amsterdam: John Benjamins, 11–26.

Barnett, Marva. 1989. *More Than Meets the Eye, Foreign Language Reading: Theory and Practice*. Englewood Cliffs, NJ: Prentice Hall.

Bernhardt, Elizabeth B. 1991. *Reading Development in a Second Language: Theoretical, Empirical and Classroom Perspectives*. Norwood, NJ: Ablex.

Carpenter, Daniel P. 2000. "Reassessing the Goal of Latin Pedagogy." *Classical Journal* 95: 391–5.

Carrell, Patricia L., Joanne Devine, and David E. Eskey, eds. 1988. *Interactive Approaches to Second Language Reading*. Cambridge, UK: Cambridge University Press.

Carroll, David W. 2004. *Psychology of Language*. 4th ed. Belmont, CA: Wadsworth.

Clifton, Charles Jr., Matthew J. Traxler, M. Taha Mohamed, Rihana S. Williams, Robin K. Morris, and Keith Rayner. 2003. "The Use of Thematic Role Information in Parsing: Syntactic Processing Autonomy Revisited." *Journal of Memory and Language* 49: 317–34.

Dillon, George L. 1978. *Language Processing and the Reading of Literature.* Bloomington: Indiana University Press.

Eskey, David E. 1988. "Holding in the Bottom: An Interactive Approach to Problems of Second Language Readers." In Patricia L. Carrell, Joanne Devine, and David E. Eskey, eds., *Interactive Approaches to Second Language Reading.* Cambridge, UK: Cambridge University Press, 93–100.

Gascoyne, Richard C., et al. 1997. *Standards for Classical Language Learning.* Oxford, OH: American Classical League.

Gernsbacher, Morton A. 1990. *Language Comprehension as Structure Building.* Hillsdale, NJ: Erlbaum.

Gibson, Edward, and Carson T. Schuetze. 1999. "Disambiguation Preferences in Noun Phrase Conjunction Do Not Mirror Corpus Frequency." *Journal of Memory and Language* 40: 263–79.

Grabe, William. 1988. "Reassessing the Term 'Interactive.'" In Patricia L. Carrell, Joanne Devine, and David E. Eskey, eds., *Interactive Approaches to Second Language Reading.* Cambridge, UK: Cambridge University Press, 56–70.

Grellet, Françoise. 1981. *Developing Reading Skills: A Practical Guide to Reading Comprehension Exercises.* Cambridge, UK: Cambridge University Press.

Hadley, Alice Omaggio. 2001. *Teaching Language in Context.* third ed. Boston: Heinle and Heinle.

Hansen, Wells. 2000. "Teaching Latin Word Order for Reading Competence." *Classical Journal* 95: 173–80.

Hoyos, B. Dexter. 1993. "Decoding or Sight-Reading? Problems with Understanding Latin." *Classical Outlook* 70: 126–30.

———. 1997. *Latin: How to Read It Fluently. A Practical Manual.* Amherst, MA: Classical Association of New England.

Jenny, Charles, Jr., Rogers V. Scudder, and Eric C. Baade. 1984. *First Year Latin.* Boston: Allyn and Bacon.

Jones, F. 1995. "Grammatical Ambiguity in Latin." *Mnemosyne* 48: 438–59.

Knudsvig, Glenn M., Gerda M. Seligson, and Ruth S. Craig. 1986. *Latin for Reading: A Beginner's Textbook with Exercises.* Rev. ed. Ann Arbor: University of Michigan Press.

Koda, Keiko. 1993. "Transferred L1 Strategies and L2 Syntactic Structure in L2 Sentence Comprehension." *Modern Language Journal* 77: 490–500.

Lawall, Gilbert, Ronald B. Palma, and David J. Perry. 2000. *Ecce Romani: A Latin Reading Program.* 3rd ed. Glenview, IL: Prentice-Hall.

Milne, R. W. 1982. "Predicting Garden Path Sentences." *Cognitive Science* 6: 349–73.

Pearcy, Lee. 1998. "Writing Latin in Colleges and Schools." *Classical World* 92: 28–42.

Pearlmutter, N. J., and M. C. MacDonald. 1995. "Individual Differences and Probabilistic Constraints in Syntactic Ambiguity Resolution." *Journal of Memory and Language* 34: 521–42.

Phillips, June K. 1984. "Practical Implications of Recent Research in Reading." *Foreign Language Annals* 17: 285–96.

Randall, John G. 1986. *Learning Latin: An Introductory Course for Adults.* Liverpool, UK: Francis Cairns.

Renfrew, Colin, and Ezra B. W. Zubrow, eds. 1994. *The Ancient Mind: Elements of Cognitive Archaeology.* Cambridge, UK: Cambridge University Press.

Seligson, Gerda M. 1960–61. "Rules for Metaphrasing." *Classical Journal* 56: 61–3.

Smith, Frank. 2004. *Understanding Reading: A Psycholinguistic Analysis of Reading and Learning to Read.* 6th ed. Hillsdale, NJ: Erlbaum.

Spivey-Knowlton, Michael, and Julie C. Sedivy. 1995. "Resolving Attachment Ambiguities with Multiple Constraints." *Cognition* 55: 227–67.

Swaffar, Janet K., Katherine M. Arens, and Heidi Byrnes. 1991. *Reading for Meaning: An Integrated Approach to Language Learning.* Englewood Cliffs, NJ: Prentice Hall.

Sweet, Waldo E., Gerda M. Seligson, and Ruth S. Craig. 1966. *Latin: A Structural Approach.* Ann Arbor: University of Michigan Press.

Taillefer, Gail F. 1996. "L2 Reading Ability: Further Insights into the Short-Circuit Hypothesis." *Modern Language Journal* 80: 461–77.

Von Berkum, Jos, Colin Brown, and Peter Hagoort. 1999. "Early Referential Context Effects in Sentence Processing: Evidence from Event-Related Brain Potentials." *Journal of Memory and Language* 41: 147–82.

Wills, Jeffrey. 1998. "Speaking Latin in Schools and Colleges." *Classical World* 92: 27–34.

CHAPTER 7

Language Acquisition and Teaching Ancient Greek
Applying Recent Theories and Technology

Kenneth Scott Morrell

In more than one state and school district, teachers of ancient Greek and Latin are having to confront the issue of proficiency and articulate learner outcomes that will serve to measure the effectiveness of their curricula (New York State Education Department; Sienkiwicz et al.). What may have been a simple, clear objective for a teacher of any foreign language, currently spoken or otherwise, to "teach students a language," is suddenly not so clear at all. We are discovering that what we teach, what students learn, and what they actually acquire may be three entirely different things, although they are certainly related as aspects of some particular "language." The following discussion attempts to clarify and simplify both the objectives and outcomes by situating the teaching of ancient Greek in the context of recent theories of second language acquisition (SLA). My goal is to outline some of the basic theories concerning the ways we acquire and use languages and then present a number of ideas about how teachers of ancient Greek can productively adapt their approaches in keeping with those theories. Because reading ancient texts represents the one language skill emphasized by all curricula for ancient Greek, this chapter will focus primarily on reading comprehension and conclude with some observations about the use of authentic texts.

The Basic Premises of Language Acquisition

Let me begin with a few brief comments concerning language. First, we must distinguish between the process of developing the use of language in general and the acquisition of a second in particular. Human beings have the innate ability to use language, and this ability is not learned. Researchers refer to this innate capacity as the language acquisition device (LAD), which includes a set of rules, universal grammar (UG), that are common to all human languages. Barring any physiological or psychological impairment, the process of developing language begins before birth, goes through a particularly intensive stage between the ages of eighteen months and six years, and continues at a slightly decelerating pace until shortly after puberty. For approximately the first ten months, infants learn to differentiate and generate the sounds of their first language (L1) based on the speech they regularly hear. Shortly before their first birthdays, these sounds become comprehensible as words; around the time they turn one, they begin to produce words; and by eighteen months they have begun to develop syntax. Most three-year-olds are grammatically correct 90 percent of the time. For this process to occur, children must perceive and comprehend examples of language in use, which usually, but not always, take the form of spoken discourse. Researchers refer to these examples as primary linguistic data (PLD) or more generally as comprehensible or comprehended input. This combination of elements—the innate LAD and UG with the input of PLD—explains why any average four-year old can be fluent in one or more languages without coaching or training of any type and without any conscious understanding of grammar.

This innate ability to use language, once developed through the acquisition of the first language (L1), allows a human being to acquire one or more second languages (L2). Because of the unique physiological circumstances under which human beings first develop the use of language, the process of acquiring one's first language as an infant differs significantly from the acquisition of a second language later in life. For example, it is virtually impossible for human beings to develop native accents in a second language after reaching puberty. However, because human beings rely heavily on their ability to use language and exercise this ability for a vast majority of their entire lives (even during sleep), humans continue to develop their linguistic skills throughout their lifetimes, unless they experience illness or injury that affects their cognitive capacities. In fact, human beings are so innately adept at acquiring language that they will naturally—some might argue unavoidably—acquire a language if they comprehend a sufficient amount of input, even if that input is flawed. How much input human beings need to become fluent in an L2 will vary from individual to individual, which accounts, in part, for the ability of some to become fluent rather quickly and the tendency of others to take much longer.

A number of factors affect one's ability to comprehend the input. Some are as trivial as momentary distractions during a conversation; others are more challenging, such as the anxiety everyone naturally feels when encountering something unfamiliar and having to negotiate situations with limited linguistic capacity and inadequate knowledge of the cultural context. Still others have to do with the processes of cognition themselves, the ability to apply lexical and grammatical knowledge to the decoding of oral and verbal input, and the varying levels of cultural knowledge one brings to a conversation or text. The fact remains, however, that the more input one encounters and comprehends, the faster and more efficient the process of language acquisition.[1]

Consequently, the "teaching" of language ultimately represents the process of creating an environment that will allow students to encounter as much input as possible in a way that will engage and facilitate their innate ability to acquire language. This environment can be solely textual, as most ancient Greek curricula are, but ideally the environment will combine textual, visual, and auditory components. The teacher is obviously a crucial component in the environment, but in ancient Greek courses his or her role has generally not been as a source of input but rather of grammatical explication. Consequently, the need for curricular materials that can supply the necessary input is even greater for ancient Greek than for modern languages.

Reading Proficiency and Integrative Methods

Most teachers would agree that at a minimum the environment for acquiring ancient Greek should foster the ability to read and understand texts by ancient authors.

The recent movement to establish curricular standards, including the national *Standards for Classical Language Learning*, mandate that we view this ability as part of a more comprehensive linguistic proficiency that includes the entire portfolio of communicative skills: listening, speaking, and writing, as well as reading. An approach designed to support the development of all four skills should incorporate at least four features. First, it should maximize comprehensible oral and verbal input and engineer the components so that each will play a supporting role in developing the full range of skills. Second, the curriculum should draw on the students' innate language facility to develop a sense for the characteristics of the language inductively. Third, students should be encouraged to express themselves orally and verbally in the target language, but the range of vocabulary and grammatical concepts should fall within workable, familiar, and predictable parameters. Expecting students one week to use the idioms from philosophical discussions on the soul and the vocabulary from descriptions of naval battles the next will tax the abilities of even the best and most committed students. Conversely, building fluency within fairly narrow domains, for example, aspects of daily life (food, school, personal relationships, the weather), that represent some of the usual and expected topics of conversation, will allow the students to develop fluency more efficiently. Most important, the approach should avoid raising the general level of anxiety among students. For example, evaluation and grading should initially focus primarily on receptive skills (reading and listening). The course should allow students to communicate creatively and experimentally with the language (speaking and writing) without fear of making mistakes that will negatively influence their grades.[2]

I will turn now to focus on the first feature of this approach: maximizing comprehensible oral and verbal input, beginning where listening and reading frequently coincide. A number of teachers have students take turns reading aloud part of the reading assignment. Because the intent of such exercises is generally to help students pronounce ancient Greek and not to comprehend spoken language, few teachers would claim that having students read aloud significantly contributes to reading comprehension. Research on the relationship between phonological capacity and the ability to comprehend written texts certainly supports their intuition (Bernhardt 38–42). Having students read aloud and practice pronouncing ancient Greek words does appear to give them some phonological competence and help in the subvocalization that inevitably takes place when students read. However, reading a text aloud actually tends to impede reading comprehension itself, partly because students must devote much of their attention and processing capacity to pronunciation, particularly in a language that has an unfamiliar system of orthographic representation (Bernhardt 77–8). The problem is not with the idea of having students develop their ability to read Greek or even comprehend spoken language but rather with conflating in one exercise the parallel but different activities of vocalization, listening, and reading.

Both reading and listening comprehension involve similar interactive processes of decoding aural and visual information and constructing meaning from the input. The two are different because the modalities of written and spoken communication differ (Bacon; Glisan; Hadley 176–81; Rubin, Hafer, and Arata;

Stevick). First, listeners tend to rely more on the "top-down" elements of the interactive process, an issue to which I will return shortly, because they are able to use nonverbal signals as well as sentential cues, such as intonation, that are often not embedded in a written text (Lund 1991). Second, the linguistic nature of the input we use to comprehend spoken language is often very different from the input we use to comprehend written texts. The development of ideas in spoken discourse tends to be more nonlinear, reflecting the interactive nature of conversation; the primary organizational unit of spoken discourse tends to be the phrase, as opposed to the sentence in written texts; and the conventions of speech allow for more latitude in grammatical continuity and consistency than those of written materials (Richards). Third, the process of comprehending spoken language is constrained by the temporal nature of speech itself. While readers are able to range over the text, moving forward and backward, listeners must cope with information as it comes with no control over a wide range of aspects that affect the process of decoding. Spoken ancient Greek with its inflected morphology, unfamiliar sound system, and variable word order poses a particularly difficult challenge for native speakers of English, who are used to processing a noninflected language with highly constrained word order.[3] Nevertheless, despite the unique characteristics of spoken language and written texts, the means of enhancing the students' ability to understand both are ultimately similar.

Making Spoken and Written Language Comprehensible

Comprehension is an interactive process that combines the mechanics of processing the linguistic input with a set of cognitive functions to derive meaning from spoken or written discourse. Under the mechanical or "bottom-up" aspects of comprehension are recognizing individual sounds and words, decoding the morphological information, and relating the words to syntactic functions. The cognitive or "top-down" components of the process include relating information from the input to the reader's background knowledge, building an intratextual schema of the discourse (which includes relating elements of the discourse to each other, for example, referring to antecedent information, predicting and confirming one's predictions about the discourse, tracking the order of elements, and making inferences), and metacognitive processes such as thinking about the information in the discourse and reflecting on the task of listening or reading and the perspective of the listener or reader.[4] One of the major differences between encountering discourse in one's native language and input in a foreign language is the relative emphasis on the decoding and cognitive processes. When engaging a written text, for example, in one's native language, one focuses the majority of one's attention on the cognitive aspects of comprehension because textual processing is nearly automatic, at least for fluent readers. When one reads a text in a foreign language as a beginning or intermediate student, paying close attention to the text itself reduces the amount of cognitive activity one can devote to deriving a meaning (Brown 1998: 198–9; Davis and Bistodeu; Grabe 241–6; Just and Carpenter 1980, 1992). When the foreign language involves an orthographic system that differs considerably from one's native language, as is the case for native English speakers who are learning ancient Greek, the overhead for processing the text is even greater (Koda 1996, 1997).

One approach to making the input more comprehensible is to create simplified examples of discourse (dialogues or textual passages) that are relatively easy to process linguistically, require little or no background knowledge beyond the range of normal human experience, and are situated in the context of daily life. *Ancient Greek Alive* by Paula Saffire and Catherine Freis is one example. An alternative method, such as *A Reading Course in Homeric Greek*, by Raymond V. Schoder, S.J., and Vincent C. Horrigan, attempts to build an environment with sufficient support for decoding and cognitive processing to make authentic discourse comprehensible for beginning students. The first approach allows students to develop comprehensional fluency quickly, but it may not always prepare them to deal with authentic input because the range of cultural phenomena is limited, and, perhaps more important, students fail to develop strategies for dealing with complex discourse. The second approach motivates the development of strategies that will support comprehension when dealing with authentic discourse, but it also overwhelms the limited capacity of the short-term memory used in comprehension and, consequently, impedes the development of fluency. Carefully integrating both models represents the ideal approach. In the beginning stages of acquisition, students should work primarily with an extensive "library" of simplified, graduated materials, but they should also experience limited authentic materials that will prepare them to cope with more complex input. As their skills develop, the simplified materials should give way to more authentic examples. Of particular importance, however, in selecting authentic materials for integration into the language environment is not only the lexical or syntactic complexity of the selection but also how well the examples conform to the range of background knowledge and interests of the students.

In designing listening and reading exercises, the objective is to provide a conceptual framework to make the cognitive functions more efficient and facilitate the process of decoding. The exercises will consist of four stages: contextualization, input, review, and application. Figure 7.1 outlines the components of the exercise and the relationship between the native and target languages.

Contextualization: Prelistening and Prereading

Contextualization includes activities that fall into two groups. The first group helps build the cognitive schemata that will provide relevant background information, establish the structural, logical, or rhetorical characteristics of the discourse readers will encounter, and set the immediate context (Swaffar 125–9). For beginning students, establishing the schemata for a passage nearly always requires using the students' native language. Subsequent elements of the contextualization process, such as previewing vocabulary, will offer the opportunity to move gradually into the target language. As the ability of the students increases and they move into advanced and sheltered language courses, the target language will figure more

Figure 7.1

Contextualization	1. Providing background information specific to culture, domain, and setting 2. Building logical and rhetorical schemata 3. Previewing lexical and syntactical elements	Native language ↓ Target language

Input	Listening or reading
	  1. Recursive presentations to reflect different modalities
	  2. Varying metacognitive framework for each iteration
		Target language

Review & application	1. Reviewing lexical and syntactic elements 2. Reviewing logical and rhetorical schemata 3. Applying information from passage and evaluating comprehension	Target language ↓ Native language

prominently in setting the context and evaluating the students' comprehension in the review and application stages.[5]

To provide students with background information, a number of curricula offer readings in English about Greek culture and history; however, the placement and content of the materials frequently diminish their role in the contextualizing process. For example, in the first chapter of *Athenaze*, a brief essay on "The Athenian Farmer" comes at the end of the unit after the Greek passage, which describes the farmer, Dikaiopolis, the main character of the narrative (Balme and Lawall). Coming at the end of the unit, the cultural material appears "supplementary," an impression that will inevitably consign the material to neglect as demands on the students' time increase during the semester. It also contains information that will prove interesting at best for most students. "The Athenian Farmer" discusses aspects of ancient agriculture that pertain fairly closely to the story, but it also provides information about the property requirements of the four administrative classifications for Athenian citizens. Although all cultural information is ultimately valuable, in the context of language acquisition, authors should focus on the task of making the passages in the target language more comprehensible. In this case, the additional political information could prove unhelpful for two reasons. First, students of a foreign language are much less certain about their abilities to comprehend a text and are more influenced by initial assumptions than more experienced or native readers, who are able to adapt and correct their preconceptions as they read.

Second, beginning students of a language who are also relatively unfamiliar with the culture are more likely to shape inaccurate expectations when cultural material is offered in an undifferentiated manner. As they begin to create a vision of Greek society based on "The Athenian Farmer," students have no idea how frequently or infrequently they will encounter the terminology for property classifications or how important those classifications are for their understanding of the society.[6] Cultural material in the form of short essays like "The Athenian Farmer" or information provided by the teacher will better enhance the student's ability to comprehend the target passage if it precedes the passage and more closely addresses the content. Here, for example, are the first two paragraphs of "The Athenian Farmer" as they might appear as a brief introduction to the reading selection, serving both to create a conceptual framework and preview some of the vocabulary students will encounter in the reading.

> Dicaeopolis (Δικαιόπολς) lives in a village in Attica called Cholleidae, about twelve miles southeast of Athens ('Αθῆναι). Athens ('Αθῆναι) and its port, the Piraeus, formed a very large city by ancient standards. However, Dicaeopolis is like most Athenians. He lives (οἰκεῖ) and works (πονεῖ) in the country (ἐν τοῖς ἀγροῖς).

> Most were farmers (αὐτουργοί). An average farm (κλῆρος) was small (μικρός), ranging in size from ten to twenty acres. What they grew on their farms depended partly on the district in which they lived. On the plain near Athens the staple products would have been vegetables and grain (σῖτος), but most of Attica is hilly; this poorer land was more suitable for grape vines, olive trees, sheep, and goats (cows were not kept for milk). All farmers (αὐτουργοί) aimed at self-sufficiency, but few would have attained it; the Athenians ('Αθηναῖοι) imported two-thirds of their grain (σῖτος). If they had a surplus, for example, of olive oil or wine, they would take it to the market in Athens (ἐν ταῖς 'Αθήναις) for sale and buy what they could not produce themselves.

Discussions that help readers recognize the rhetorical, structural, or logical features of the language and teach the strategies of comprehension come next. These activities are valuable not only because they enhance a student's ability to comprehend passages in a foreign language but also because many of the skills are transferable to other academic contexts and, more important, by developing such a repertoire of strategies, students believe they are developing their ability to comprehend passages in the target language. A positive sense of progress and development helps to overcome anxiety some students feel when acquiring a foreign language and to lower the "affective filter" that impedes the acquisition of language.[7] A crucial component in this process is drawing attention to function words that indicate the formal organization of the text. For a course in ancient Greek, the student's ability to decode the significance of particles is particularly crucial for understanding not only the logical progression of the text but the meaning of words.

Particles frequently receive inadequate attention because teachers often assume that the content of the text will allow students to understand the meaning of the particles. For beginning students, however, who are often unsure about the meaning of content words, let alone the particles, so much effort goes into processing content words that little attention remains for particles. By gaining a feeling for the significance of the particles during the prelistening or prereading process, students can then begin to use the particles and the logical structure they represent to guess at the meaning of unfamiliar words. This aspect of the contextualizing component should also alert students to other complexities that might affect comprehension, ranging from syntactical issues (e.g., changes in voice, person, subject, and shifts in tense) to structural discontinuities (e.g., intrusions by the narrator and elliptical or parenthetical comments) and potential problems associated with multivalent uses of language such as irony and sarcasm (Swaffar).

The third part of contextualization focuses on building vocabulary and facilitating lexical processing. This element is particularly important for listening exercises because processing speech requires a greater degree of anticipation. With regard to written texts that accommodate a more nonlinear approach and allow students to range over the passage and even consult notes, instructors and textbooks often provide extensive vocabulary notes, assuming that they will necessarily facilitate comprehension as the students work through the text. Although notes might aid in textual processing, they do not necessarily enhance comprehension because they tend to distract students from creating cognitive schemata for comprehension (Johnson 1982). There are two other common problems associated with glosses. First, they tend to emphasize the more context-bound, specific meanings of words, which may prove confusing for beginning and intermediate students, who often associate a word with the first definition they encounter and persist in using that definition whenever the word appears without allowing the word to convey different ideas based on the context. Second, authors assume that a student acquires a word after being exposed to it a certain number of times and fail to consider that students not only acquire different sets of words depending on their interests and background knowledge but they acquire them at different rates. Glosses do have their place. For example, glosses are helpful for words that students will seldom if ever encounter again. They also help when students are unlikely to derive the meanings of the words through structural analysis and contextual clues. However, when possible, teachers might first try providing visual clues in the form of graphics, using synonyms or antonyms, or constructing a definition in the target language from words and expressions already familiar to the students.

With the primary aim of establishing the contextual parameters of the passage and facilitating lexical processing without eliminating all opportunities for guessing at the meaning of words from context, the vocabulary activities should begin with reviewing words that students should recognize and know from previous work. For new words that students will encounter in the passage, the teacher should differentiate between words that will begin appearing with more frequency and those that are more specialized and appear in more restricted contexts. In presenting new words, teachers should build cognitive schemata, so students can see how words relate to each other within semantic categories through activities such as semantic mapping (Devitt; Johnson and Pearson). Activities should begin with nouns and adjectives, which students tend to learn more easily and retain longer, and then branch out to include other parts of speech and allow students to derive the meanings from their background of the nominal elements (Swaffar; Laufer). Visual materials are particularly helpful for beginning students. For example, I frequently draw and label pictures of objects during the contextualization, allow students to refer to the pictures while they hear or read a selection, and then erase the labels during the review and ask them to identify the objects or provide new labels. As students become more fluent, the contextualization can make greater use of the target language itself.

At this point in the contextualizing process, students should be able to infer what the speaker's or author's objectives are and offer predictions about what they will encounter in the passage (Richards). Asking students to predict the direction and content of the passage based on background knowledge, structural clues, and a preview of the vocabulary provides teachers with the opportunity to adjust incorrect assumptions and preconceptions as well as review lexical information that will help students decode the selection. The final element of contextualization is the assignment of a task. Receptive activities such as listening and reading always involve a particular intention on the part of the listener or reader as he or she approaches a speech act or text.[8] Depending upon the type of passage, these assignments should focus the intention of the listener or reader as well as promote the development of particular microskills and condition a response that will indicate students' understanding and sustain their attention.[9] For example, an assignment might ask the students to listen or skim for particular elements or information, such as the names of the characters and places where events take place. Yet another assignment might emphasize the skill of distinguishing among major and minor constituents in the passage by asking students to identify the main idea and suggest an appropriate title or headline for the passage. Another type of assignment might focus on "bottom-up" decoding skills by having students identify types of word, such as adjectives, verbs, or participles. To focus on developing the students' lexical capacity, one might have students approach a passage with the task of identifying synonyms or antonyms for a list of words.

Input

With background knowledge, accurate preconceptions about the nature of the passage, information about the vocabulary they will encounter, and an assignment or objective in mind, students are ready to listen or read. As noted earlier, it is important for teachers not to conflate vocalization, listening, and reading in a single exercise. If students are working on listening skills, they should not have access to the written text, and when students are reading for meaning, they should not have to read the passage aloud. This does not mean, however, that reading a text aloud has no place in the process of developing reading comprehension. In fact, having the students hear the text as they read along in class will help them better subvocalize as they read the text outside of class. Of primary importance, if the ultimate objective is to increase comprehension, is to work through the passage more than once. Varying the assignments and the mechanics of the exercise not only exposes the students to the same input more than once but also promotes a higher level of attention, encourages flexibility, and develops the students' sense of being able to work confidently with language in different contexts and settings. One way for teachers to alter the way students hear or read a text from one iteration to another is to take different approaches in maintaining the cognitive and lexical "scaffolding," which allows the listeners and readers to comprehend the text more efficiently. This process nearly always calls for some metacognitive commentary by the students or the teacher, that is, a discussion about the process of reading and comprehending the text. Students, for example, can participate by occasionally summarizing or paraphrasing events, taking notes either individually or as a group, drawing illustrations, or periodically anticipating what will happen next. Teachers, on the other hand, can assist by providing brief and focused information about specialized terms, helping students through difficult syntactic constructions, and demonstrating strategies for deriving the meaning of words from context or working around unknown expressions. While certain types of information prompted by the metacognitive comments will require explication in the native language, the teacher should try to use the target language as much as possible. In explaining the meaning of words, for example, the teacher should use other words in the target language from the same semantic category, periphrases, or illustrations, and, whenever possible, draw connections with similar words or forms of the same word in the passage.

Above all, the comments and actions of the teacher should reflect the primary objective of the exercise: to comprehend the passage. In each component of the exercise, teachers should be continually aware of the fact that when students appear to know what the words mean, it does not necessarily follow that they know what the passage "says," and once the students seem to know what the passage "says," they are not always aware of what it "means." Focusing on comprehension should not create the impression in the minds of students that once they "comprehend" a passage, the passage no longer has any value in the process of acquiring the language. Nor should the pace of the curriculum push students so intensively that they do not have the opportunity to work through passages more than once during a semester. Periodically reviewing passages not only builds fluency but helps to underscore the fact that we understand texts differently each time we encounter them.

Review and Application

Contemporary models of listening and reading suggest that comprehension is such a complex, interactive process that relying on one type of review or evaluation will not provide an adequate measure of how well students of foreign languages are succeeding (Swaffar; Swaffar and Bacon; Wolf). Exercises during the review should parallel the activities of the contextualizing component and reflect the range of operational modes at work in comprehending a passage. Teachers might begin, for example, with exercises to review the "bottom-up" process of decoding by posing a series of questions designed to confirm the students' having recognized and understood certain elements in the text. Simple recognition questions might take a variety of forms: true or false ("The Corinthians captured Dikaiopolis, but Philippos escaped." "True or false?"), multiple choice ("Where did Dikaiopolis finally stop and rest? Megara, Eleusis, or Athens?"), cloze ("They stayed the entire _____ in the ditch."), or direct content ("What did the Corinthians accuse Dikaiopolis and Philippos of being?"). These questions, which teachers can pose in the target language, ultimately serve two other important purposes. First, questions that call for students to respond with single words or short phrases offer the learners the chance to reply in the target language, and, second, such questions also provide the teacher with an opportunity to review significant lexical elements. As students work through recognition activities with a focus on lexical items, they are in a better position to gauge for themselves which items require further attention (Paribakht and Wesche; Wesche and Paribakht). From recognition questions, the teacher might move to more open-ended activities: having students paraphrase the passage; asking them to respond to a free recall protocol, which prompts students to record what they remember about certain topics (Bernhardt); having them draw a story board with captions to depict the events; having them continue with the story or recast the story from a different perspective; or assigning roles for a dramatic reenactment. At this point in the review, the native language should become the primary means of expression for the students. Depending upon the nature of the students' responses, they might well want to recast their responses in the target language with the instructor's help.[10] Finally, a third type of question (inference or problem solving) might engage the students' ability to apply information from the passage. See Cohen (211–54) for more strategies for assessing comprehension.

In concluding this description of a listening or reading exercise, the issue of anxiety requires at least brief attention. From the students' perspective, review and application ultimately take two forms: on a daily basis students expect to review the content of a passage and apply the information they obtain; however, they also realize that on less frequent but more formalized occasions they will have to perform many of the same activities under controlled conditions as part of the evaluation that will determine, at least to a certain extent, their grades. The more closely these forms resemble each other, the lower the level of the students' anxiety. Not only will they have a clear and accurate preconception of what the examinations will entail but they will also view daily exercises as ongoing opportunities to practice and prepare (Young).

A Sample Reading Exercise Based on Lysias 1

The Role of Authentic Texts

Although most issues in research on the acquisition of foreign languages are far from settled, both theorists and practitioners are close to consensus on the need to use authentic texts as frequently and early as possible.[11] While it is true that using authentic texts for listening and reading exercises will require teachers to provide more schematic and lexical support for the students, students benefit from the exposure to authentic texts because they represent a richer source of information about the culture and a wider variety of linguistic phenomena, generally engage the attention of the students, and require them to develop more robust strategies for deriving meaning than those they develop through restricted exposure to simplified input. In addition, using authentic texts is the ideal springboard for incorporating the *Standards for Classical Language Learning* into the classroom. As students read authentic texts, they interpret and discuss texts (Communication), explore cultural attitudes (Culture), expand their knowledge through reading ancient sources (Connections), compare their own culture with the ancient world (Comparisons), and recognize that the cultural diversity of the ancient world has practical applications today (Communities).

In selecting authentic texts for use with beginning students, I have relied on three basic criteria: the adaptability of the text primarily to listening and reading exercises; the length and coherence of the text; and, perhaps most important, how engaging the text is and how well it will motivate students to continue exploring the text. Although in theory any text that tells a story will work, among the texts that most successfully meet these criteria are some of the narrative passages from the Attic orators. Whether or not actual litigants delivered some of the speeches as we have them today is beyond recovery; nevertheless, the logographers worked with the constraints of oral delivery in mind. Because the narrative passages in particular were designed to persuade the jurors by depicting a series of events as plausibly as possible, they are generally paratactic in structure and follow a linear progression, allowing the students to follow the story with comparative ease. They also represent a major source of information about the daily lives of Athenians and tend to hold the attention of the students.

To demonstrate ways of using authentic texts as just discussed, I have provided here a sample reading exercise based on a passage from Lysias 1, which I have used with students beginning as early as the second semester.[12] The portion of the text used in this exercise comprises sections 7 through 10. Because the narrative actually begins in chapter 4, the students have usually had at least one exercise and received information about those elements of the Athenian legal system that pertain to the case (for example, the nature of the charges, the objectives of the speaker, the composition of the audience) and the facts of the case itself.[13]

Text

ἐν μὲν οὖν τῷ πρώτῳ χρόνῳ, [7] ὦ 'Αθηναῖοι, πασῶν ἦν βελτίστη· καὶ γὰρ οἰκονόμος δεινὴ καὶ φειδωλὸς [ἀγαθὴ] καὶ ἀκριβῶς πάντα διοικοῦσα· ἐπειδὴ δέ μοι ἡ μήτηρ ἐτελεύτησε, ἣ πάντων τῶν κακῶν ἀποθανοῦσα αἰτία μοι γεγένηται. [8] ἐπ' ἐκφορὰν γὰρ αὐτῇ ἀκολουθήσασα ἡ ἐμὴ γυνὴ ὑπὸ τούτου τοῦ ἀνθρώπου ὀφθεῖσα, χρόνῳ διαφθείρεται· ἐπιτηρῶν γὰρ τὴν θεράπαιναν τὴν εἰς τὴν ἀγορὰν βαδίζουσαν καὶ λόγους προσφέρων ἀπώλεσεν αὐτήν. [9]

πρῶτον μὲν οὖν, ὦ ἄνδρες, (δεῖ γὰρ καὶ ταῦθ' ὑμῖν διηγήσασθαι) οἰκίδιον ἔστι
μοι διπλοῦν, ἴσα ἔχον τὰ ἄνω τοῖς κάτω κατὰ τὴν γυναικωνῖτιν καὶ κατὰ τὴν
ἀνδρωνῖτιν. ἐπειδὴ δὲ τὸ παιδίον ἐγένετο ἡμῖν, ἡ μήτηρ αὐτὸ ἐθήλαζεν· ἵνα
δὲ μή, ὁπότε λοῦσθαι δέοι, κινδυνεύῃ κατὰ τῆς κλίμακος καταβαίνουσα, ἐγὼ
μὲν ἄνω διῃτώμην, αἱ δὲ γυναῖκες κάτω. [10] καὶ οὕτως ἤδη συνειθισμένον
ἦν, ὥστε πολλάκις ἡ γυνὴ ἀπῄει κάτω καθευδήσουσα ὡς τὸ παιδίον, ἵνα τὸν
τιτθὸν αὐτῷ διδῷ καὶ μὴ βοᾷ. καὶ ταῦτα πολὺν χρόνον οὕτως ἐγίγνετο, καὶ
ἐγὼ οὐδέποτε ὑπώπτευσα, ἀλλ' οὕτως ἠλιθίως διεκείμην, ὥστε ᾤμην τὴν
ἐμαυτοῦ γυναῖκα πασῶν σωφρονεστάτην εἶναι τῶν ἐν τῇ πόλει.

7. In the beginning, gentlemen of Athens, she was the best of all women, for
she was a skilled housekeeper, thrifty, and carefully attended to the household
affairs. Then my mother died, and her having died was the cause of all my ills,
because my wife accompanied her during the funeral procession and, having been
seen by that man, in time is ruined. He watched for the servant who goes to the
marketplace and [through her] conveying messages [to my wife] destroyed her.
First, however, gentlemen, because I should explain this to you, my modest house
has two stories, with those rooms upstairs, the women's quarters, equal in size to
the rooms below, the men's quarters. When we had a baby, the mother nursed it,
and in order that she did not have to risk going down the ladder whenever she
needed to give him a bath, I occupied the upstairs quarters, and the women, the
downstairs. And so we had grown accustomed to the arrangement, so that my
wife would often go downstairs to sleep with the baby, so she could nurse it and
it wouldn't cry. So it was for some time, and I never felt any suspicion, but was
so foolishly disposed to believe that my wife was the most temperate of all the
women in the city.

Prereading

Step 1: Building the Schemata for Comprehension

I begin by having the students review the events from sections 4 through 6. Over
the course of the semester, students take turns providing a summary of previous
passages. This helps the students to reorient themselves and practice recalling
information. During this review, I will occasionally ask them to refer to the text
and identify terms that refer to the key events, particularly if they will appear in
the next assignment; for example, in the current passage, students will see the verb
"διαφθείρω" ("destroy or corrupt") used again, so I have them locate where the
author has used this word in the previous section. We might also take time to review
basic information about the courts, context of the speech and speaker's objectives,
and, at this particular juncture in the narrative, the convention of marriage and
the members of an Athenian household as depicted in Lysias 1. During this step,
I also try to use as many expressions from the text as possible when referring to
different aspects of the background information; for example, when discussing the
courts and the audience, I refer to "ὦ ἄνδρες" ("gentlemen") and "ὦ 'Αθηναῖοι"

("men of Athens"), which the students have encountered in the first assignment and will see again repeatedly.

Step 2: Preview of the Selection

I begin this step by having students anticipate what the next section of the narrative might contain, on the basis of their understanding of the context and the objectives of the speaker. After responding to their expectations, I narrow their attention by sketching the basic details: Euphiletos will first tell the jurors how he felt about his wife. Next comes the death of his mother, what happened during one part of the funerary ritual, and how Eratosthenes made contact with Euphiletos's wife through a female slave. Then, in the third part of the passage, Euphiletos describes his house, which has two stories and sections for men and women, the birth of his child, and the changes in their living arrangement to accommodate the newborn. To condition the students to recognize the shifts in topic as they occur in the text, I alert them to the rhetorical markers in the text: the speaker signals the beginning of the first section with "ἐν μὲν οὖν τῷ πρώτῳ χρόνῳ," (literally, "in the first time," but more idiomatically, "at the beginning"), the second part with "ἐπειδὴ δέ," ("then"), and the third section with "πρῶτον μὲν οὖν" ("first").[14]

Step 3: Preview of Lexical Elements

Now that the students have a general idea of what they will encounter in each of the three thematically distinct sections, we begin the preview of lexical items by anticipating the types of words we are likely to encounter. In the first section, Euphelitos describes how he felt about his wife. After telling the students that he speaks of her in very complimentary terms, I ask them to suggest what attributes might endear her as a wife from Euphiletos's perspective and gradually narrow the discussion to focus on aspects of managing a household. Building on "οἶκος" ("house") and "οἰκῶ" ("I inhabit"), which are two of the basic vocabulary items from the elementary text, we review "οἰκία" ("household") and "οἰκειότης" ("marriage") from the previous exercise, and then consider "οἰκονόμος" ("manager of the household") and "διοικέω" ("dealing with household affairs"), and "οἰκίδιον" ("little house"), which they will encounter in the current selection. For the next two sections, we review common words for familial relationships, including "γυνή" ("wife"), "μήτηρ" ("mother"), "παῖς" ("child"), and "παιδίον" ("little child"), and then focus on transitions in life by discussing expressions for death and dying (for example "ἀποθνήσκω" and "τελευτάω"), which students will encounter in the second section, and birth, which not only looks back to the previous exercise but appears again in the third section of the current passage. There are two more lexical domains that I discuss with students prior to reading the assignment. The first deals with domestic architecture and the second with the effects of a baby on the household, particularly with regard to the care the child requires. For introducing domestic architecture, I draw a sketch of the house as Euphiletos describes it and pose questions I want students to consider as they read the passage, for example, where would they get water, and how would they get from the first to the second floor.[15] At this point, I leave the parts of the sketch unlabeled because I will have students make their own drawing and furnish labels as part of the review exercises. Finally, I ask the students to describe some of the tasks associated with caring for an infant in order to introduce words related to breast-feeding ("θηλάζω" and "τὸν τιτθὸν δίδωμι") and bathing ("λόω") and behaviors commonly associated with infants, which will alert them to "βοάω" ("cry").

In summary, the primary objectives of the process of contextualizing is to prepare the students to comprehend the text. This includes helping them to have a clear understanding of the context and build the necessary schemata of background information, reviewing lexical items that they have had before and introducing new words by drawing connections to other words related by constituent elements, thematic associations, or semantic groupings, and motivating them to develop beneficial strategies for approaching the text, for example, anticipating and guessing the meaning of words from context.

Reading

Step 1: Skimming

I like to begin the actual reading by having students skim the passage for specific information or to get the basic gist. For this passage, I first have students quickly skim the passage to locate the rhetorical markers I mentioned during the pre-reading, so they will have a clear idea of when the change in topics occur. I might also have them locate some of the lexical items we discussed. Next, I have them scan the text to locate the section where he describes his "little house." I prefer to work through this section with the students, so they clearly understand one part of the passage that will serve as a semantic anchor for the rest of the passage.

Step 2: Careful Reading for Meaning

As noted earlier, the mechanics of reading the passage will differ from passage to passage. I occasionally read the passage aloud while the students follow silently in their texts in order to acquaint them with the phonology of the words, which tends to help them retain the meanings (Laufer; Devitt). In addition, I use the opportunity of reading the passage aloud to group words into phrases that will help the students decode the passage. I then allow the students to work through the passage at their own pace and encourage them to raise their hands when they reach a section or word they do not understand. I frequently have students work in teams, so students can help each other with lexical items. If the class as a whole does not understand a word, we will often work together at deriving the meaning from context, applying a variety of strategies beginning with the analysis of the stem, suffixes, and prefixes. For example, in the section about the death of Euphelitos's mother, students will encounter the word "ἐκθορά" ("funeral procession"), which they are usually able to understand once I show them how it is related to the verb "φέρω" ("carry"). We also look to see if there are potential synonymous relationships among words or if there are rhetorical markers that indicate contrasting or antonymous relationships. We approach questions concerning syntax the same way, focusing on understanding the meaning of the passage, not using problems as pretexts for lengthy grammatical explications. Finally, whenever possible, I try to use the target language when responding to lexical and syntactical questions. Also of use are illustrations on the board, acting out the meanings or situations, replacing pronouns with proper names or making the antecedent connections clearer, rephrasing sentences with altered word order that makes comprehension easier, and referring back to words, phrases, or passages in previous assignments that will provide students with comparative insights when dealing with a lexical or grammatical difficulty.

Review and Application

The exercises in this part of the process should reflect the primary objective of the reading, which is to obtain information, both of a specific nature with regard to Euphiletos's defense and of a more general nature concerning aspects of Athenian society. As outlined earlier, teachers should vary the types of exercises to emphasize the different modalities of comprehension. One way of beginning the review component is to ask a series of questions to determine how well students identified certain elements of the text. For example, I might write a list of eight attributes on the board or give students a similar list on a handout and ask them to identify the four attributes Euphiletos assigns his wife, requiring them to recall not only what he said about his wife in the first section of the passage but also pick up the adjective "σωφρονεστάτη" ("most temperate" or "of soundest mind") he uses in the final sentence. A second activity might involve the sketch of Euphiletos's house that they drew as part of the prereading activities. For example, they could label the parts of the house using a list of vocabulary items provided for them. Both activities would offer the class the chance to review the lexical items introduced in the prereading as well as demonstrate how well they understood the passage. The next activities should explore how well they are able to recall the main ideas of the passage. For example, students might write a paragraph recalling what they understood about the passage, paraphrasing the selection, or providing a precis. As noted earlier, for evaluating the level of comprehension, I generally have students paraphrase or summarize first in English. We can then recast their work in Greek. I might also ask them to provide a title, list the main ideas, or draw a storyboard for the passage. A third type of review activity would require the students to apply the information they obtained from the passage. One approach is to have the students discuss what this passage suggests about the lives of married women in Athens, speculate on what Eratosthenes might have said in his messages to the slave or how he convinced her to convey the messages to Euphiletos's wife, consider the role this part of the narrative plays in Euphiletos's defense and the impact it might have had on the audience based on how the class felt, or asking students to draft a rebuttal to Euphiletos's narrative.

Reflection on the Standards

The use of authentic texts is especially well suited for integrating the goals of the *Standards of Classical Language Learning* into the beginning language classroom. At every stage of the reading process, goal 1, Communication, is fostered at the prereading, reading, and review and application stages by exploration of lexical, grammatical, and discourse structures. Students demonstrate knowledge of vocabulary, basic morphology and syntax, and narrative structures, read and understand the passage, and reinforce their comprehension of the passage through a variety of postreading activities (standard 1.1). In addition, students listen to oral reading of Greek, respond to simple questions, and write a summary of the passage as part of the language learning process (standard 1.2). Furthermore, information about the culture is at the heart of reading authentic texts. In Lysias 1, students observe the practices of Athenians in court and reflect on the interaction of men and women in ancient Athens (standard 2.1), and they develop an understanding of the Athenian οἶκος ("house") (standard 2.2). Through reading an authentic text such as Lysias 1, moreover, students can expand their knowledge of social relations in ancient Athens and connect their knowledge of Athenian law to modern legal systems (standard 3.2). After reading Lysias 1, students have the opportunity to compare and contrast Athenian courtroom procedure and rules for evidence with American courts and can reflect on how gender shapes expectations and interactions within a marriage in both ancient Athens and the modern world (standard 4.2). Finally, by exploring issues of gender and status in ancient Athens, students can recognize the continuing relevance of these issues in the modern world (standard 5.2).[16]

The Role of Technology: *Perseus*

As noted earlier, having students encounter authentic materials as often and early as possible allows them to acquire the language more efficiently. However, providing students with authentic texts presents the teacher with certain problems. First, teachers must often devote a considerable amount of time to creating the conceptual infrastructure students need to reach a satisfactory level of comprehension. Second, the number of available printed texts and commentaries severely restricts the options for teachers who would like access to enough variety to support student-centered curricula, which allow the teacher to take the student's individual background into consideration as it relates to the student's prior knowledge, experience in formulating effective strategies for approaching a second or foreign language, and interests. Compiling an anthology of appropriate readings and managing the distribution to students generally requires more time and energy than most teachers can afford. Even if a set of commercially available texts could provide the required variety, there still remains the issue of cost, if teachers require students to purchase more than one text, or the issue of copyright and the expense of duplication.

Electronically based resources, which are rapidly growing in number and quality as well as availability via the web, offer a compelling solution. Computer applications for use in the acquisition of foreign languages fall into three broad categories: packages that attempt to individualize instruction by creating an interactive environment in which students respond to questions and receive immediate feedback on the correctness of their responses;[17] databases of authentic language in textual, audio, and video formats;[18] and word-processing or authoring systems, lexica, and applications that check for spelling and grammatical errors that assist beginning and intermediate students as they write compositions by making lexicographical and grammatical information readily available along with examples of usage and expressions suited to a variety of contexts.[19]

By far the most significant online resource for the study of ancient Greek is *Perseus* (www.perseus.tufts.edu). Representing the texts of forty major authors, the database contains nearly eight million words of ancient Greek. Thousands of images of topography, artifacts from daily life, vases, sculpture, architecture, and coins complement the textual database. *Perseus* also offers a set of tools for analyzing and studying Greek texts; for example, a student can obtain a morphological analysis of any word, including the lexical lemmata and lists of the possible grammatical attributes. They can also access the lexical information from Liddell and Scott's *Greek-English Lexicon*. *Perseus* provides users with statistics on the frequency of words, which will help teachers decide which words merit ongoing attention in contextualizing and evaluative activities and those that require only incidental clarification. Because *Perseus* will generate a list of occurrences for any word, teachers can design activities that will allow students to generate meanings through examining the same word in more than one context, and for teachers and students who wish to begin with English expressions and find corresponding words or phrases in Greek, students can use *Perseus* to search the lexicon for Greek words that contain particular English words in their definitions. The scope of textual materials in *Perseus*, along with the basic lexical and morphological support, give teachers greater latitude in designing student-centered curricula (see Mahoney; Mahoney and Rydberg-Cox). With very basic, widely available graphic applications, teachers can also use the library of digital images to supplement listening and reading exercises with visual aids.

Conclusion

Developing a full argument for the adoption of a whole-language or four-skills approach to ancient Greek would go well beyond the scope of this chapter. The comments and strategies presented here will serve, I hope, as an invitation to draw on the work of cognitive psychologists, linguists, and colleagues in modern languages who continue to develop and refine our understanding of how human beings acquire and use language. Perhaps of more immediate, practical value, they are intended to situate the teaching of ancient Greek within the current standards for instruction in foreign languages, which are exerting a significant formative influence on the evolution of curricula in the United States. In the final analysis, however, creating aural, textual, and even visual course materials, finding ways of conveying lexical and syntactic information in the target language, generating contexts that allow students to acquire a knowledge of the grammar more inductively, and, finally, developing conversational fluency as a means of helping students develop communicative strategies for oral and verbal discourse will serve to invigorate any teacher of ancient Greek and the discipline as a whole, because these approaches ultimately make better use of Aristotle's λόγος (*Politics* 1253a1–15), the communicative impulse of human beings and their innate ability to acquire language.

Notes

1. For a discussion of the human capacity for acquiring and using language, see Crain and Lillo-Martin 3–70 and Pinker 262–6. For an overview of the differences between the processes of acquiring L1 and L2, see Brown 2000: 49–77. With regard to age differences, see Krashen 1985: 12–3.

2. The views and curricular perspectives in this chapter most closely conform to the Natural Approach as developed by Krashen (1981, 1982, 1985, 1994) and Krashen and Terrell. Briefly summarized, the Natural Approach attempts to adapt the way human beings acquire L1 to the acquistion of L2. The highly inductive methods as well as components of the underlying theory continue to be the objects of considerable debate among both theorists and practitioners. See, for example, Barasch and James. Proponents of inductive approaches have received additional support from a recent interest in constructivism as an epistemology with application to the acquisition of foreign languages. See Reagan. On the standards, see Abbot, Davis, and Gascoyne and Gascoyne et al. The goals for teaching ancient languages and the interest in approaches that emphasize all four communicative skills have attracted recent critical attention. Carpenter proposes a set of objectives for Latin programs that do not include the reading and comprehension of ancient texts. Ball and Ellsworth disparage attempts to view Latin as a viable means of communication and argue that "academic politics" and an "obsession with the real" lie behind the movement to develop a four-skills approach for Latin instruction. Abbott and Davis make a spirited response.

3. For a study involving students of German who are native speakers of English, see Lund 1991. See also Stevick 282–3.

4. See Bernhardt's (168–71) theory of second language reading and Swaffar's description of the interactive process. Barnett 1989: 9–35 surveys bottom-up, top-down, interactive, and reading/writing models. Many of the models stem from work done by Miller. For a helpful schematic representation of the reading process, which organizes the elements according to Miller's typology and the "higher-level" and "lower-level" framework, see Devitt 460.

5. See Barnett's (1988) controlled study involving more than two hundred fourth-semester students of French. To develop reading strategies, her students (153) "discussed and practiced reading strategies in English before applying them to French texts; students became conversant in English and French with such terms as context, skim, scan, and guess. They were encouraged to predict as they read and to analyze their reading styles; they were also tested on some of these reading strategies."

6. See Bernhardt's (127, 147) work on the influence of initial assumptions and general background knowledge. See also Swaffar 129–30.

7. There is increasing evidence that a student's reading skills in his or her native language contribute significantly to the ability to comprehend texts in a second language. See

Fecteau. See Barnett 1988: 57–8 for the significance of the students' perceived use of reading strategy, Krashen 1985: 3–4 for a summary of the affective filter, and Lee for a discussion of the role of affect in reading.

8. Because spoken discourse generally takes place in a more dynamic context influenced by the immediacy of the speaker and hearer and the nature of the information, the intention usually plays a greater role for listeners than for readers. See Dunkel 101–3. For an overview of task-based approaches to foreign language texts, see Knutson.

9. Lund 1990 identifies six types of functions or intentions that listeners have as they encounter spoken language: identification (for example, recognizing words, categories of words, or morphological information), orientation (recognizing the type of discourse, the speaker, the context), main idea comprehension, detail comprehension, full comprehension, and replication. He also outlines nine modes of responding: doing (responding physically as practices in total physical response), choosing ("The listener selects from alternatives such as pictures, objects, graphics, texts, or actions."), transferring (for example, drawing a picture), answering (providing answers to questions about the text), condensing, extending (providing text that goes beyond what the listener heard), duplicating, modeling, and conversing. Richards 228–30, for example, identifies thirty-three microskills for conversational listening and eighteen for academic listening. While Richards's taxonomy is neither canonical nor exhaustive, it does illustrate the complexity of the listening process and does introduce ways of designing listening exercises that can incrementally develop the students' listening skills.

10. For the purposes of reviewing or evaluating reading comprehension, questions that ask students to respond in the target language, particularly those at the beginning and intermediate stages, generally fail to provide accurate assessment. See Bernhardt 191–219, Swaffar 125, and Wolf 484.

11. For a discussion of the role of authentic text in SLA, see Devitt 462–3. For the use of authentic texts in developing listening skills see, for example, Bacon 545–6, Gilman and Moody 333, and Richards 234, and in fostering reading comprehension see Barnett 1989: 145, Hadley 188–92, and Swaffar 139–40. For the role of literary texts as part of a whole language approach in secondary and university settings, see Adair-Hauck, Crooker and Rabiteau, Maxim, and Weist.

12. Depending on the interests of the students and their proficiency, other possible narratives include Antiphon 1.14-20, Lysias 3.5-20, 12.4-18, and [Demosthenes] 54.3-12. Using the generic knowledge structures of Graesser and Clark, Brown 1998: 196–7 provides theoretical support for using narratives.

13. This passage contains two textual issues that are instructive with regard to the approach outlined in this section. When students encounter [ἀγαθή], I generally take a moment to discuss what the brackets mean and then use this as an example to illustrate the problems nonnative speakers encounter when processing a text. Apparently confused about φειδωλὸς, someone in the manuscript tradition presumably believed that φειδωλὸς was a noun and needed a modifying adjective to match the preceding phrase οἰκονόμος δεινή. This helps the students to see how a reader's expectations and the impulse to infer meaning from context work. It is, in fact, a "mistake" I hope students will also make. The second is a syntactical problem in the sentence: ἐπειδὴ δέ μοι ἡ μήτηρ ἐτελεύτησε, ἣ πάντων τῶν κακῶν ἀποθανοῦσα αἰτία μοι γεγένηται. This sentence has plagued editors for decades. From the grammatical perspective, the problem is a subordinate temporal clause introduced by ἐπειδὴ followed by a relative clause, which is also a subordinated structure. In short, this sentence does not have a main clause as the text currently reads. Editors have proposed a number of explanations. I follow Wilamowitz-Moellendorff, who

suggested that this was an example of anacoluthon (see *Hermes* 58 [1923] 63 n. 1). What is important in the context of the present discussion is the fact that the "sentence" conveys a clear meaning, which students should be able to derive. As noted earlier, language from direct communicative contexts is filled with inconsistencies of this nature. Such linguistic phenomena should motivate students to remain flexible in their "bottom-up" textual processing and focus on the meaning.

14. Note that rather than just draw the students' attention to the particles, I have allowed the particles to remain in their context as part of a prepositional phrase. This is meant to motivate students to process information in phrases rather than as individual words.

15. For a discussion of the house in light of excavations, see Morgan and Morris.

16. For further activities and suggestions for integrating the Standards with reading, see Arens and Swaffar, Weist.

17. The selection of available CALL software for ancient Greek is much more limited than it is for Latin. See Johnson et al. for reviews of several applications, including the Electronic Workbook by Mastronarde, Gramma by Burian and Blackwell, and JACT Greek by Neuburg. Information about applications is available from Centaur Systems, 407 N. Brearly Street, Madison, WI 53703-1603; telephone: 608-255-6979; fax: 608-255-6949; URL: www.centaursystems.com; and Greek-Language.com, 303 Forbush Mountain Drive, Chapel Hill, NC 27514; URL: greek-language.com.

18. For the study of ancient Greek, the *Thesaurus Linguae Graecae* represents the most comprehensive collection of electronic texts. The CD is available from the TLG Project, 3450 Berkeley Place, University of California Irvine, Irvine, CA 92697-5550; telephone: 949-824-7031; fax: 949-824-8434; e-mail: tlg@uci.edu; URL: www.tlg.uci.edu/. The Packard Humanities Institute distributes CDs with Latin literary texts, Greek documentary papyri, and Greek inscriptions. For further information address inquiries to Packard Humanities Institute, 300 Second Street, Suite 201, Los Altos, CA 94022; telephone: 650-948-0150; fax: 650-948-4135; e-mail: phi@packhum.org. For resources on the web, see the Stoa Consortium, www.stoa.org, the home of the *Suda On-Line*, URL: www.stoa.org/sol, and *Diotima: Women and Gender in the Ancient World*, URL: www.stoa.org/diotima.

19. Currently no applications solely of this type are available for ancient Greek. Examples for French are Antidote and Le Correcteur Pro. For further information about software for foreign language instruction, contact World of Reading, Ltd., P.O. Box 13092, Atlanta, Georgia 30324-0092; telephone: 404-233-4042 or 800-729-3703; fax: 404-237-5511; e-mail: polyglot@wor.com; URL: www.wor.com; or WorldLanguage.com, 2130 Sawtelle Blvd., Suite 304A, Los Angeles, CA 90025; telephone: 310-996-2300 or 800-900-8803; fax: 310-996-2303; e-mail: moreinfo@worldlanguage.com; URL: www.worldlanguage.com.

Works Cited

Abbott, Martha G., and Sally Davis. 1996. "Hyperreality and the Study of Latin: Living in a Fairy Tale World." *Modern Language Journal* 80: 85–6.

Abbott, Martha G., Sally Davis, and Richard Gascoyne. 1998. "National Standards and Curriculum Guidelines." In Richard A. LaFleur, ed., *Latin for the Twenty-first Century: From Concept to Classroom*. Glenview, IL: Scott Foresman–Addison Wesley, 44–58.

Adair-Hauck, Bonnie. 1996. "Practical Whole Language Strategies for Secondary and University-Level Students." *Foreign Language Annals* 29: 253–71.

Arens, Katherine, and Janet Swaffar. 2000. "Reading Goals and the Standards for Foreign Language Learning." *Foreign Language Annals* 33: 104–19.

Bacon, Susan M. 1989. "Listening for Real in the Foreign-Language Classroom." *Foreign Language Annals* 22: 543–51.

Balme, Maurice, and Gilbert Lawall. 2003. *Athenaze: An Introduction to Ancient Greek.* 2nd ed. Oxford: Oxford University Press.

Ball, Robert J., and J. D. Ellsworth. 1996. "The Emperor's New Clothes: Hyperreality and the Study of Latin." *Modern Language Journal* 80: 77–84.

Barasch, Ronald M., and C. Vaughn James. 1994. *Beyond the Monitor Model: Comments on Current Theory and Practice in Second Language Acquisition.* Boston: Heinle and Heinle.

Barnett, Marva A. 1988. "Reading through Context: How Real and Perceived Strategy Use Affects L2 Comprehension." *Modern Language Journal* 72: 150–62.

———. 1989. *More Than Meets the Eye: Foreign Language Reading: Theory and Practice.* Englewood Cliffs, NJ: Prentice Hall Regents.

Bernhardt, Elizabeth B. 1991. *Reading Development in a Second Language: Theoretical, Empirical, and Classroom Perspectives.* Norwood, NJ: Ablex.

Brown, Carol M. 1998. "L2 Reading: An Update on Relevant L1 Research." *Foreign Language Annals* 31: 191–202.

Brown, H. Douglas. 2000. *Principles of Language Learning and Teaching.* 4th ed. Englewood Cliffs, NJ: Prentice Hall Regents.

Carpenter, Daniel P. 2000. "Reassessing the Goal of Latin Pedagogy." *Classical Journal* 95: 391–5.

Cohen, Andrew D. 1994. *Assessing Language Ability in the Classroom.* Boston: Heinle and Heinle.

Crain, Stephen, and Diane Lillo-Martin. 1999. *An Introduction to Linguistic Theory and Language Acquisition.* Oxford: Blackwell.

Crane, Gregory R., ed. *The Perseus Digital Library.* Available at www.perseus.tufts.edu.

Crooker, Jill, and Kate Rabiteau. 2004. "Enriching the Latin Curriculum by Adapting Authentic Passages." *Classical Outlook* 82: 14–8.

Davis, James N., and Linda Bistodeau. 1993. "How Do L1 and L2 Reading Differ? Evidence from Think Aloud Protocols." *Modern Language Journal* 77: 459–72.

Devitt, Seán. 1997. "Interacting with Authentic Texts: Multilayered Processes." *Modern Language Journal* 81: 457–69.

Dunkel, Patricia A. 1986. "Developing Listening Fluency in L2: Theoretical Principles and Pedagogical Considerations." *Modern Language Journal* 70: 99–106.

Fecteau, Monique L. 1999. "First- and Second-Language Reading Comprehension of Literary Texts." *Modern Language Journal* 83: 475–93.

Gascoyne, Richard C., et al. 1997. *Standards for Classical Language Learning.* Oxford, OH: American Classical League.

Gilman, Robert A., and Loranna M. Moody. 1984. "What Practitioners Say about Listening: Research Implications for the Classroom." *Foreign Language Annals* 17: 331–4.

Glisan, Eileen W. 1988. "A Plan for Teaching Listening Comprehension: Adaptation of an Instructional Reading Model." *Foreign Language Annals* 21: 9–16.

Grabe, William. 2000. "Reading Research and Its Implications for Reading Assessment." In A. J. Kunnan, ed., *Fairness and Validation in Language Assessment: Selected Papers from the Nineteenth Language Testing Research Colloquium, Orlando, Florida.* Cambridge, UK: Cambridge University Press, 226–62.

Graesser, A. C., and L. F. Clark. 1985. *Structures and Procedures of Implicit Knowledge.* Norwood, NJ: Ablex.

Hadley, Alice Omaggio. 2001. *Teaching Language in Context.* 3rd ed. Boston: Heinle and Heinle.

Johnson, Dale D., and P. David Pearson. 1984. *Teaching Reading Vocabulary*. 2nd ed. New York: Holt, Rinehart, and Winston.

Johnson, Patricia. 1982. "Effects of Building Background Knowledge." *TESOL Quarterly* 16: 503–15.

Johnson, William A., et al. 1995. "Computer Assisted Instruction (CAI) in the Learning of Greek and Latin." *Bryn Mawr Classical Review* 95.02.11. On-line. Available at http://ccat .sas.upenn.edu/bmcr/1995/95.02.11.html.

Just, Marcel Adam, and Patricia A. Carpenter. 1980. "A Theory of Reading: From Eye Fixations to Comprehension." *Psychological Review* 87: 329–54.

———. 1992. "A Capacity Theory of Comprehension: Individual Differences in Working Memory." *Psychological Review* 99: 122–49.

Knutson, Elizabeth M. 1997. "Reading with a Purpose: Communicative Reading Tasks for the Foreign Language Classroom." *Foreign Language Annals* 30: 49–57.

Koda, Keiko. 1996. "L2 Word Recognition Research: A Critical Review." *Modern Language Journal* 80: 450–60.

———. 1997. "Orthographic Knowledge in L2 Lexical Processing: A Cross-linguistic Perspective." In James Coady and Thomas Huckin, eds., *Second Language Vocabulary Acquisition*. Cambridge, UK: Cambridge University Press, 35–52.

Krashen, Stephen D. 1981. *Second Language Acquisition and Second Language Learning*. Oxford: Pergamon Press.

———. 1982. *Principles and Practice in Second Language Acquisition*. New York: Pergamon Press.

———. 1985. *The Input Hypothesis: Issues and Implications*. London: Longman.

———. 1994. "The Input Hypothesis and its Rivals." In Nick C. Ellis, ed., *Implicit and Explicit Learning of Languages*. London: Academic Press.

Krashen, Stephen D., and Tracy D. Terrell. 1983. *The Natural Approach: Language Acquisition in the Classroom*. Hayward, CA: Alemany Press.

Laufer, Batia. 1990. "Why Are Some Words More Difficult Than Others? Some Intralexical Factors that Affect the Learning of Words." *International Review of Applied Linguistics* 28: 293–307.

Lee, James F. 1999. "Clashes in L2 Reading: Research Versus Practice and Readers' Misconceptions." In Dolly Jesuita Young, ed., *Affect in Foreign Language and Second Language Learning*. Boston: McGraw-Hill.

Liddell, Henry George, and Robert Scott. 1940. *A Greek-English Lexicon*. Revised by Henry Stuart Jones and Roderick McKenzie. Oxford: Clarendon Press.

Lund, Randall J. 1990. "A Taxonomy for Teaching Second Language Listening." *Foreign Language Annals* 23: 105–15.

———. 1991. "A Comparison of Second Language Listening and Reading Comprehension." *Modern Language Journal* 75: 196–204.

Mahoney, Anne. 2001. "Tools for Students in the Perseus Digital Library." *CALICO Journal* 18: 269–82.

Mahoney, Anne, and Jeffrey A. Rydberg-Cox. 2002. "Vocabulary Building in the Perseus Digital Library." *Classical Outlook* 79: 145–9.

Maxim, Hiram. 2002. "A Study into the Feasibility and Effects of Reading Extended Authentic Discourse in the Beginning German Language Classroom." *Modern Language Journal* 86: 20–35.

Miller, George A. 1988. "The Challenge of Universal Literacy." *Science* 241: 1293–9.

Morgan, Gareth. 1982. "Euphiletos' House: Lysias 1." *Transactions of the American Philological Association* 112: 115–23.

Morris, Ian. 1998. "Remaining Invisible: The Archaeology of the Excluded in Classical Athens." In S. Joshel and S. Murnaghan, eds., *Women and Slaves in Greco-Roman Culture*. London: Routledge, 193–220.

New York State Education Department. 1986. *Latin for Communication: New York State Syllabus*. Albany: New York State Education Department.

Paribakht, T. Sima, and Marjorie Bingham Wesche. 1997. "Vocabulary Enhancement Activities and Reading for Meaning in Second Language Vocabulary Acquisition." In James Coady and Thomas Huckin, eds., *Second Language Vocabulary Acquistion*. Cambridge, UK: Cambridge University Press, 174–200.

Pinker, Steven. 1994. *The Language Instinct*. New York: Morrow.

Reagan, Timothy. 1999. "Constructivist Epistemology and Second/Foreign Language Pedagogy." *Foreign Language Annals* 32: 413–25.

Richards, Jack C. 1983. "Listening Comprehension: Approach, Design, Procedure." *TESOL Quarterly* 17: 219–40.

Rubin, D., T. Hafer, and K. Arata. 2000. "Reading and Listening to Oral-Based and Literate-Based Discourse." *Communication Education* 49: 1–24.

Saffire, Paula, and Catherine Freis. 1999. *Ancient Greek Alive*. 3rd ed. Chapel Hill, NC: University of North Carolina Press.

Schoder, Raymond V., and Vincent C. Horrigan. 1985. *A Reading Course in Homeric Greek*. Chicago: Loyola University Press.

Schulz, Renate A. 1991. "Second Language Acquisition Theories and Teaching Practice: How Do They Fit?" *Modern Language Journal* 75: 17–26.

Sienkewicz, Thomas J., Danetta Genung, Carol Ihlendorf, and Sue Robertson. 1999. "Latin Teaching Standards: Process, Philosophy and Application." *Classical Journal* 95: 55–63.

Stevick, Earl W. 1984. "Similarities and Differences between Oral and Written Comprehension: An Imagist View." *Foreign Language Annals* 17: 281–3.

Swaffar, Janet K. 1988. "Readers, Texts, and Second Languages: The Interactive Processes." *Modern Language Journal* 72: 123–49.

Swaffar, Janet K., and Susan Bacon. 1993. "Reading and Listening Comprehension: Perspectives on Research and Implications for Practice." In Alice Omaggio Hadley, ed., *Research in Language Learning*. Lincolnwood, IL: National Textbook.

Weist, Vanisa D. 2004. "Literature in Lower-Level Courses: Making Progress in Both Language and Reading Skills." *Foreign Language Annals* 37: 209–23.

Wesche, Marjorie Bingham, and T. Sima Paribakht. 2000. "Reading-Based Exercises in Second Language Vocabulary Learning: An Introspective Study." *Modern Language Journal* 84: 196–213.

Wilamowitz-Moellendorff, Ulrich von. 1923. "Lesefrüchte." *Hermes* 58:57–61.

Wolf, Darlene F. 1993. "A Comparison of Assessment Tasks Used to Measure FL Reading Comprehension." *Modern Language Journal* 77: 473–89.

Young, Dolly Jesuita. 1991. "Creating a Low-Anxiety Classroom Environment: What Does Language Anxiety Research Suggest?" *Modern Language Journal* 75: 426–39.

CHAPTER 8

Ancient Greek in Classroom Conversation

Paula Saffire

This chapter covers four topics: (1) *why* to use conversational ancient Greek in a beginning course in the language, (2) *how* to do it, (3) *obstacles* to overcome, and (4) *future possibilities*. I shall concentrate on *how*, giving specific recommendations as well as a transcript of classroom conversation. I begin with the question *why* because unless teachers are convinced that the enterprise is worthwhile, it will hardly matter *how*. My remarks are based principally on direct observation or reports by students and teachers, and are bolstered by the research of scholars.

I have used spontaneous, conversational ancient Greek in the classroom for over twenty years, originally at the University of Massachusetts at Amherst (1972–74) and recently at Butler University (1989–present). Other professors who have done this are Eliot Youman at Mercer University, Joel Farber at Franklin & Marshall College, Catherine Freis at Millsaps College, Jeffrey Wills at the University of Wisconsin, and David Kovacs at the University of Virginia. Information was gleaned through conversations, remarks overheard, student questionnaires, and letters. (As others of you try this method, I would appreciate hearing about your experience.)

All the professors just mentioned used conversations from my textbook *Ancient Greek Alive* (Saffire and Freis).[1] This beginning ancient Greek textbook provides scripts for using conversational ancient Greek during the first two weeks of class. On the first day students learn to greet each other, and ask and report on each other's names. On the second day students learn to understand and produce short sentences about what they see, know, and have. Until the third day, transliteration is used for any Greek that needs to be written on the blackboard. On the third day the Greek alphabet is introduced. For homework, students are asked to read the first pages of the book, which are simply the scripts of what has been spoken in class. Conversation and other oral practices are the primary mode of education for the first two weeks. After that, conversation is phased out, almost entirely. The two weeks provide an introduction to Greek grammar, which helps the students learn throughout the year. (See the end of the chapter for three sample lessons.)

Why Use Conversational Ancient Greek

There are no longer native speakers of ancient Greek. The point in teaching students to hear and speak ancient Greek must be to make them good receivers of written communication, that is, good readers. My goal of using conversational Greek to help students become better readers is consistent with standard 1.2 of the *Standards for Classical Language Learning*: "Students use orally, listen to, and speak Latin or Greek as part of the language learning process."

Before listing the advantages of using conversation to teach, I shall begin with an appeal to imagination: Imagine that there has been some sort of nuclear holocaust and you are the only person left in the world who knows English. The libraries are full of books in English, and people want to read them. They ask you to teach them English. Would you ever in your wildest dreams teach them to read only, without teaching them to speak? Would it not seem the most effective, natural, and enjoyable method to teach your students to speak English in order to teach them to read? And if this is so, do not the same arguments hold for ancient Greek or Latin as well? To be sure, it will not be as easy for you, since you are not a native speaker. But it will still be the best method for your students.

The natural method, of teaching by speaking, provides many advantages. I shall begin with the psychological advantages. These alone would make using conversational ancient Greek worthwhile. In addition, there are pedagogical advantages, which will be described afterward.

Relaxation in Class

The first day of ancient Greek is often an intimidating experience for students. Usually they are confronted with a strange language, a strange script, and strange rules (declension or conjugation). The oral method reduces the strangeness. Most students find this a relaxing way to begin their study of ancient Greek. Leon Galis, a philosophy professor who learned ancient Greek at Franklin & Marshall by the oral approach after having taken Greek in two different grammar-translation courses, commented in a letter to me that he had been skeptical about the oral approach to begin but soon saw the wisdom of the method, finding it to be the "most engaging" and "least intimidating" way to learn Greek.

A caution: while most students find this nonintimidating, a totally visual learner may be frightened. Very few students are totally visual. These students reveal themselves by the way they move their eyes as they make conversation, as if picturing something in writing. Sometimes they will actually write something and look at it before they are willing to risk speaking. They need to be reassured that learning will soon become primarily visual (Barbe and Swassing; Scarcella and Oxford; chapters 2 and 3).

Relaxation saves energy, which can be used for learning. Specifically, relaxation lowers what Krashen calls the "affective filter," the emotional screen that causes students to filter out much of what has been heard in class (Krashen 1982: 30–3; Krashen and Terrell 19, 37–9, 46). The affective filter is related to the distinction between *input*, what the teacher tries to put into the student's mind, versus *intake*, what the student actually takes in (Gass and Madden 3). Anxiety is the most important factor in raising the affective filter. Lowering anxiety will not be enough in itself to guarantee learning, of course, since, as Gardner (1988, 2002) points out, it is but one of four types of individual differences that directly affect achievement: intelligence, language aptitude, motivation, and situational anxiety.[2]

Relaxation in Reading

When students begin by speaking ancient Greek, this both paves the way for and enhances relaxation in reading. In the first place, relaxation is a habit, and once students have learned to relax speaking, they will carry that relaxation into reading. Second, when their first reading is classroom scripts, they need only decipher script to sound without simultaneously hunting for meanings, since they are reading material they have already spoken or heard. A Millsaps student made the following comment on an evaluation: "The part of the textbook which helped me most was the scripts. Learning the sound before the letters made it easier to read on sight." Finally, since oral Greek allows for a rapid and natural acquisition of vocabulary, by the time students begin reading stories they already have mastered a significant amount of vocabulary, which means they are not burdened by a host of unfamiliar words that they must learn as they read.

The traditional method of teaching reading—by rules, paradigms, and isolated sentences—often produces a competent but tense mode of reading—"cryptoanalytic decoding," as Krashen calls it (1985: 91, citing Newmark). It seems likely that the newer method, of giving reading passages in easy ancient Greek, will prevail. This method allows for more relaxation in reading.

Enjoyment

Experience shows me that students enjoy very much communicating out loud in ancient Greek. Why? Because it makes Greek come alive and, as William Blake said, "Life delights in life." Genuine communication is simply enjoyable for humans. Enjoyment is no trivial matter; we ought not to underrate it. If relaxation conserves energy, enjoyment generates it. And an enormous amount of energy is needed for students to absorb the patterns of ancient Greek. We teachers will be asking students to learn, for example, a verb that has about 120 forms. If we can boost their energy for learning by giving them an enjoyable experience, they will have a far better chance of success. Gardner (1988: 137) stresses the connection between enjoyment and learning: "It is equally reasonable . . . that happy experiences in language learning situations and success in learning the language will foster positive attitudes and enhance motivation." Krashen goes even further with what he calls *the pleasure hypothesis*: "those activities that are good for language learning are regularly perceived by students to be pleasant" (1994). In other words, effective language teaching can be "Eat your ice cream" not "Take your medicine."

Confidence in Progress

Conversational ancient Greek produces not only enjoyment but confidence and a sense of progress. In the beginning, progress in oral ancient Greek is far more rapid than progress in reading can be. At the end of the two weeks, Judy, who was taking beginning Hebrew simultaneously in a reading-only course, told me, "We're barely finishing the alphabet in Hebrew. I can't believe how much I've learned in

Greek already." And I overheard Vera say, "I'm so excited. Speaking was really a good idea. I have so much confidence."[3]

The Competitive Edge

I am not sure how important this factor is, but perhaps we should not underestimate it. During the second week, Judy told me that her friend, who was taking French, asked what she did in Greek class. "What did you tell her?" I asked. Flashing me a radiant smile, eyes sparkling, she said, "I told her, 'Oh, we speak just the way you do.'" I could see she was delighted not to be perceived as disadvantaged. It is perhaps relevant to note that Latin was overtaken by foreign languages in enrollment in the United States only after the Berlitz method, with its oral approach, became an accepted method of teaching. As Thompson et al. (22–3) report:

> Prior to the mid–nineteenth century, foreign language study in the United States was almost totally confined to the study of classical languages (Latin and Greek). The methodology of choice was Grammar-Translation. . . . The era of immigration (1840–1910) saw the introduction of modern foreign languages (particularly German and French) to public and private school curricula, but the Grammar-Translation method remained the most common . . . through the 1940's. . . . No modern foreign language overtook Latin until after World War II.

(For historical trends in teaching Latin, see Kitchell; Wills.) Although the intellectual climate in this country is not as favorable as before to the reading of Latin and Greek texts, it seems that providing a more enjoyable learning experience—which the oral method does—will increase enrollments.

Class Solidarity

Speaking ancient Greek offers a chance for a great deal of student interaction. After teaching students to say "What is your name?" and "My name is—" in ancient Greek on the first day, I have them go around the room introducing themselves to each other in pairs. At other times they will be shaking hands or giving and taking books with the appropriate, "I give you the book," "I take the book." And I am often asking them questions about each other, as I shift persons of the verb. ("Do you see me?" "Oh friend, does Kate see me?") This promotes a sense of class solidarity. Students know each other and, because they have been taking risks together, they have a feeling of support for and from each other. Like relaxation and enjoyment, a feeling of class solidarity can liberate some extra energy for learning Greek.

Humor

One final benefit is that a lot of humor is generated. Why I am not sure. But I observe that there is a lot of laughing in classes full of conversational ancient Greek.

I guess that mistakes and difficulties seem funny. The tension of speaking is dissipated in laughter at mistakes. This is a friendly laughter, since all are in the same boat together. It enhances enjoyment as well as class solidarity.

Humanistic Development

Nothing so fosters humanistic development, in my opinion, as reading the great Greek texts, which is the goal of learning Greek. But students will not be ready to read these with ease for quite a while. In the meantime, one of the benefits of conversation is that it helps create an atmosphere that nourishes the self. Moskowitz not only talks about warmth in the classroom but gives ways to attain it. The aim of a humanistic classroom is to produce self-actualizing persons:

> Self-actualizing persons accept themselves and others, are natural and spontaneous rather than conforming, have a mission in life and a strong sense of responsibility, are independent and look to themselves for their own growth, experience pleasurable, awesome feelings related to everyday life, have great empathy and affection for humanity, are not prejudiced, and are creative in their approach to things. (Moskowitz 12)

This may seem like a tall order; but, in truth, there is no reason that a college classroom should not foster the growth of the self as it fosters learning.

The foregoing are psychological benefits. They are combined with the genuine and solid educational benefits that I will now describe.

Rapid and Secure Acquisition of Vocabulary

As mentioned earlier, using conversational ancient Greek enables students to learn a large amount of vocabulary, naturally and firmly, in a short time. This in turn enables them to start reading interesting stories quickly. Late in the second semester, Stuart lamented to me, "In the beginning we learned vocabulary so easily. Now we have to *drum* it into our heads from a list." He was stating in a concrete way what Krashen and Terrell have pointed out in the abstract: that vocabulary is best learned orally and contextually, and that there is no evidence that rote learning helps much. As put by Krashen and Terrell (156),

> the Natural Approach is based on the premise that . . . new words are acquired when they are heard in an utterance or in a sentence that is comprehensible. . . . It may be argued that a Natural Approach to vocabulary acquisition is impractical, in that classroom time is limited and that only a small range of topics can be discussed. Thus, some intervention in the form of more direct teaching, such as rote learning or vocabulary exercises, is necessary. There is no evidence, however, that such intervention helps much. It appears to be the case that

"memorized" or "drilled" vocabulary does not stick; words learned by rote or drill do not enter permanent memory storage. True vocabulary acquisition with long-term retention occurs *only with meaningful exposure in situations in which real communication takes place.*[4]

In terms of quantity alone, it is possible to present an extraordinary amount of ancient Greek in a short time by speaking. Reading, on the other hand, is very slow in the beginning. As Peterson (87) says, "no other type of language input is as easy to process as spoken language, received through listening." A two-minute interchange from the fourth day of my beginning Greek class is transcribed later in this chapter. During those two minutes, 155 Greek words (based on 13 lexical entries) were used by teacher and students, 149 correctly. (The teacher spoke at normal conversational pace, the students much more slowly.) Imagine how many Greek words could be *read* in two minutes by the fourth day of class. Considerably less!

By using ancient Greek conversationally, my students acquire in two weeks a *working* vocabulary of over 50 words—not precariously, by studying and reading them several times, but naturally and firmly, by repeated use, having heard these words probably 80 times on average. (In the two-minute interchange, the phrase τὰ γράμματα was used 24 times.) I once overheard Vera and Cammie talking in the hallway. "Don't you wish we were still speaking Greek?" Vera asked. To which Cammie replied, "Everything I learned by speaking I remember."

Higher Levels of Proficiency

Why would anyone teach students to understand or produce spoken ancient Greek? Lightbown and Spada summarize research that shows that learners who interacted with each other in the target language produced greater quantity and a greater variety of speech than if they interacted only with the teacher. In another experiment, Pica, Young, and Doughty found that "modifications in interaction led to higher levels of comprehension than modifications in input " (cited in Lightbown and Spada 86). Researchers such as Merrill Swain (1985, 1995, 2000), moreover, argue that comprehensible input alone is insufficient in attaining higher levels of proficiency. It is only when learners are required to produce the language that they are forced to test their knowledge of the language in the real world. Finally, linguists and language educators alike argue that an integrated skills approach to language teaching that involves listening, speaking, reading, and writing leads to more proficient language learners (Poole 77).[5]

Reading Aloud Is Smoother

One other benefit of beginning with oral ancient Greek is that students read aloud more smoothly, without fear and hesitation. This was pointed out to me by Joel Farber. After teaching by the usual method for thirty years, Farber adopted the conversational approach. He reports that his students read aloud better than he has ever seen. This makes sense. Reading aloud combines two tasks: decipherment of text and production of sounds; while conversation is simply the production of sounds, a single task. If students master the single task first, they will be more confident and competent when they begin to combine it with another.

Natural Previews: Natural, Nonsystematic Learning in Anticipation of the System

This is the most important benefit of using conversational ancient Greek in the beginning: *students are able to pick up a large amount of grammatical information unsystematically*. This learning is comparatively effortless and will stand them in good stead for the rest of the term. As the formidable array of paradigms unroll, they will find in each paradigm reassuring islands of familiarity. And they will have mastered basic concepts (such as aspect) from the beginning in an informal way. You could say they have had a "natural preview."

On the very first day, my students learn, by echoing, to say τί ἐστι τὸ ὄνομά σου, which will make learning the enclitic rules less daunting later. And they learn γιγνώσκωμεν ἀλλήλους ("let's know each other") versus γιγνώσκομεν ἀλλήλους ("we know each other"), from which they learn to distinguish a subjunctive meaning from an indicative and to understand how important endings are. (Also, the hortatory "we" subjunctive can now be used in stories, although subjunctives will not be systematically introduced until months later.)

During their first two weeks, my students learn, in a nonsystematic way: (1) some cases of first, second, and third declension nouns, (2) forms of personal pronouns, (3) some enclitic patterns, (4) some present forms and infinitives of verbs following the patterns of ἀκούω, βούλομαι, and δείκνυμι, (5) some aorist forms and the aorist infinitive of μανθάνω, (6) "we" subjunctive of γιγνώσκω, and (7) patterns of contract verbs.

I cannot stress enough how valuable this "natural preview" method of unsystematic learning is to students, as opposed to the usual "lock-step" method.

> Specifically, under lock-stepping a student is exposed to a very small amount of the foreign language. The student studies that quantum until able to understand it, orally and visually. After the student has acquired the capacity to actually reproduce and manipulate that quantum, the student advances to the next quantum. . . . Lock-stepping is most obvious in old-fashioned textbooks with their straighforward cognitive-code approach. It is also obvious in audio-lingual texts. . . . Two questions arise: Is lock-stepping necessary? And is it desirable? Experience inclines us to answer both questions in the negative. (Harvey 32)

The "natural preview" method is useful for language *acquisition*, which need not be conscious, versus the conscious learning of rules. For an interesting discussion of Krashen's views on acquisition and learning, see Hadley (61–4). A teacher devoted to systematic learning may not be able to see the charm of the natural preview. But experience has shown that it works. The following written comments are by two of Catherine Freis's students at Millsaps College:

> It's comforting to see that nothing will sneak up on you. When approaching a new chapter you can honestly say that you've seen the material, even if only in one word.

> It's a wonderful technique, to learn so much in the first week and then spend the rest of the time discovering all the things you already sort-of know. It was very scary, coming in every day and having to pay such close attention and learning with our ears. I'm not an auditory person, and I felt panicked, but it was worth it in the end. It made everything that was to come later seem less threatening and overwhelming.

How to Use Conversational Ancient Greek

Assuming that readers are convinced that using oral ancient Greek is worth trying, the next question is: how to do it? Here I draw on my years of experience, with support from learning theory. My method is a product of intuition, observation, and experimentation. My conversational method has many points of contact with Krashen and Terrell's Natural Approach, the chief difference being that I do not allow for a "latent period," in which the teacher produces sounds but students do not.

Like the Natural Approach, my method uses genuine communication, has a low affective filter, makes use of some sort of natural order, and produces utterances slightly beyond the current level of competence in order to educate. However, Krashen and Terrell (20) allow time for a "silent period" (which can be months) between hearing and producing the language; and I do not, for several reasons. (1) My time is limited. Younger students have far more time to learn language basics than college Greek students. (2) I have not found it to be necessary. Students are able to respond, without anxiety, from the beginning. (3) I believe that production enhances learning, from the beginning.[6]

Some of the principles I have arrived at for using conversational ancient Greek follow.

Genuine Communication, not Drill

The most important rule is: *use conversation for genuine communication*. Ask questions with unknown answers, questions that, whenever possible, are of genuine interest. Some questions will be limited to classroom experience—for example, "Is the poem short?" "Is the poem hard?" But the closer one can come to emotional issues, the more interesting and lively the class will be. "Do you like your doctor?" "Are you afraid of your doctor?" Genesee (5) says: "It is now universally recognized that language is acquired most effectively when it is learned for communication in meaningful and social situations." And in a personal communication Genesee noted that we would never ask someone in normal conversation "What color is my tie?" Why do it, then, in the classroom? As Canale and Swain (33) note, "communication activities must be as meaningful as possible and be characterized (at increasing levels of difficulty) by aspects of genuine communication such as its basis in social interaction, the relative *creativity and unpredictability of utterances*, its purposefulness and goal-orientation, and its authenticity" (italics mine). In my view, questions with known answers should be avoided. They are at best boring, at worst patronizing or insulting.

Because I plan my conversations in advance—I use scripts from *Ancient Greek Alive* and occasionally produce variations spontaneously—I often miss out on the sense of novel communication. One year, on the ninth day of class, I asked one of my students, who is a mother, "When your child is sick, do you call the doctor?" This was a new question, which I had never asked anyone before. And I was genuinely excited at the fact that in a mere nine days this question and its answer could be understood by all my students. My students have this excitement all the time. For them, all of the communications are new.

If simple exposure—number of times a linguistic item is heard—were what teaches the language, language tapes and drills would work. But studies have shown that (1) it is interaction, not mere exposure, that teaches, and (2) the more meaningful the interaction, the better it teaches. In other words: drills alone won't work well (Wong and VanPatten). And besides, they are, as Krashen and Terrell (14) note, "excruciatingly boring."[7]

The reason drill does not work may be that students speak but do not "rehearse." Information needs to be transferred from short-term memory to long-term memory for learning to take place. Information in short-term memory is "is lost within about one minute unless it is rehearsed, repeated, or meaningfully encoded. If the information is rehearsed and is meaningful, it can be transferred" (Padilla and Sung 45). It is universally recognized that meaningful interactions have far more effect on language learning than drills. It is my belief that drills have no place, ever, in the language classroom.

Variation

Variety keeps students happy and attentive; they enjoy the unexpected. In the first two weeks of Greek, I teach with conversation (the mainstay) and storytelling. I have my students memorize a poem and act out a skit. For the skit, I have students practice reading each part out loud, then have each group do a performance. The skit is given with uncontracted verb forms (which are used for the first eight days of class). Then I introduce verb contraction, and have students rewrite and reenact the skit with contracted forms. Young (429) reports that skits can be very anxiety-producing and recommends that students practice before performing in class—which is just good, common sense. I have not seen skit-anxiety in my students; perhaps the age of the students is relevant. Students remember virtually *everything* from the skit, for months to come.

Deagon's remarks (69) on Latin apply also to Greek: "A final word on variety. It is the single most lacking element in college-level approaches to Latin, yet it is one of the things students appreciate most about any language course." (For detailed suggestions, not all suitable for the college classroom, see Brown and Palmer 23.) One must beware of claiming a variety which is not there. Allen (6) reports, "I recently visited a Russian class where the teacher spent 55 minutes on pattern drills. When I asked her if she thought there was enough variety in her lesson, she replied, 'Oh yes, we drilled the affirmative, the negative, the interrogative, and all the tenses.' The students, of course, thought of the class as one, single tedious activity."

Liveliness

I wanted things to be truly "alive" the first time I taught Greek by the conversational method. Because χελώνη (turtle) is a perfect A-group noun, I decided to buy a live turtle and bring it to class. The salesman at the pet store informed me, alas, that turtles carry salmonella, and the state university would not allow me to do this. I contented myself with an inflated turtle and, in later years, with my lame drawings of turtles on the blackboard. But the principle remains: be as lively as you can, with at least a lively style of delivery, and whatever else imagination provides.

Bodily Action

It is a known principle that there are three basic modes of learning—by seeing, by hearing, and kinesthetic (linked with bodily action, which can include writing). Individuals differ with respect to their favored modes. Linking conversation with bodily motions will make it more memorable for all, in particular for those whose favored mode is kinesthetic. Great success is reported for Asher's total physical response (TPR) method, which uses a multitude of commands for bodily action (Asher 1982; Richards and Rodgers 73–80; Strasheim); TPR is valuable as a technique in teaching by the Natural Approach because it provides a lot of comprehensible input and also reduces stress. Using the body to learn is effective. A friend recently told me that he took a Hebrew class many years ago. The only words he now remembers are the ones that he learned with an accompanying physical action. In my ancient Greek class I often use language linked with bodily action on. "Give me your hand." "Give her the book." "Show him your tongue." The last always gets a laugh, since it is breaking a taboo to stick out one's tongue in the classroom.

Gentle and Sparing Correction of Mistakes

Correct mistakes gently, positively, and only when absolutely necessary. When a two-year-old child says, "I want a piece cake," the parent doesn't respond "No, you got it wrong. You can't say 'a piece cake,' you must say 'a piece of cake.'" That would be demoralizing. Parents might respond with a delighted "Yes, you want *a piece of cake*?" This sort of response leaves the child's self-esteem intact and at the same time models the correct language. I first learned of the "yes" method of correction from a talk given by Dennis Kratz at the University of Massachusetts in the early 1970s, and this has been a benefit to me and my students ever since. Krashen and Terrell (87) give examples of the "yes" method of correction: pointing to a blouse, the teacher says, "This woman is wearing a red." When a student mispronounces the word *blouse*, the teacher responds, "*Yes, that's right*, she's wearing a red blouse." Or the teacher might expand to model correct language. 'What is the man doing in the picture?" "Run." "*Yes, that's right*, he's running" (italics mine).

Teachers are apt to assume that learning will be impaired if mistakes go uncorrected. This is not so. Obvious mistakes need not be corrected. One can simply pass on to the next student. As Krashen (1982: 117) says, "Error correction is not of use for acquisition." Interestingly enough, as Krashen and Terell (27) point out, error correction does not seem to help in children's language acquisition (first language). They cite a study showing that parents often correct their children's speech for content but rarely for grammar. A parent will let "Her curl my hair" pass uncorrected but will correct to "Wednesdays" if their child says, "Walt Disney comes on television on Tuesdays."

Perhaps we ought to change our attitude about errors entirely. As Stevens (268) argues,

> if the atmosphere of the classroom is non-threatening, and their attempts to speak are met with encouragement and understanding (in the literal sense) children will produce communicative language, even if it is replete with grammatical errors. These should be considered to be creative mistakes, indicating a transition period between non-language and acceptable speech.

Or, as Genesee notes (4), "errors in language use are no longer seen as bad but rather as indications of the learners' active efforts to master a complex linguistic system."[8] Krashen (1994) notes that there may be many more spoken errors in a natural method classroom than in a traditional classroom (with language drills), but that actually the natural method students are *talking*, while the others are not. (And talking produces more learning than does parroting.)

Most errors need not be corrected. If any do, this should be done in a gentle, positive way—with the "yes" of the parent's response, rarely with a "no." It is important that students not feel fear in the classroom, as this will raise the "affective filter" and detract from their ability to learn a language. Safety is created over a long period of time. It can be destroyed by a single overcritical response.

Participation

Make sure to include all the students, although no student should be forced. Keep student responses brief and easy unless the student shows particular talent for continuation. In the transcript that follows, during two minutes and seven seconds, there were nine student responses. Kate, a talented student, responded four times, and each of the other five students, with some prompting, completed a single response.

Scholars who study language anxiety recommend not calling on students randomly (e.g., Daly 11; Young 433). There is the question of trade-off. Is there not a way to guard against anxiety for the few (who can be told privately that they will not be called on) without sacrificing learning for the majority (who might benefit from the healthy tension of expecting to be called on at any time)? Of course, every student should have the "right to pass" (Moskowitz 29). But if Padilla is right, random calling may keep students rehearsing, which will contribute significantly to their learning.[9]

Note Grammatical Patterns

There is no point in insisting on spoken ancient Greek only, as has been the technique in some intensive language programs. This is partly a matter of time. We teach ancient Greek, at least at the college level, at a point in students' lives where they do not have several years to acquire the language. (The opposite situation holds for those learning foreign languages in elementary or middle school.) And we are sometimes teaching sophisticated students who already have some sense of system in languages. As Ausubel notes, it enhances learning—even when one is teaching only by the oral method—to stop and present in a systematic way what has been imbibed nonsystematically, through conversation. From the very beginning, I will stop to give charts of what learning can be gleaned from our conversations—with transliteration—the first few days and then in Greek script once the alphabet has been learned.

Early zealots of some oral methods insisted that the native language never be used. But, as Ausubel (422) points out regarding the inductive process of discovering linguistic regularities, "this type of discovery learning . . . is exceedingly wasteful and unnecessary when we deal with older learners who are perfectly capable of comprehending abstract syntactic propositions." And again, "actually, it is both unrealistic and inefficient for the older student to attempt to circumvent the mediating role of his native language when he is learning a second language." Munsell and Carr's analogy is relevant here. They suggest that it may be easier to learn a language by being taught some rules just as it is easier to learn chess by being taught the rules rather than by watching countless games. "We cannot imagine trying to learn basketball, monopoly, bridge, or quantum mechanics simply by watching people do them, trying them, and creatively constructing the rules. It is much easier to start with conscious exposition of the rules and build one's skill upon that foundation" (499).[10]

Make the Process Conscious

As Krashen and Terrell (73) say, whenever possible students should be informed as to the relationship between the goals and the methodology that will be used. During the first two weeks I tell my students that I am giving them as much nonsystematically as I feel they can hold, and that my purpose is for them (1) to absorb language without tension and (2) to learn enough vocabulary so they can be reading interesting stories right away. I start with the singular and third person plural of Greek verbs of the ἀκούω pattern but give only the singular for verbs of the βούλομαι and δείκνυμι patterns. When a student asks, "What about the 'they' form?" I answer, "I don't want to burden you now with too many forms. For now I'm giving you just as much as we need to talk and to read interesting stories."

It is good also to discuss learning strategies with the students so they can become conscious of their methods of learning. This is called "metacognitive awareness" and has been shown to help students learn. For metacognitive awareness, see chapter 2. For making students aware of learning strategies in general, see Oxford; for making them aware of language anxiety, see Crookall and Oxford. A good example of a teacher creating awareness of reading strategies can be found in Richards (92–3).

Repetition, Sequencing

These are obvious principles that are followed when presenting a language in writing, and that also need to be followed when presenting a language through conversation. There should be enough repetition so that earlier material is learned well. And material should be learned with only a few new items at a time—nothing overwhelming. And it should be graded in such a way that there is some logic to what is learned first and what is learned next.[11]

Transcript

An example will illustrate many of the features just discussed. The transcript that follows is from an audiotape of the fourth day of my beginning ancient Greek class at Butler University, September 4, 1992. The textbook script for day 4 (see the end of the chapter) from *Ancient Greek Alive* (Saffire and Freis) is the matrix upon which the classroom embroidery is worked. One should be aware that skill in embroidery increases over time, and that even the most rudimentary embroidery will please beginning students.

The transcript was made during my fifth year of teaching ancient Greek by conversation. Time of the tape is two minutes and seven seconds. The teacher (I) speaks at normal speed, students considerably more slowly. In general, I barely slow down when I speak Greek. Others report that their students need them to speak considerably more slowly than normal. Slowing is one feature of "teacher talk." (See discussion on p. 174.) Too much slowing down can make learning harder. As Peterson (92) points out, "the teachers should not slow their speech because the students' short-term memory capacity is too short to remember sentences when they are extended by slow speech."

Pronunciation is with uncontracted vowels. Mistakes are in bold face. Self-corrections are underlined.[12]

Teacher: ὦ φίλη (looking at Cammie, pointing to alphabet on blackboard)
ὁράεις ταῦτα τὰ γράμματα;

Cammie: ναί, ὁράοι— (Cammie pronounces the omega as if it were oi.)

Teacher: (with an intonation of approval, as a prompt not a criticism)
"ὁράω"—

Cammie: τότα—

Teacher: (with the same intonation) "ταῦτα"—

Cammie: τὸ γράμματα.

Teacher: "τὰ γράμματα. "ταῦτα τὰ γράμματα."
καὶ σύ, Eric, ὁράεις ταῦτα τὰ γράμματα;

Eric: ναί, ὁράεις—

Teacher: "ὁράω"— (pause) "ταῦτα τα—"

Eric: ταῦτα τὰ— (pause)

Teacher: "τὰ γράμματα"—

Eric: τὰ γράμματα.

Teacher: καὶ σύ, ὦ Judy, ἐθέλεις γράφειν ταῦτα τὰ γράμματα; ἐθέλεις
γράφειν ταῦτα τὰ γράμματα;

Judy: ναί, ἐθέλω γράφειν ταῦτα τὰ γράμματα.

Teacher: καὶ— And you know . . . If I say ἔχω with one of those "to do"
forms, with an infinitive, it means "are you able to?" It sounds like "do
you have to?" but it really means "do you have the power to . . . ?" ἔχεις
γράφειν ταῦτα τὰ γράμματα; ὦ Shelley, ἔχεις γράφειν ταῦτα τὰ
γράμματα;

Shelley: ἔχω γράφειν ταῦτα τὰ γράμματα.

Teacher: Yes, "ἔχω γράφειν ταῦτα τὰ γράμματα." ἔχεις λέγειν ταῦτα
τὰ γράμματα; λέγειν means "to say." Vera, ἔχεις λέγειν ταῦτα τὰ
γράμματα;

Vera: ναί, ἔχω λέγ—?

Teacher: "λέγειν"—

Vera: ταῦταυ? ταῦτο?

Teacher: "ταῦτα"—

Vera: ταῦτα τὰ γράμματα.

Teacher: ὦ Cammie, Vera ἔχει λέγειν ταῦτα τὰ γράμματα; Vera ἔχει
λέγειν;

Cammie: ναί, Vera λέχει—

Teacher: (in prompting tone) "ἔχει"—

Cammie: ἔχει λέγειν **ταῦτο**—ταῦτα τὰ γράμματα.

Teacher: καὶ σύ, ἔχεις λέγειν ταῦτα τὰ γράμματα; καὶ σύ (pause), ἔχεις λέγειν;

Cammie: ναί, **ἔχοι**—

Teacher: "ἔχω"—

Cammie: Oh, ἔχω. ἔχω λέγειν ταῦτα τὰ γράμματα.

Teacher: πάντα τὰ γράμματα; πάντα τὰ γράμματα; All of them?

Cammie: ναί, πάντα τὰ γράμματα. (Cammie laughs at her own confidence.)

Teacher: εὖγε. λέγωμεν—what is λέγωμεν, with that -ωμεν ending? What is λέγωμεν?

Class (at more or less the same time): "Let's!"[13]

Teacher: "Let's say." λέγωμεν πάντα τὰ γράμματα. Πάντες ἅμα. OK? All to-gether. (Class proceeds to read the alphabet out loud from the blackboard.)

Reflections on Transcript

I will restrict myself to a few brief comments.

1. The amount of ancient Greek actually processed in two minutes is phe-nomenal. It would take at least five times as long for students to read this much ancient Greek, and they would not learn it as well because there would be no production.

2. This is far from boring to students. Speaking ancient Greek is challeng-ing, and the kernel utterances keep changing slightly. The process goes from (1) ὁράω ταῦτα τὰ γράμματα, to (2) ἐθέλω γράφειν ταῦτα τὰ γράμματα, to (3) ἔχω γράφειν ταῦτα τὰ γράμματα, to (4) ἔχω λέγειν ταῦτα τὰ γράμ-ματα. As Krashen and Terrell point out (76), the instructor can weave repetitions naturally so they don't sound like repetitions.

3. We can see a student absorbing correction in the two-minute interchange. Cammie (who is an A+ student) begins by mispronouncing ἔχω and also ταῦτα. In the end, after being gently corrected a second time, she makes the sound of ἔχω correctly, and without any prompting, pronounces ταῦτα correctly on her second time around. This is learning in action!

4. No one has been left out. Eric has the most difficulty of all. He is never shamed. He goes at his own slow pace. Because he learns primarily by visual means, he will be able to "catch up" once the material is learned primarily through reading. As Rubin points out (49), some students are not comfortable unless they have something written

in front of them. (Eric is aware that he is a visual learner. The teacher has discussed with him the fact that visual learning will soon be of prime importance.)

5. There is repetition of the old and sequencing of the new here. The progression of kernel sentences—see item 2—goes from the better known (ὁράω, ἐθέλω γράφειν) to the less known (ἔχω, *I have*, now given the meaning *I am able*) to the unknown (λέγω, a new vocabulary word). The first and second person are the most familiar. They are used over and over again before the less familiar third person singular—ἔχει—is slipped in, probably for the second time in the course.

6. Learning is natural and effortless. In two minutes, students have learned a new usage (ἔχω) and a new vocabulary word (λέγω), have reused the infinitive (learned the day before), and have reviewed the hortatory subjunctive (learned on the first day), as well as having heard familiar words over and over. Multiply this by about twenty, and you can imagine *how much* students can learn, and *how well* they can learn it, in a single class period.

How to Create Scripts

The best way to learn to ride a bicycle is get on and try it. The best way to learn to teach by speaking Greek is to plan a few short conversations and try them. I do not use guidelines or rules to create scripts. I simply create them intuitively, and then refine constantly, using observation and reason. I use reason to elucidate the principles (given earlier) that underlie the scripts I create, and also to weigh options for the optimal ordering. I use observation to see what works and what does not.

For example, it might seem most orderly and economical to teach all three uses of αὐτός at once. However, this does not work. Some students will not remember the three uses, or will confuse one with the other. It is simply a matter of empirical observation that it is best first to use αὐτός in oblique cases as a pronoun (which happens naturally in the course of most rudimentary conversations), next to introduce it as *the same*—using many examples in class ("Do you have the same book?" "Does she have the same name?"), and finally, only when the first two uses are firmly grasped, to introduce it as emphatic ("The doctor *himself* is coming").

The easiest way to begin a course with conversational ancient Greek is to use the scripts in *Ancient Greek Alive*. However, if a different textbook is being used for the course, it may be best to make up initial conversations based (if possible) on the vocabulary that comes earliest in that book, using the scripts from *Ancient Greek Alive* as a model. Jeffrey Wills began an introductory Greek class at the University of Wisconsin with scripts from *Ancient Greek Alive*, though students were going to use a different textbook for the course. He reports that students were nervous over not making progress in their assigned textbook.

Obstacles to Overcome

Greek teachers may be reluctant to take on the challenge of using conversational ancient Greek. Once the benefits of using conversational Greek have been shown and the method absorbed, why would a teacher choose not to try it? I shall voice the major objections and give a response to each.

1. *"It won't work."* Answer: It *does* work. Comments by students and teachers show that it works. A Millsaps student wrote this comment on her evaluation: "I *love* the oral beginning of the course. I think every language course would benefit by beginning this way." Eliot Youman at Mercer University said that his students were better prepared for second-year Greek because they started with conversation. All the professors I know who have used the conversational method have returned to it.

2. *"It takes too much class time."* Answer: It takes very little class time. After two weeks, I phase out speaking almost entirely. But what has been learned during those two weeks makes systematic learning easier throughout the term.

I doubt that it is possible at all to teach students ancient Greek as firmly through reading alone as through reading and speaking. But if it were possible, one would have to add far more than eight hours of additional reading to the course—eight hours being the amount of time I devote to conversation in the first two weeks.

3. *"It is too much work for the teacher."* Answer: It is extra work. But it is not overwhelming, as all the teachers who have tried it agree. And it gets easier as time goes by. I confess that even now, well past my tenth year of conversational ancient Greek, I am relieved when the first two weeks are over, and I can begin teaching in the usual, mostly visual way. Why, then, do I begin with conversation? I believe that teaching involves a contract similar to that of parenting. (For the concept of implicit contracts, see the *Crito*, of course.) When we agree to be teachers, we agree to put the good of our students on a par with our own. I am willing to sacrifice some of my energy for the sake of my students.

I might add that there are rewards for the extra energy put in. In the first place, teaching the forms later is easier, and so in the end energy is saved. Also, students' appreciative comments along the way are nourishing and can boost a teacher's energy and morale. Finally, if the retention rate goes up—and it seems to—that also gives satisfaction. It may give a teacher more work, but it is the kind of work we welcome.

4. *"I'll never be able to do it."* Perhaps you will never be able to talk like Socrates. But you *will* be able to use "teacher talk," which is a variant of "foreigner talk," and that is all it takes. It is well known that people use a special language in talking to children and foreigners. Berko-Gleason (16) asserts, "The language spoken to infants the world around has great similarities: it consists of short, repetitive, well-formed utterances, has a limited and redundant vocabulary, deals with topics of interest to young children, and is delivered at a rate that is approximately one-half as fast as speech to adults." Gass and Madden (4–5) characterize foreigner talk as having the following: slower rate of speech, louder speech, longer pauses, common vocabulary, few idioms, greater use of gestures, more repetition, more summaries of preceding utterances, shorter utterances, and more deliberate articulation.

Gass and Madden (4–5) trace the evolution of the understanding of "foreigner talk." First there were observations about caretaker speech, known as "baby-talk," then as "motherese," then as "caretaker speech." Krashen and Terrell (34) mention caretaker speech, foreigner talk, teacher talk, and interlanguage talk (the talk of second language learners with each other). Caretaker talk is (1) motivated by the caretaker's desire to be understood, (2) is simpler than adult language, and (3) is about the here and now. The others resemble it. If native speech is more paratactic than written language (Richards 72), foreigner talk is even more so. Wesche and Ready (110–1) characterize "foreigner talk" as being characterized by simplification, well-formedness, explicitness, regularization, and redundancy. It is very important that we classics teachers not be ashamed of using language that is below the standards of the texts we will want our students to read. We should embrace "caretaker speech" as a great help to our students.

5. *"I'll make mistakes."* Answer: Yes, but what is wrong with that? In the first place, your mistakes will almost always go unnoticed, and, besides, will do no harm. In the second place, it might be good for students to see you making mistakes. This will free them to make mistakes; and they will learn far more by trying and making mistakes than by not trying. (See Cammie in the transcript.) Finally, by trying to find ways to communicate with them, you will be modeling one of the traits of a good learner—"creative guessing," as Rubin calls it. She notes that good language learners are not inhibited (47), and they often are willing to appear foolish (43). Teachers would do well to model this behavior for their students and be willing risk-takers.

Future Possibilities

What lies ahead for the use of conversational ancient Greek? How long should it be used in class? For what purposes? What other oral techniques should be used with it? How will teachers become proficient? I bring these questions forward without having answers. Perhaps there will be some community discussion, which will move us all along.

How Long?

Until now, I have phased out conversation almost entirely after the first two weeks. I *do* make forays back into spoken Greek when it is particularly appropriate. For example, when we learn comparatives, I draw horses and turtles on the blackboard and ask about bigger and smaller. And I do drawings with conversation when we get to οὗτος, ὅδε, and ἐκεῖνος. But after the first two weeks, conversations in ancient Greek are short and sporadic, and are never again the primary mode of learning. Why not? In a nutshell: time. I have been unable to shake my conviction that college students should master the paradigms of common nouns and the entire normal verb during the first year of Greek. And it seems to me there is not time for them to do this and keep talking.

Another reason is that once we begin systematic learning, with complete paradigms, our ability to read ancient Greek forms rapidly outpaces our ability to produce them. (Both forms and accent shifts are difficult.) And finally, it becomes harder and harder to find conversational contexts for all the words, as the vocabulary becomes more abstract.

In spite of all these objections, I am now having second thoughts about stopping conversation in ancient Greek. My students regret it when we stop. Katie and Stuart asked me, months after we stopped speaking Greek, "Couldn't we keep speaking right to the end?" I miss the speaking, too—especially when I remember how high-spirited my students were in those early days. I note that on my second-semester evaluations last year, three out of five students responded "speak more Greek" for "ways the course might be improved."

As for the goal—to have my students learn all of the important paradigms—is it the right one? It is hard for me to loosen my standards. But if anything will change them, it will be a question asked by Stephen Fineberg at an informal meeting of classicists in 1992: "What if we aimed not to produce a reader in a year, but to give our students a pleasant, confidence-building experience in learning a foreign language, one which makes them receptive to learning more about the culture?" If we take this as our aim, then the oral method should definitely be continued throughout the year.

The motivation of the students is relevant here. Students who ardently want to begin reading a text (and this includes most graduate students) will appreciate speed. But many students (certainly those fulfilling a language requirement) are not in a hurry; and we may be doing them a disservice by speeding them along beyond their capabilities.

Is it true that there is not enough time to keep speaking? What takes up time during my classes? Presentation of new grammar, careful translation of reading passages, and some review. Some classicists have suggested that we eschew translation entirely (as is done in some modern foreign language classrooms); we might talk about the texts but we should never directly translate them. Dropping translation would certainly free up time for speaking, but so far that feels like dropping my standards. I have been trained to translate precisely in order to show myself (and others) that I have understood the Greek precisely. This is training I value and want to provide for my students.

One way to generate extra time for speaking is to hurry the rest and squeeze in some conversation. Another solution, suggested by my students, is to add an hour and a credit to the course. Why couldn't Greek be like science, they asked me, with an hour of lab in which there was only speaking?

If the aim were to produce the best reader in two or three years—and this aim is wholly appropriate for secondary school—then it would be wise to continue speaking ancient Greek far into the course, probably for several years. However, if the aim is to produce the best reader in one year (or even one semester, as is still done in some colleges), I can say only this much with assurance: the two weeks spent introducing ancient Greek through classroom conversation will actually shorten the time it takes to teach students the basic grammar in a year, and will make the whole experience far more enjoyable to boot.

For What Purposes?

My two main pedagogical purposes in using ancient Greek conversationally during the first two weeks are (1) to introduce firmly a lot of vocabulary in the beginning, and (2) to plant unconscious seeds in the beginning that will help students later to learn grammatical patterns. But seeing my students' distress at ending conversation, and also being encouraged by Jeffrey Wills's enthusiasm and determination, I have begun to work on devising complex conversations.

Even if the conversational Greek were less complex than the Greek being learned, it would still spark morale. And why not work to improve my Greek? My students remain "iffy" for a long time on the imperfect as habitual past. Would I not teach them better—and maybe even save time in the end—by devoting some classroom conversation to "When you were a child did you use to . . . ?" with a lot of practice with the imperfect? Or what about questions based on Moskowitz (217–8): "If you could have honeycakes for dinner, how many times would you have them in a week?" "If you could have a dog, how many would you have?" Why not design such questions to fit vocabulary and use them to teach future potential conditions along with povsow and numbers? (See Wills and Strasheim for other ideas for oral activities.)

I did try a little conversation as vocabulary review at the end of the year, after my students lamented the loss of conversation. I am not sure that the conversations taught them a lot of vocabulary, but they did turn out to stimulate some rather interesting exchanges. I asked Katie whether she had a brother and whether her brother was a thief. Answering in the affirmative for both gave her a chance to "debrief" about how her brother took things from her room. I asked Martha whether she was a messenger (ἄγγελος). She paused and answered in slow, thoughtful tones, "I don't know," thinking of the meaning "angel"—which got us off into a short discussion (in English!) of the mystics' statement "I am God."

What Other Oral Techniques?

For certain students, memorizing poetry is inspiring. For the majority, conversation and skits work the best. I would continue with having students create short skits. Giving them their choice of topic works best. They reveal their personalities in their skits, and this interests the class. Also, I would have them turn their reading stories into skits and then act them out in class. We classicists can start scouring the modern foreign language books for interesting oral assignments. Not all will be suitable. For one, our primary aim is not to produce speakers, as is theirs, but readers. For another, Greek and Latin are simply harder than these languages (it would be interesting to analyze why), and many of the activities will be too difficult. (See Wills and the "Speaking and Listening" and "Grammar" sections of the annotated bibliography.) There is no point reinventing the wheel. Let us see what ideas have worked for others so that we may adapt them when possible, or at least use them for inspiration.[14]

How to Become Proficient

If it were merely a question of speaking Greek in class for two weeks—which in itself would be highly beneficial to students—proficiency is not a problem. This is attested by the teachers who have used *Ancient Greek Alive*. They all agree that speaking Greek is "not that hard." But can we speak Greek at higher levels of complexity? Can we use all the forms we have been taught to read? Can we exhibit all the possibilities of syntax in our speech? How?

I have tried speaking out loud to myself, keeping up a running commentary on what I am doing. That has not worked well; my vocabulary is not adequate. I have tried imagining speaking to other classicists in Greek. I can do that for simple thoughts, but eventually find myself stymied. Someone once told me that he thought it was the "dirty little secret" of classicists that we do not know our language as well as modern foreign language teachers know theirs. I have never been one to fall prey to shame. Yes, I cannot speak Greek as well as they—or even I, myself—can speak French. There is some excuse in that Greek is harder; there is more excuse in the fact that I was never taught; and finally the greatest excuse is that I will never have the chance to interact with native speakers of ancient Greek, as I did with the French.

But what is the point of excuses? Let us simply do what we can. I have learned an enormous amount from using Greek with my students. I expect I could learn much more from using Greek with my colleagues. I look forward to the day when we all teach ourselves to speak Greek as many Latinists are now developing their oral skills.[15] I know that, like my students, the forms I have heard (and spoken) I do not forget. Why not inaugurate a cooperative venture? We could have informal self-tutoring sessions at annual classics meetings. Ahead of time we would each choose some vocabulary, forms, and usages to try to slip into conversation. If we do our job well enough, our project will self-destruct. The next generation of classicists will be able to teach by speaking with far less difficulty than we have.

The Read-and-Speak Method

The most exciting experiment I have read about was tried by Harvey, teaching French by the read-and-speak method at the University of Utah. Since there was a control, the success of the method seems acceptably established. Out of seven sections of beginning French students, one was chosen to try a method with massive amounts of easy readings in French (three hundred pages during the first quarter, a thousand pages by the end of the third quarter) and encouragement to speak in class. The "normal" sections used the grammar book from the beginning. The experimental section did not read the grammar book until April, by which time they covered the entire grammar text in five weeks. By the end of the year they significantly outperformed other students on standardized tests, and in addition found the method pleasant. (See also Day and Bamford; Maxim.)

I would love to try this experiment. It is not possible now; but someday it might be. This would take an enormous amount of cooperation. (We could think of it as a sort of Argonaut expedition.) First of all, we would have to teach each other to speak Greek, as described earlier. Second, we would have to generate the passages in easy Greek. The readings must be interesting. Krashen and Terrell (132) note that "a text is appropriate for a reader if it meets two criteria. First, it must be at an appropriate level of complexity. Second, the reader has to find it interesting.") Right now there is nowhere near a body of 300, let alone 1,000, pages of *easy interesting* ancient Greek. The stories need not be about the Greeks any more than the French readings need be about the French. I still jot down interesting stories from all over the world, in the hopes of someday adapting them in ancient Greek. What a worthwhile project it would be if we classicists created a bank of easy readings to charm and interest students of ancient Greek.

Conclusion

It would be foolish to claim that conversational ancient Greek is a new "super-method," complete in itself and able to work miracles. But it is a method that is marvelously potent, as is being demonstrated in modern foreign language classrooms. It was once used in teaching the classical languages, and, with some effort and courage on our part, it can be used again.

There are many examples that show that it is possible to use an ancient language for speech: (1) Hebrew, once used only in fixed language for prayer, is now the everyday, living speech of Israel. That was an experiment in speaking an ancient language that worked, and on a massive scale! (2) I am told that Sanskrit is still spoken in some ashrams in India. (3) Latin is still spoken in the Vatican. (I learned this in a game of Diplomacy played in Jerusalem. While everyone else disappeared into corners to make their "top secret" plans, the two Vatican-trained priests conversed loudly and openly, secure from prying because the rapidity of their Latin made eavesdropping impossible.) (4) I knew a Russian who was taken prisoner in Poland, and whose only mode of communication with his fellow prisoner was via Latin.

The benefits of conversational ancient Greek are many and great. The single drawback is the extra energy it takes; and there is ample compensation for that. Fear and perfectionism are the greatest enemies of the oral method. It is natural to be afraid of making errors. But if we teachers wait until we are good at speaking ancient Greek before trying it, it will probably never happen. It is as John Henry Cardinal Newman said: "A man would do nothing if he waited until he could do it so well that no one would find fault with what he has done." Taking a risk for a good cause is something to admire. We will help our students far more by daring to speak ancient Greek with them than by maintaining a safe and error-free silence.

—χαίρετε, ὦ φίλοι.
—χαῖρε, ὦ φίλε. χαῖρε, ὦ φίλη.

—γιγνώσκομεν ἀλλήλους;

     <πάντες ἅμα> *all together*
     <αὖθις> *again*

—οὐ γιγνώσκομεν ἀλλήλους.
—γιγνώσκωμεν ἀλλήλους.

    | γιγνώσκο**μεν**
    | γιγνώσκω**μεν**

    Endings are important. Listen for them.

—τὸ ὄνομά μου ____ ἐστιν.
—τί ἐστι τὸ ὄνομά σου; λέγε μοι· τί ἐστι τὸ ὄνομά σου;

    <εὖγε> *good! well done!*

—τί ἐστι τὸ ὄνομα αὐτοῦ; λέγε μοι.
—τί ἐστι τὸ ὄνομα αὐτῆς; λέγε μοι. λέγε ἡμῖν.

—οἶσθα;
—οὐκ οἶδα.

    | οὐ γιγνώσκομεν
    | **οὐκ** οἶδα

—ἐρώταε: "ὦ φίλε, τί ἐστι τὸ ὄνομά σου;"

This is a day for getting acquainted. By asking and answering in Greek, learn the names of your partners in this enterprise of learning ancient Greek.

The ancient Greek you are learning is called Attic Greek. It is the Greek that would have been spoken in Athens in the fifth century B.C.

Homework: Meet or telephone a classmate and have a conversation in ancient Greek, or teach someone who does not know Greek what you learned today.

*To teachers: See Words to Teachers [in *Ancient Greek Alive*] on the use of scripts, particularly on the importance of transliterating Greek sounds during the first few classes. Students are not expected to read scripts beforehand, though they will read them after class starting on the fourth day. Boxes (represented here by vertical lines) contain important information for rapid review. Usually you will use a script a day. Exception: the lesson on the Greek alphabet may take two days.

—γιγνώσκω σε. (To another student) καὶ γιγνώσκω σε. (To another) καὶ γιγνώσκω σε. ὦ φίλε, γιγνώσκεις με; —Ah (with a sigh to the class), ὁ — γιγνώσκει με. —καὶ σύ, ὦ φίλη, γιγνώσκεις με; —Ah, ἡ — γιγνώσκει με.

—ὁράω σε. (To another student) καὶ ὁράω σε. (To another) καὶ ὁράω σε. ὁράεις με; —Ah, (to class) ὁ — ὁράει με. —καὶ σύ, ὁράεις με; —Ah (to class) ἡ — ὁράει με.

—καὶ σύ, ὁράεις αὐτόν; ὁράεις αὐτήν; λέγε μοι· ὁράεις αὐτήν;

—ὦ φίλη (drawing a turtle on the board), ὁράεις τὴν χελώνην; ὁράεις αὐτήν; λέγε ἡμῖν. ὁράεις αὐτήν; καὶ γιγνώσκεις αὐτήν; λέγε ἡμῖν.

—ὦ φίλε, ὁράεις με; (Hiding face behind a paper) καὶ νῦν ὁράεις με; οὐχί. νῦν οὐχ ὁράεις με.

—καὶ σύ, ὦ φίλη, ὁράεις τὴν χελώνην; καὶ σύ, ὦ φίλε, ὁράεις αὐτήν; Ah, (to class) ἡ — καὶ ὁ — ὁράουσι τὴν χελώνην. ὁράουσιν αὐτήν.

—ὦ φίλε, γιγνώσκεις αὐτόν; τί ἐστι τὸ ὄνομα αὐτοῦ; —καὶ σύ, γιγνώσκεις αὐτόν; καὶ ὁ — καὶ ἡ — γιγνώσκουσιν αὐτόν.

οὐ γιγνώσκω	γιγνώσκουσι τὴν χελώνην	Α καὶ Β
οὐκ οἶδα	γιγνώσκουσιν αὐτήν	καὶ Α καὶ Β
οὐχ ὁράω		

—ὦ φίλε, ἔχω ὄνομα. <Demonstrate ἔχω>
ἔχω γλῶτταν, ἔχω χεῖρα, ἔχω βιβλίον

—ἔχω ὄνομα. καὶ σύ, ἔχεις ὄνομα; τί ἐστι τὸ ὄνομά; σου;
—τὸ ὄνομά μου — ἐστιν. —τί ἐστι τὸ ὄνομά σου;

—καὶ ὁ — ἔχει ὄνομα; νή τὸν Δία ἔχει ὄνομα. —καὶ ἡ — ἔχει ὄνομα;
— νή τὴν κύνα ἔχει ὄνομα. —καὶ ἡ — καὶ ὁ — ἔχουσιν ὄνομα.

νή τὸν Δία   by Zeus
νή τὴν κύνα   by the dog

I	ἔχω	γιγνώσκω	ὁράω
You	ἔχεις	γιγνώσκεις	ὁράεις
He, she, it	ἔχει	γιγνώσκει	ὁράει
They	ἔχουσι(ν)	γιγνώσκουσι(ν)	ὁράουσι(ν)

Homework: Learn the three ways of negating: οὐ, οὐκ, οὐχ. How do you say these sentences in Greek?

| I know the turtle. | You have the turtle. | (S)he sees the turtle. |
| I don't know the turtle. | You don't have the turtle. | They don't see the turtle. |

—ὦ φίλη (writing **a** on the blackboard), τί ποιέω; —γράφω γράμμα. γιγνώσκεις τοῦτο τὸ γράμμα; γιγνώσκεις τοῦτο;

—καὶ νῦν, ὦ φίλε, (writing alphabet) τί ποιέω; —γράφω γράμματα. γιγνώσκεις ταῦτα τα γράμματά; γιγνώσκεις ταῦτα;

τὸ γράμμα	τοῦτο τὸ γράμμα	τοῦτο
τὰ γράμματα	ταῦτα τὰ γράμματα	ταῦτα

γράφω γράμματα μικρά. ὦ φίλη, γιγνώσκεις τὰ γράμματα τὰ μικρά; λέγε ἡμῖν· γιγνώσκεις τὰ μικρὰ γράμματα;

—καὶ νῦν ἀναγιγνώσκω τὰ γράμματα. (Reading alpha, beta, etc.) ἀναγιγνώσκω πάντα τὰ γράμματα τὰ μικρά. καὶ σύ, ὦ φίλε, ἐθέλεις ἀναγιγνώσκειν τὰ γράμματα;

τὰ μικρὰ γράμματα	Both mean:	γιγνώσκω	*know*
τὰ γράμματα τὰ μικρά	*the small letters*	ἀναγιγνώσκω	*read*

—ἐγὼ (pointing to self) ἐθέλω ἀναγιγνώσκειν τὰ γράμματα. καὶ σύ, ἐθέλεις ἀναγιγνώσκειν τὰ γράμματα; ἀληθῶς ἐθέλεις ἀναγιγνώσκειν τὰ γράμματα; εὖγε. ἀναγιγνώσκμεν τὰ γράμματα. πάντες ἅμα.

—καὶ σύ, ὦ φίλη, ἔχεις γράφειν τὰ μικρὰ γράμματα; ἔχεις γράφειν πάντα τὰ γράμματα τὰ μικρά; λέγε ἡμῖν.

ἔχω βιβλίον	I **have** a book.
ἔχω γράφειν	I **am able** / have the ability to write.

—καὶ σύ, ὦ φίλη, ἔχεις ἀναγιγνώσκειν ταῦτα τὰ γράμματα; βούλεαι ἀναγιγνώσκειν τὰ γράμματα; ἐγὼ βούλομαι. καὶ σύ;
—Ah, (to class) ἡ — βούλεται ἀναγιγνώσκειν ταῦτα τὰ γράμματα.

—καὶ σύ, ὦ φίλε, βούλεαι ἀναγιγνώσκειν ταῦτα; Ah, (to class) ὁ — βούλεται ἀναγιγνώσκειν τὰ γράμματα. καὶ ἡ — καὶ ὁ — βούλονται ἀναγιγνώσκειν τὰ γράμματα.

ἐθέλω	βούλομαι	Learn both verb patterns.
ἐθέλεις	βούλεαι	βούλομαι has more force. It is a full-fledged *I want.*
ἐθέλει	βούλεται	ἐθέλω is weaker, more like *I am willing.*
ἐθέλουσι(ν)	βούλονται	(The original "you want" form was βούλεσαι.)

—καὶ νῦν, ὦ φίλοι, ἀναγιγνώσκωμεν ἐκ τοῦ βιβλίου.

(Turn to p. 1 of textbook. Students take turns reading.)

—ὦ φίλε (pointing to page one of book), ὁράεις γράμματα μικρά; —ὁράεις πολλὰ γράμματα μικρά; πάντα τὰ γράμματα μικρά ἐστιν; ναί, πάντα τὰ γράμματα μικρά ἐστιν. πάντα τὰ γράμματά ἐστι μικρα.

Actually the Greeks did not use small letters at all. They used only the letters we call capitals. Small letters were developed as cursive in ninth century Europe. They are used now because they are easier to read. For the same reason, we use word division, although the Greeks did not. (Another practice that would make reading easier would be to drop all smooth breathing signs.)

—καὶ σύ, ὦ φίλε (writing ? on board), ὁράεις τοῦτὸ; οἱ Ἕλληνες (pointing to ?) γράφουσι τοῦτο; οὐ γράφουσι τοῦτο.

The Greeks used the symbol ; for questions, not our question mark. They did not have quotation marks (which are used for clarity in our stories in made-up Greek). Where we use a colon, the Greeks used a raised dot.

The Greek period and comma have the same form as our own.

ἔργα ~Read aloud the scripts of days # 1–4. (Do you have any questions? Keep reading and rereading until you can understand these pages perfectly.)

~Write the alphabet once in small and large letters.

~Rewrite the following passage, substituting forms of βούλομαι for forms of ἐθέλω (which are shown in bold print):

ἐθέλω γράφειν τὰ γράμματα. καὶ σύ, ἐθέλεις γράφειν τὰ γράμματα; ἡ χελώνη οὐκ ἐθέλει γράφειν τὰ γράμματα. ὁ — καὶ ἡ — ἐθέλουσι γιγνώσκειν τὸ ὄνομά μου.

Notes

1. This textbook was first used under the name *Beginning Ancient Greek* by Paula Reiner at the University of Massachusetts in the early 1970s. It was next used at Butler University as *Ancient Greek Alive*, by Paula Reiner, in 1992. Many of the remarks in this essay were first given in my talk "Ancient Greek in Classroom Conversation," Reiner 1992. Some of the comments can be found in Saffire and Freis 269 and are reprinted with permission of the University of North Carolina Press.

2. The views of Krashen are mentioned throughout this chapter. The single most important view of Krashen and Terrell is that language *acquisition* is what counts—acquisiton being an *unconscious* process by which we are able to use language naturally for meaningful communication—and that *large amounts of comprehensible input* are what promotes acquisition, not information about the language, that is, not grammar lessons. See, for example, Krashen 1981: 1–3; 1982: 10–1; Krashen and Terrell 18–9. As Krashen says (1985: 1), "'Acquisition' is a subconscious process identical in all important ways to the process children utilize in acquiring their first language, while 'learning' is a conscious process that results in 'knowing about' language." For an excellent summary that raises good (and for the most part answerable) objections to Krashen's hypotheses, see Shannon 8–16. I have respect for Krashen's views because I arrived at almost all of them independently as I worked out ways of teaching ancient Greek by conversation.

There is disarmingly little that is actually new in the way languages are taught in a Natural Approach classroom. As Richards (136) notes, an observer might not be aware of the teaching philosophy at all in a Natural Approach classroom. "What characterizes the Natural Approach is the use of familiar techniques within the framework of a method that focuses on providing comprehensible input and a classroom environment that cues comprehension of input, minimizes learner anxiety, and maximizes learner self-confidence." As he remarks later (141), the Natural Approach is "evolutionary rather than revolutionary in its procedures. Its greatest claim to originality lies not in the techniques it employs but in their use in a method that emphasizes comprehensible and meaningful practice activities, rather than production of grammatically perfect utterances and sentences."

3. The names of my students have been changed. Gender is as indicated. I was fortunate to have Vera and Cammie in my beginning Greek class, two returning students in their forties who were vociferous in expressing their appreciation, as younger students rarely are. Comments from my Butler students were oral and spontaneous. Millsaps students wrote their comments on an evaluation form at the end of first-semester Greek.

4. Italics mine. For an evaluation of Krashen on reading for comprehended input, see Coady, especially 227–8, on negative evidence in an experiment by Tudor and Hafiz: the experimental group read far more and became better at reading and writing, but their vocabulary base remained relatively unchanged. For the importance of frequency for vocabulary acquisition, see Ellis as well as Oxford and Scarcella. For the view that it is meaningful communication and not brute number of repetitions that stimulates learning see the following: (1) Brown 41: "Nativists who claim that the relative frequency of stimuli is of little importance in language acquisition might, in the face of evidence thus far, be more cautious in their claim. It would appear that frequency of *meaningful* occurrence may well be a more precise refinement of the notion of frequency." (2) Berko-Gleason 20 (cited by Brown 42): "While it used to be generally held that mere *exposure* to language is sufficient to set the child's language generating machinery in motion, it is now clear that, in order for successful first language acquisition to take place, *interaction*, rather than exposure, is required; children do not learn language from overhearing the conversations of others or from listening to the radio, and must, instead, acquire it in the context of being spoken to." Although one must proceed with caution when applying patterns from first- to second-language learning, this is one observation that seems to apply to both.

5. In addition to the studies cited in Lightbown and Spada, Harvey offers convincing evidence that speaking improves one's language proficiency. John Rassias at Dartmouth is also working with a speaking-intensive method. (From a summary of research on Rassias's method by Florence L. Walters by Edward F. Wolff: "students taught via the Rassias Method scored statistically-significantly higher than the traditionally taught students. . . . Specifically, their listening scores were 33% higher, speaking scores 60% higher and grammar scores 30% higher. Dr. Walters found the last result to be especially interesting since the classes using traditional methods spent more time covering grammar. This confirms, she said, that students learn language more effectively by usage than by analysis." My thanks to Helene Rassias, personal communication, for supplying this information.)

Asher 1981a reports good results with the total physical response method (an oral approach, using spoken cues for bodily action). However, his results—greater skill in reading as well as listening—are often in comparison with results of the audiolingual method rather than grammar-translation. The only negative findings I have seen for an oral-aural approach are reported by Corbett and Smith (249), who say that the listening strategy may not have worked at Purdue because it was simply added into a standard course without any course adjustment.

6. There is much debate on the "silent period." Asher 1981b: 50–1, 67, criticizes teachers for insisting that students talk before they are ready. But others find that speaking should not wait for language learning but should be used to assist it. Harvey (36) remarks that intake invites output (speech), and that memory traces are laid down no less when students speak than when they hear. He asks, "Why should speech—which is at once motor and conceptual—be the one activity where conscious effort is futile or even counter productive?" And he notes that "experiments have shown that self-generated information is more likely to be retained than information generated by others."

7. I might as well own up, at this point, to my allergy to boredom. With my extreme taste for liveliness, I am probably at the far end of any spectrum. I was traumatized by the unbelievably boring language tapes I was supposed to endure—and respond to—in my French labs in college in the 1960s. The drills made me want to scream. I simply walked out of the language lab, never to return. Although almost no one teaches by a purely audiolingual method any more, the audiolingual drill is still used as one tool out of many. I know this is true for ancient Greek because in asking colleagues whether they used Greek out loud in the classroom, I was sometimes told, "Oh yes, in drills." For an account of the audiolingual method and some objections, see Hadley 110–3; Richards and Rodgers 50–69, especially "The Decline of Audiolingualism."

8. See Brown 215–33 for an account of error as the result of learner's developing interlanguage system.

9. More recent research (Gregersen and Horwitz) points to the connection between perfectionism and anxiety. In particular, "anxious and non-anxious students differ in their personal performance standards, procrastination, fear of evaluation, and concern over errors" (562). To overcome certain students' perfectionism, Gregersen and Horwitz recommend building a supportive learning environment in which mistakes are a normal part of the learning process. They also recommend stressing learning and improvement over perfect performance of various assignments and reassuring students that they will receive the help they need to succeed.

10. The debate about how to present grammar is a long one. Peckett (8) offers a fairly stringent requirement for explanation: "only then, when your pupils can imitate you in producing the grammar in such a way that you believe it is the result of logical thought rather than imitation, can you discuss the grammar in English. At that point, encourage them to make up their own rule; and if they cannot do this, go back to producing examples until they can." On the other hand, Scarcella and Oxford (172) note: "because Krashen believes that the memorization of rules has little effect on language development, he encouraged others to downplay grammar in language classrooms. This severe downplaying of grammar was perhaps a necessary antidote to the grammatical overexposure language learners experienced in the heyday of the cognitive approaches to language teaching. However, the pendulum is now swinging back to a more reasonable point, a state at which grammar is again considered an essential element of language learning." Current research recommends "a focus on form" within a meaningful context. See Doughty and Lightbown and Spada.

11. Krashen 1982: 68–9 is against *grammatical* sequencing when the teacher gives comprehensible input for (unconscious) acquisition, though there will be sequencing of some sort since the conversation gradually incorporates more and more that is new.

12. This tape was played during my APA talk (Reiner). The conversation can be found in Saffire and Freis 270–271. I have found that beginning with uncontracted forms and then learning to contract them works better than beginning with contracted forms. (Neither way is fully satisfactory.) Although I am a proponent of restored pronunciation at the advanced level, I believe that beginners should have clear pronunciation for each Greek letter, unique

if possible. For this reason I recommend using the old-fashioned pronunciations, "f" for phi, "th" for theta, and "ch" as in the Scottish *loch* for chi. I try also, usually without success, to pronounce eta ("Ann") and omega ("awe") in a distinctive way. For further arguments see Saffire and Freis 6.

13. This is the "random volunteered group response" recommended by Krashen and Terrell (86). It works fine, allowing many individuals to speak at once without feeling coerced (as in choral repetition).

14. Another approach that integrates speaking into the classroom is Adair-Hauck and Donato's PACE model, a story-based approach to teaching grammar in a Standards-based language curriculum (2002a, b).

15. See, for example, the summer Latin program at the University of Kentucky (www.uky.edu/AS/Classics/aestivumeng.html) and the University of Kentucky Institute for Latin Studies (www.uky.edu/AS/Classics/institute.html), both organized by Terence Tunberg. In addition, Septentrionale Americanum Latinitatis Vivae Institutum and the North American Institute for Living Latin Studies (NAILLS), founded in 1996 to promote oral Latin in North America (www.latin.org/), is organized by Nancy Llewellyn. The latter website provides links to other organizations throughout the world that promote speaking Latin.

Works Cited

Adair-Hauck, Bonnie, and Richard Donato. 2002a. "The PACE Model: A Story-Based Approach to Meaning and Form for Standards-Based Language Learning." *French Review* 76: 265–76.

———. 2002b. "The PACE Model—Actualizing the Standards through Storytelling: 'Le Bras, la Jambe et le Ventre.'" *French Review* 76: 278–96.

Allen, E. D. 1974. "The Teacher as Catalyst: Motivation in the Classroom." In Frank M. Grittner, ed., *Student Motivation and the Foreign Language Teacher: A Guide for Building the Modern Curriculum.* Skokie, IL: National Textbook, 1–10.

Asher, James J. 1981a. "Comprehension Training: The Evidence from Laboratory and Classroom Studies." In Harris Winitz, ed., *The Comprehension Approach to Foreign Language Instruction.* Rowley, MA: Newbury House, 187–222.

———. 1981b. "The Extinction of Second-Language Learning in American Schools: An Intervention Model." In Harris Winitz, ed., *The Comprehension Approach to Foreign Language Instruction.* Rowley, MA: Newbury House, 49–68.

———. 1982. *Learning Another Language through Actions: The Complete Teacher's Guidebook.* 2nd ed. Los Gatos, CA: Sky Oaks.

Ausubel, David A. 1965. "Adults versus Children in Second-Language Learning: Psychological Considerations." *Modern Language Journal* 48: 420–4.

Barbe, Walter B., and Raymond H. Swassing. 1979. *Teaching through Modality Strengths: Concepts and Practices.* Columbus, OH: Bloser.

Berko-Gleason, Jean. 1982. "Insights from Child Language Acquisition for Second Language Loss." In Richard D. Lambert and Barbara F. Freed, eds., *The Loss of Language Skills.* Rowley, MA: Newbury House, 13–23.

Brown, H. Douglas. 2000. *Principles of Language Learning and Teaching.* 4th ed. White Plains, NY: Addison Wesley Longman.

Brown, J. M., and A. S. Palmer. 1988. *The Listening Approach.* New York: Longman.

Canale, Michael, and Swain, Merrill. 1980. "Theoretical Bases of Communicative Approaches to Second Language Teaching and Testing." *Applied Linguistics* 1: 1–47.

Coady, James. 1997. "L2 Vocabulary Acquisition through Extensive Reading." In James Coady and Thomas Huckin, eds., *Second Language Vocabulary Acquistion: A Rationale for Pedagogy*. Cambridge, UK: Cambridge University Press, 225–37.

Corbett, S., and W. F. Smith. 1981. "Listening Comprehension as a Base for a Multiskill Approach to Beginning Spanish: The Purdue Experiment." In Harris Winitz, ed., *The Comprehension Approach to Foreign Language Instruction*. Rowley, MA: Newbury House, 223–51.

Crookall, David, and Rebecca L. Oxford. 1991. "Dealing with Anxiety: Some Practical Activities for Language Learners and Teacher Trainees." In Elaine K. Horwitz and Dolly J. Young, eds., 1991. *Language Anxiety: From Theory and Research to Classroom Implications*. Englewood Cliffs, NJ: Prentice Hall, 141–50.

Daly, J. 1991. "Understanding Communication Apprehension: An Introduction for Language Educators." In Elaine K. Horwitz and Dolly J. Young, eds., *Language Anxiety: From Theory and Research to Classroom Implications*. Englewood Cliffs, NJ: Prentice-Hall, 3–13.

Day, Richard R., and Julian Bamford. 1998. *Extensive Reading in the Second Language Classroom*. Cambridge, UK: Cambridge University Press.

Deagon, Andrea W. 1991. "Learning Process and Exercise Sequencing in Latin Instruction." *Classical Journal* 87: 59–70.

Doughty, Catherine. 1998. "Acquiring Competence in a Second Language: Form and Function." In Heidi Byrnes, ed., *Learning Foreign and Second Languages: Perspectives in Research and Scholarship*, New York: Modern Language Association, 128–56.

Ellis, Rod. 1994, "Factors in the Incidental Acquisition of Second Language Vocabulary from Oral Input: A Review Essay." *Applied Language Learning* 5: 1–32.

Gardner, Robert C. 1988. "Attitudes and Motivations." *Annual Review of Applied Linguistics* 9: 135–48.

———. 2002. "Social Psychological Perspective on Second Language Acquisition." In Robert B. Kaplan, ed., *The Oxford Handbook of Applied Linguistics*. New York: Oxford University Press, 160–9.

Gass, Susan M., and Carolyn G. Madden. 1985. Introduction to Susan M. Gass and Carolyn G. Madden, eds., *Input in Second Language Acquisition*. Rowley, MA: Newbury House, 3–16.

Genesee, F. 1991. "Pedagogical Implications of Second Language Immersion." Paper presented at the annual meeting of the Spanish Association of Applied Linguistics, San Sebastrian, Spain, and circulated privately.

Gregersen, Tammy, and Elaine K. Horwitz. 2002. "Language Learning and Perfectionism: Anxious and Non-Anxious Language Learners' Reactions to Their Own Oral Performance." *Modern Language Journal* 86: 562–70.

Hadley, Alice Omaggio 2001. *Teaching Language in Context*. 3rd ed. Boston: Heinle and Heinle.

Harvey, J. E. 1987. "Beginning French via the Read-and-Speak Method," *Foreign Language Annals* 20: 31–7.

Kitchell, Kenneth F., Jr. 1998. "The Great Latin Debate: The Futility of Utility." In Richard A. LaFleur, ed., *Latin for the Twenty-first Century*. Glenview, IL: Scott Foresman–Addison Wesley. 1–14.

Krashen, Stephen D. 1981. *Second Language Acquisition and Second Language Learning*. Oxford: Pergamon.

———. 1982. *Principles and Practice in Second Language Acquisition*. Oxford: Pergamon.

———. 1985. *The Input Hypothesis: Issues and Implications*. London: Longman.

———. 1994. *From Theory to Practice: The Natural Approach*. Video conference program, February 23. McGraw-Hill Satellite Teleconference.

Krashen, Stephen D., and Tracy D. Terrell 1983. *The Natural Approach: Language Acquisition in the Classroom*. Oxford: Pergamon.

Lightbown, Patsy, and Nina Spada. 1999. *How Languages Are Learned*. Rev. ed. Oxford: Oxford University Press.

Maxim, Hiram. 2002. "A Study into the Feasibility and Effects of Reading Extended Authentic Discourse in the Beginning German Language Classroom." *Modern Language Journal* 86: 20–35.

Moskowitz, G. 1978. *Caring and Sharing in the Foreign Language Class: A Sourcebook on Humanistic Techniques*. Rowley, MA: Newbury House.

Munsell, Paul, and Thomas Carr. 1981. "Monitoring the Monitor: A Review of Second Language Acquisition and Second Language Learning." *Language Learning* 31: 493–502.

Oxford, Rebecca L. 1990. *Language Learning Strategies: What Every Teacher Should Know*. Boston: Heinle and Heinle.

Oxford, Rebecca L., and Robin C. Scarcella. 1994. "Second Language Vocabulary Learning Among Adults: State of the Art in Vocabulary Instruction," *System* 22: 231–43.

Padilla, Amado M., and Hyekyung Sung. 1990. "Information Processing and Foreign Language Learning." In Amado Padilla, Halford H. Fairchild, and Concepcion M. Valadez, eds., *Foreign Language Education: Issues and Strategies*. Newbury Park, CA: Sage, 41–55.

Peterson, Pat Wilcox. 2001. "Skills and Strategies for Proficient Listening." In Marianne Celce-Murcia, ed., *Teaching English as a Second or Foreign Language*. 3rd ed. Boston: Heinle and Heinle, 87–100.

Poole, Deborah. 2002. "Discourse Analysis and Applied Linguistics." In Robert B. Kaplan, ed., *The Oxford Handbook of Applied Linguistics*. New York: Oxford University Press, 73–84.

Reiner, Paula. 1992. "Ancient Greek in Classroom Conversation," Paper presented at the annual meeting of the American Philological Association, New Orleans, December 30.

Richards, Jack C. 1990. *The Language Teaching Matrix*. Cambridge, UK: Cambridge University Press.

Richards, Jack C., and Theodore S. Rodgers. 2001. *Approaches and Methods in Language Teaching*. 2nd ed. Cambridge, UK: Cambridge University Press.

Rubin, Joan. 1975. "What the 'Good Language Learner' Can Teach Us." *TESOL Quarterly* 9, 1: 41–51.

Saffire, Paula, and Catherine Freis. 1999. *Ancient Greek Alive*. Chapel Hill: University of North Carolina Press.

Scarcella, R., and Oxford, R. 1992. *The Tapestry of Language Learning: The Individual in the Communicative Classroom*. Boston: Heinle and Heinle.

Shannon, S. 1994. "Introduction." In Ronald M. Barasch and R. and C. V. James, eds., *Beyond the Monitor Model: Comments on Current Theory and Practice in Second Language Acquisition*. Boston: Heinle and Heinle, 7–20.

Stevens, F. 1983. "Activities to Promote Learning and Communication in the Second Language Classroom." *TESOL Quarterly* 17, 2: 259–72.

Strasheim, Lorraine A. 1987. *Total Physical Response*. Amherst, MA: Classical Association of New England.

Swain, Merrill. 1985. "Communicative Competence: Some Roles of Comprehensible Input and Comprehensible Output in its Development." In Susan M. Gass and Carolyn G. Madden, eds., *Input in Second Language Acquisition*. Rowley, MA: Newbury House, 235–53.

―――. 1995. "Three Functions of Output in Second Language Learning." In Guy Cook and Barbara Seidlhofer, eds., *Principle and Practice in Applied Linguistics: Studies in Honor of H. G. Widdowson*. Oxford: Oxford University Press, 125–144.

―――. 2000. "The Output Hypothesis and Beyond: Mediating Acquisition through Collaborative Dialogue." In James P. Lantolf, ed., *Sociocultural Theory and Second Language Learning*. Oxford: Oxford University Press, 97–114.

Thompson, Lynn, Donna Christian, Charles W. Stansfield, and Nancy Rhodes. 1990. "Foreign Language Instruction in the United States," In Amado Padilla, Halford H. Fairchild, and Concepcion M. Valadez, eds., *Foreign Language Education: Issues and Strategies*. Newbury Park, CA: Sage, 22–35.

Wesche, M. and D. Ready. 1985. "Foreigner Talk in the University Classroom." In Susan M. Gass and Carolyn G. Madden, eds., *Input in Second Language Acquisition*. Rowley, MA: Newbury House, 89–114.

Wills, Jeffrey. 1998. "Speaking Latin in Schools and Colleges." *Classical World* 92: 27–34.

Wong, Wynne, and Bill VanPatten. 2003. "The Evidence is IN: Drills are OUT." *Foreign Language Annals* 36: 403–23.

Young, D. J. 1991. "Creating a Low-Anxiety Classroom Environment: What Does Language Anxiety Research Suggest?" *Modern Language Journal* 75: 426–37.

CHAPTER 9

Teaching Writing in Beginning Latin and Greek
Logos, Ethos, and *Pathos*

John Gruber-Miller

Teachers have long felt that composition in the Greek and Latin classroom is beneficial. It helps students master the intricacies of Greek and Latin morphology and, at more advanced levels, provides a way to understand ancient prose styles. Teachers realize too that there is an important, if not completely understood, connection between reading classical languages and writing them. Yet teachers also realize that there are so many subskills to master that they wonder how there will be time to spend writing Latin and Greek. Instead of asking their students to write, they "help" their students out by giving them textbook sentences to compose. Too often, what passes for writing is really another way to say translation.

When I was first learning Latin, I was asked to translate into Latin sentences such as "The teacher's horse is in the field" or "The advice of the teacher having been heard, we shall read the book" (Ullman, Henderson, and Henry 86, 250). From our students' point of view, this model has little to recommend it. Students are asked to translate individual sentences into Latin or Greek that are not part of any connected narrative or exposition; that have no audience except one, the teacher; and that have as their primary purpose to learn morphology, syntax, and vocabulary. Once students do write, what they remember is the humiliation of going to the blackboard and having their sentences critiqued, erased, and largely rewritten rather than the success of learning Greek or Latin. As a result, students have little motivation to write in Latin or Greek. Instead of the joy of expressing ideas, it is the anguish of being unsuccessful. It is no wonder that some in our field consider composition a waste of time.[1] Yet if we want our students to learn Latin and Greek as something more than a puzzle to decode, offering them the opportunity to write is a great way to accomplish that end.

This is not to say that writing as a means of learning the nuts and bolts of a language is not important. Writing reinforces these basic language skills. But writing connected prose shows students how discourse is structured and how to read Greek and Latin with greater understanding. Writing also offers the possibility of exploring our own ideas, feelings, thoughts, and values, and making comparisons with the ancient world. As classicists, we have been reluctant to imagine writing Latin and Greek as much more than a means to an end. We have been so concerned to help our students learn vocabulary and syntax that we have neglected the rhetorical training recommended by the ancients. As Aristotle and Cicero realized, composing texts requires the triad *logos, ethos,* and *pathos*—roughly corresponding to what modern students of rhetoric refer to as text, writer, and audience. What we have been teaching our students is only a weak form of *logos*, and we have not helped them develop the writer's voice or sense of audience. Our students as "composers" of textbook sentences have been deprived of opportunities to choose topics to write about and to select an audience to read their writing. In addition, since we have focused on accuracy, writers have spent time on grammar and vocabulary, at least at some elementary level, but they have not learned how to make use of invention, arrangement, or diction to develop their writing. Without knowing their audience, our students cannot hope to develop a voice or select and arrange content. In short, our students have been denied the opportunity to use Greek and Latin to communicate (see chapter 1, this volume), and in the process have not nurtured some of the skills needed for reading classical languages.

In the rest of this chapter, I argue that if we keep in mind the classical model for composing (*ethos*, *logos*, and *pathos*), we may come to a richer, more flexible way of incorporating a writing component in beginning Greek and Latin. Throughout most of the rest of the chapter, I focus on choices that student writers can make (with the assistance of their teachers) to inform their writing, choices in topic, genre, or perspective that will allow them to present their own point of view or the point of view of specific characters from the ancient world (*ethos*). In addition, I present ways to help students to work with words, not only basic vocabulary and sentence-level syntax but also word choice, cohesion devices, and organization (*logos*). Finally, I offer ways for student writers to write for multiple audiences and to receive feedback from those audiences in order to improve their writing (*pathos*). In all the examples that follow, communication is the primary goal. Basic language skills are important too: within a communicative context, students are motivated to learn these basic skills as the result of sharing their ideas with multiple readers. I also present ways for structuring assignments so that students can build upon their knowledge and language skills to create step-by-step, complete written texts (the writing process). But first, I want to address reasons why beginning Greek and Latin students should write and how they should do so.

Reasons for Writing

I am not going to say that writing is not one of the hardest tasks that language students face in learning a language. It is. It involves an enormous range of skills from forming letters and writing words to mastery of the morphology and syntax of sentences to organizing thoughts into a coherent whole.[2] Yet there are many reasons to make the effort, some of which teachers have implicitly known for years: (1) writing contributes to students' ability to communicate; (2) it helps students to reinforce the basic code of the language; (3) it aids in developing reading skills; and (4) it provides an opportunity for implementing the *Standards for Classical Language Learning*.

First, we should not underestimate the importance of communicating in another language. It provides students with motivation and investment in the language. If students can write to classmates, friends, or pen pals, they feel that what they are doing is not just learning a special code that must be analyzed but a tool that allows them to communicate with other people just like any other language. Once they start writing stories to share with the rest of class, writing letters to pen pals, and writing inscriptions commemorating their accomplishments, they can begin to be invested in the language as a means to communicate. In short, they have a purpose for writing and an audience to read what they write.

Attention to the writer's triad—*logos, ethos,* and *pathos*—helps students go beyond composing textbook sentences and create interesting and meaningful discourse. In fact, language students are capable of creating a variety of text types (e.g., descriptive, narrative, and expository) even in beginning language classes (Valdés, Haro, and Echevarriarza; Way, Joiner, and Seaman). After perhaps some initial reluctance, students want to write because they have ideas to share, stories to tell, satire to write. They can develop a voice (*ethos*) because they have some choice in whose perspective they tell their story from. By writing from another's point of view (one possible *ethos*), moreover, they can begin to understand Greek and Roman culture from the point of view of various individuals in the culture. By writing for an audience that wants to read their work, they know that they must pay attention to their readers' needs for a clear, well-organized, and interesting text (*pathos*). And by paying attention to sentence-level syntax as well as discourse patterns, they read with greater understanding of how ancient texts are structured and arranged (*logos*).

Second, writing to communicate reinforces the acquisition of language (Harklau). According to recent research in second language acquisition, learners acquire language through a dynamic process in which they make hypotheses about the appropriate rules, test them by comparing their language production with others', and then revise their own system (McLaughlin; McLaughlin and Heredia; Ellis). More and more evidence suggests that producing the language—output, as the researchers name it—is crucial for reaching higher levels of proficiency in a language (Nobuyoshi and Ellis; Pica; Pica et al. 1989; Swain and Lapkin). Only through output do learners test their understanding of the language and have the opportunity to receive feedback on their progress thus far. Merrill Swain, in her study of English-speaking students in French-immersion programs in Canada, maintains that

> comprehensible output . . . is a necessary mechanism of acquisition independent of the role of comprehensible input. Its role is, at minimum, to provide opportunities for contextualized, meaningful use, to test out hypotheses about the target language, and to move the learner from a purely semantic analysis of language to a syntactic analysis of it. (252)

Simply knowing that one will be expected to produce may be the "trigger that forces the learner to pay attention to the means of expressions needed in order to successfully convey his or her intended meaning" (249).[3] Once students understand the meaning of the utterance, it may be possible for them to pay more attention to form. Most important for writing, since learner language develops through both performance and feedback, written feedback has the potential of making a more vivid, clear, lasting, and personal impression than oral feedback (Chastain). In other words, writing helps students do what we always thought it did: get control of the rule system of the language. What is crucial is that this negotiation of meaning and form occurs in the context of meaningful discourse.[4]

Third, research on reading and writing has pointed to the interaction and interdependence of the two. Early studies of reading and writing relationships, reviewed by Stotsky and Belanger, suggested the reciprocal relationship of reading and writing:

1. Better writers tend to be better readers.

2. Better writers read more than poorer readers.

3. Better readers tend to produce more syntactically mature writing than poorer readers.

Further studies (Carson; Grabe; Krashen 1984; Leki 1993) have noted additional parallels. Good readers and good writers attend to the global meaning of the text instead of being bogged down with word- and sentence-level grammatical and print code concerns. Good readers and writers are flexible, utilizing strategies not hierarchically or linearly but interactively in reading and recursively in writing. We also know that writing activities can be useful for improving reading comprehension and retention of information (e.g., summarizing, paraphrasing, and outlining) (Stotsky). In addition, direct instruction in sentence, paragraph, and discourse structure for writing results in significant improvement in reading (Belanger). In short, reading builds knowledge of various kinds to use in writing, and writing consolidates knowledge in a way that builds schemata to read with (Bereiter and Scardamalia; Leki 1993; Sternglass 1988).

It is no surprise that writing reinforces reading, since they draw upon the same cognitive text world. Both reading and writing are acts of composing, of making meaning with text (Tierney and Pearson; Zamel 1992). Writers have usually been thought to be engaged in a constructive process when they compose, but readers are too. Both reading and writing share common generative cognitive processes involved in meaning construction in both composing and comprehending text: both reading and writing emphasize background knowledge, both draw on a common data pool of written language, both utilize similar transformations of background knowledge into text, and both employ common processing patterns in text production as individuals read and write (Carson; Kucer). To put it another way, the process of reading and writing is similar to reading a palimpsest or viewing developing film. At the beginning, active readers gather ideas and make hypotheses about the text they are reading just as writers gather ideas and form a hypotheses before they write. They then develop a "draft," identifying purpose, audience, style, and organizational patterns. Throughout the process, they make use of three types of schemata—what Patricia Carrell terms linguistic (language knowledge), content (topic knowledge), and formal (rhetorical knowledge)—to help make sense of the emerging text. They also continue to revise these "drafts," changing perspective, and revising hypotheses (Kauffmann; Straw). In short, reading and writing involve the negotiation of meaning between reader, writer, and text. Just as the writer must take into account his audience, so, too, a reader must try to negotiate the meaning of the writer. In short, readers and writers construct text from this common pool of cognitive, linguistic, and cultural schemata.

Writing also gives readers a way to focus their reading. Instead of reading to learn grammar or to pick out the main ideas of a text, writing offers a unique way for readers to make personal connections with a text. For example, we might ask students to engage in writing before reading a text by writing from their own experience and background knowledge about an idea or experience in the text they are about to read. Such an activity helps students anticipate what they are going to read by activating knowledge of vocabulary, linguistic structures, content, and formal schemata (Spack). We might also ask our students to respond to the content of a text by writing annotations, summaries, responses in the forms of letters, inscriptions, or minidramas to help students become more engaged with the text and better able to understand the reading. In short, writing is a way of reading better "because it requires the learner to reconstruct the structure and meaning of ideas expressed by another writer. To possess an idea that one is reading about requires competence in regenerating the idea, competence in learning how to write the ideas of another" (Squire 1983, cited in Sternglass 1986: 2).[5]

Fourth, writing offers teachers ways to implement all five goals of the *Standards for Classical Language Learning*. As we just saw, writing contributes to general language proficiency, reinforces reading skills, and encourages students to communicate with each other (Communication goal). Writing, moreover, helps students gain knowledge of Greek and Roman culture (goal 2). For example, students can see the world through others' eyes by composing election notices, giving a guided tour of an ancient monument, or imagining what they hear when eavesdropping in a house or the theater (see examples that follow). Writing can also help students make connections with other disciplines (goal 3), such as art, by using vase-paintings or sculptures as springboards for stories, drama, or poems (e.g., see "Working with picture sets" or "Comparison" hereafter). Furthermore, writing assignments, such as letter writing, election notices, or epitaphs (examples follow), provide points of departure in making comparisons between the ancient and modern world (goal 4), whether the topic is letter-writing conventions, politics, or attitudes toward death. Finally, writing for different audiences, whether in the school or beyond, is an ideal way for students to participate in wider communities (goal 5). In particular, writing from the point of view of a marginal character or creating minidramas that represent characters from different walks of life (see hereafter) encourage students to use their knowledge of Greek and Roman cultures in a world of diverse cultures.

The Writing Process

If any story sums up the importance of the composing process, it is the story, preserved in Plutarch's *On the Glory of the Athenians* (Moralia 347f), of Menander writing one of his comedies. Approached by a friend not long before his play would commence production, he was asked how his play was coming along. Menander replied, "I have indeed composed it: the plot is worked out, but I've still got to add the lines." Whether this brief anecdote is true or not, it brings into relief the importance of the writing process: invention and arrangement, the planning that precedes the actual writing, are just as important as writing down the words. And once the script was written, it was no doubt revised during rehearsal, perhaps all the way up until it premiered at the City Dionysia or Lenaea. In short, writing for Menander was a many-layered process that included prewriting, writing, and revising and editing. To focus on any one phase alone would not truly represent the playwright's composing process.

If writing is a process, for the ancients and for us, one might reasonably ask why we have "lost" this knowledge. One possible explanation is that when Erasmus and other Renaissance humanists decided to model their Latin prose on Cicero, they created a fundamental change in how we view composing in Greek and Latin. Up until the Renaissance, Latin was taught as a living language used to communicate everything from basic necessities of life to philosophical reflections on creation, life, and death. What Erasmus and his colleagues did in choosing Cicero as the exemplar of good Latin was to tip the balance from communication to imitation. Learning Latin and Greek became more concerned with following a pattern of correct usage, style, and diction and less likely to be a medium of communication (Ganss; Kitchell). It became more concerned with careful imitation of polished models, echoing their structure, thoughts, turns of phrase, and arguments. In the long run, this approach, especially at the beginning and intermediate level of learning Greek and Latin, led to an emphasis on correct form, translation of teacher-composed sentences, and the finished product.[6]

A process approach, on the other hand, instead of focusing on the end product, takes into account the steps involved in writing. At first this process was thought to be a linear one (Emig), moving from prewriting to writing to revising to editing. But further research (Hillocks; Krapels; Krashen; Reichelt 1999, 2001; Roca de Larios, Murphy, and Marín; Silva) revealed that writers rarely go directly from point A to point B. Instead, scholars realized that writing is a recursive process in which writers plan, write, reread, get new ideas, plan some more, rewrite, and finally edit. The composing process, according to Vivian Zamel (1983) is "non-linear, exploratory, and a generative process whereby writers discover and reformulate their ideas as they attempt to approximate meaning." In addition, communication within a specific context and for a specific audience gives the writer a purpose other than imitating a master or getting a grade.

Where did this distinction between product and process originate? Researchers (Grabe and Kaplan; Krapels; Krashen; Roca de Larios et al.; Silva) studying the composing process, first of experienced and successful writers and then of novice or less skilled writers, discovered that less skilled writers tend to view their writing as a product: their composing is mechanical and formulaic, they are inhibited by concerns with correctness and form; they cannot easily get beyond the surface structure, they revise at the word level, and they get bogged down when they cannot think of alternative vocabulary or structures to express themselves. They think they have an audience of one (the teacher) and hence are less concerned about making their message clear to the reader. More skilled writers, on the other hand, use a process approach. They view their writing from a more global approach, they plan more and have more flexible plans: they are willing to change their ideas as they write, and they revise their essay's structure accordingly. At the same time, more skilled writers scan back through their texts in order not to lose a sense of the whole. Furthermore, they rescan in order to plan and decide if what they have written corresponds to what they intend to say. Moreover, when good writers revise, they are willing to revise whole chunks of discourse to add content. Finally, good writers are more concerned with the reader. They spend time thinking about the effect they want to make on the reader, what background knowledge the reader needs to have, what might interest the reader. In short, more skilled writers are more successful in converting their ego-centered "writer-based" prose into "reader-based" prose, from prose that is personal and reflects the interior monologue of a writer thinking on paper to prose that pays attention to the reader (Flower).

So what are the benefits of a process approach to writing in the classroom? First, a process approach more closely reflects the reality of writing. It encourages teachers and students to see writing as a communicative act rather than simply an exercise to learn correct structure or correct grammatical forms. Because students are encouraged to write for an audience broader than the teacher, attention to structure and form are important in conveying ideas. Hence they have a reason for using a particular rhetorical structure or correct grammar. Just as important, a process approach allows writers to focus on individual parts of rhetorical problems. By submitting their drafts to peers at one or more stages in the writing process, students can tackle such global rhetorical problems as audience, topic, development, logic, and even local-level rhetorical problems such as spelling, sentence structure, and word choice in some systematic manner (Roen). Finally, a process approach helps students realize that there may be several ways to convey ideas and that they are in some part responsible for shaping the way others will view reality. In short, writing once again becomes a creative act that involves *ethos*, *logos*, and *pathos*, that encourages writers to write with purpose.

Making the Process Work: Sequencing Activities

As Plutarch's anecdote about Menander shows us, writing is a many-layered process. If first-language writers such as Menander go through a recursive process of prewriting, writing, revising, and editing, second language writers have even more to manage. Not only do second language writers need time to develop a point of view and choose how they will present their story but also they need a chance to recall and rehearse basic vocabulary, morphology, and syntax. Just as important, they need to understand how culture affects the text they will write. With so many cognitive demands, beginning second language writers need time to activate linguistic, cultural, and rhetorical schemata as well as time to develop ideas. In this section, I present two scenarios demonstrating how I have successfully sequenced writing activities to lead up to a free, unguided composition. At the end of the section, I offer additional examples of prewriting activities. Throughout this section, I show how prewriting activities can include invention strategies that help students brainstorm topics and develop ideas for a composition while at the same time introducing appropriate cultural background, suggesting relevant vocabulary, and reviewing relevant linguistic structures and sentence-level syntax.

Sequence Based on a Picture (Adapted from Tittle)

Choose a picture from daily life or mythology, for example, students in school, people at the harbor, soldiers marching into town, Odysseus blinding Polyphemus, or Psyche gazing at Cupid. A basic picture with only a few people, objects, or actions will keep the vocabulary manageable and the writing focused. For this example, I have chosen a drawing from *Athenaze* (Balme and Lawall), chapter 4, page 36, showing women drawing water from a fountain.[7] This same exercise (with a different picture) could be used later in the course, but with richer possibilities since students by then will know more vocabulary and syntax.

Task 1: Recognition

Ask students to list in Greek all the objects or features in the picture. In other words, "Who is in the picture? What is in the picture?" After each student compiles a list, he or she should then get together with a partner to check for details that they may have left out or for vocabulary they did not remember. A representative list for "Women drawing water" might be

ἡ γυνή	woman
αἱ γυναῖκες	women
ἡ θυγάτηρ	daughter
ἡ μήτηρ	mother
ἡ ὑδρία	water jar
ἡ κρήνη	spring, fountain

Task 2: Description

Now ask students to write short descriptions answering the questions "What is happening in the picture? Where is it happening? When is it happening?" Since the recognition task was to elicit noun vocabulary, this task is designed to get students to concentrate on other parts of speech. Since this task may be more difficult, it may be useful for students to collaborate on this task from the outset.

Examples:

ἐν τῇ κρήνῃ	at the spring
πρωί	early
ἡ κρήνη ἐστι καλή.	The fountain is beautiful.
πολλαὶ γυναῖκες πάρεισιν.	Many women are present.
αἱ γυναῖκες λέγουσιν.	The women are talking.
ἀλλήλους χαίρουσιν.	They are greeting each other.
τας ὑδρίας φέρουσιν.	They are carrying water jars.
τὰς ὑδρίας πληροῦσιν.	They are filling the water jars.

Task 3: Expansion

For the third task, students now write a four- to five-sentence paragraph using the vocabulary and descriptions they compiled in the first two tasks. This task allows students to organize their material into a cohesive and coherent composition: they will have to make decisions regarding the order of the sentences, combining ideas into a single sentence (e.g., using μέν and δέ), and providing links from sentence to sentence (cohesion devices such as pronouns and conjunctions). This stage is crucial since researchers have found that the overall quality of a composition depends upon discourse features, especially those for cohesion, more than on morphology and syntax (Chiang 1999, 2003). They will have the opportunity to personalize their narrative in the next task. After completing task 3, students should have an opportunity to read the paragraphs of other groups.

Task 4: Elaboration

After writing a fact-based narrative based on the picture in task 3, students now have the chance to develop personalities, create dialogue, and elaborate on their previous paragraph. One way to accomplish this task is to ask students to answer the question "What are the characters talking about?" Another way to approach this task is to ask the students to consider each sentence written in task 3 and add a sentence or two that makes a conjecture, gives an explanation, or describes follow-up or related events. Either approach allows students to create a more interesting narrative, one that goes beyond simple description to include characterization and motivation for what is happening in the picture. The exercise has progressed from mere description to one of imagination and personal interaction. Finally, students should provide a title for the composition. After each group has completed its paragraph, the groups should share their narratives with other groups, either on paper, on a computer screen, or on an overhead projector.

Sequence Based on a Reading Passage

Another sequence of activities that lead to a free, unguided composition could be based on a reading passage. This example is based on the *Oxford Latin Course*, part 2, chapter 18, in which Quintus and his father make the journey from Venusia to

Rome. The ultimate goal of this sequence is to write a letter home from Flaccus or Quintus to mother and daughter telling about the trip. First, the instructor might talk about travel by land in the Roman world, showing pictures of Roman roads, carts, shoes, and satchels. Then the class might brainstorm to come up with vocabulary relevant to describe a trip (verbs of motion, words related to spending the night). After the class has read the story in chapter 18, then students in small groups would test each other's comprehension by writing four or five questions in Latin about one portion of the passage. All the questions from each group could then be gathered on the board or overhead so that the rest of the class could respond to the questions, either in writing or in speech. After reading the story, students should brainstorm what questions Horatia or Scintilla might have about the trip. Then they would write a letter home to Horatia or Scintilla describing what happened on the trip. Once again, it is important for writers to add details about their characters' feelings during the trip or to describe encounters with other travelers on the way (task 4: elaboration). Finally, before revising the letter home, students could learn to pay attention to the cohesion of their letters by completing a paragraph in which the connectives (expressions of time or place, adverbs) are missing and they fill in the missing blanks from a list of expressions at the bottom of the page. In short, such a sequence gives students the building blocks to activate topic knowledge, linguistic knowledge, and rhetorical schemata before embarking on a free composition. At the same time, the final composition allows students to integrate culture, vocabulary, syntax, and cohesion devices from a particular point of view for a particular audience.

Although these two sequences are meant as examples of how a teacher might sequence activities, there are many other types of prewriting, writing, and revision activities that could be combined into a sequence. Of course, some of these activities may be used independently to practice specific grammatical points, cohesion techniques, or discourse strategies, but students more often recognize the need for learning these elements of writing and reading well if these activities are part of a larger project that has communication with others as its goal.[8]

Other Prewriting Activities

Identify and List Items in a Picture or a Text

For example, if students are writing about a three-dimensional space, they might receive a floor plan or a drawing and then label the rooms or the items in a room. If students are writing an election advertisement, they can read sample texts and pick out the key words they would use to support their candidate or to denigrate the opposition.

Brainstorm

To choose the same examples: if students are writing about what happens in different rooms in a house, they might brainstorm about what happens in each room. Questions such as "Who spends time in this room? What do they do in this room?"

might elicit answers about the kitchen such as *servi laborant, coquunt, urnas quaerunt.* If they are writing an election advertisement, they could brainstorm about what various candidates would promise if elected.

Semantic Mapping

Beginning with a specific word, idea, or concept, students brainstorm vocabulary and phrases related to the main idea. These words and phrases are then written on the board or overhead and organized visually into groups that belong together. Students can then offer headings for each group of items, discuss which ideas are more important, and even create an outline for a composition. By graphically organizing ideas and vocabulary, students and teachers explore ways to elicit vocabulary, to understand ancient culture, and to structure a text.[9]

Strategic Questioning

The basic questions "who, what, where, when, how, and why?" provide many ways to get writers to begin thinking about what to write and about basic vocabulary at the same time. Another set of questions can focus on a common rhetorical arrangement: situation—problem—solution/response—evaluation/result (Tribble 86–91). What is the situation? Who is involved? What is the problem? Who or what does it affect? How do various people respond? What is the result? This organizational pattern is evident not only in narrative texts but also in texts that analyze a process or argue a point. Finally, a third set of strategic questions may derive from Aristotle's "topics," asking questions related to definition, comparison, relationships, circumstances, or testimony (Reid 6–7).

Attention to *Logos*: Controlled Writing

Controlled writing is writing that helps students make the transition from working only with memorized material to more authentic, communicative writing. In this section, I offer examples of transformations, sentence builders, sentence combining, text completion, and guided composition.[10] Depending on focus, these exercises can be used either as prewriting or as revision activities. Since each of these activities focuses primarily on one aspect of the rhetorical triad—sentence-level syntax and discourse structure (*logos*)—none of these activities should be an end in themselves; they should be part of a sequence of activities that lead to a more open-ended composition.

Transformation

Transforming a passage is a useful way for students to get a handle on new grammar within a complete rhetorical context. Students can transform the number of the subject from singular to plural, the tense from present to past (or future), the mood from indicative to subjunctive (or optative), or from direct to indirect statement (question or command). For example, after students have learned the imperfect and aorist tenses, it is often useful to go back to an earlier passage in a textbook, usually one that describes an event clearly, and ask students to transform it into the past, paying special note when to use the imperfect or aorist (e.g., *Athenaze*, chapter 5, page 63, the three paragraphs beginning ὁ δὲ πάππος . . .). After they are finished, either in groups or individually, students should explain the reasons for their choices.

Sentence Builders

Students can be guided to create sentences that tell a story, describe a situation, or form an argument. Without having to spend time thinking of words, they can compose a coherent paragraph in the present, future, or past. It is very helpful to provide a context for the activities, such as "a typical day" or "what I did yesterday." The following example offers ways of developing cohesion (adapted from Magnan 126).

Mane	ego	librum legere	emptum ire
deinde		laborare	cum amicis colloqui
meridie		me exercere	musicam audire
vespere		studere	in theatrum ire

After students have formed a short paragraph about themselves, they then expand the content of the paragraph by using connectives and adding a second subject.

Mane	ego	librum legere	sed meus amicus	emptum ire
deinde		laborare	dum mea amica	cum amicis colloqui
meridie		me exercere	et meus amicus	musicam audire
vespere		studere	quod mea amica	in theatrum ire

As students become comfortable with these phrases, they may wish to add to the list of activities in order to be more representative of what they and their friends do with their time. After such controlled practice, then students could write a more open-ended paragraph comparing typical activities of the writer and a friend. Some questions that might focus the paragraph: Do you work harder than your friend? Do you and your friend have different likes and dislikes? Do you and your friend get along because your schedules are compatible? For another approach to writing about oneself, see Scott (53).

Sentence Combining

Sentence combining offers writers practice at recognizing possibilities in writing. One area that language students frequently do not recognize is the reason why authors choose gramatically similar constructions, such as adjectives, participles, or relative clauses, and when to use them. The following sentences are based on the passage "Vilbia" in the *Cambridge Latin Course*, unit 3 (Phinney and Bell 26). Students need to combine the following sentences into a coherent paragraph, deciding when to use adjectives, participles, or relative clauses.

Vilbia et Rubria pocula sordida lavabant.

hae puellae in culina tabernae garriebant.

hae puellae erant filiae Latronis.

Latro tabernam tenebat.

hic erat vir magnae diligentiae sed minimae prudentiae.

Vilbia pulchra et obstinata erat.

haec patrem flocci non faciebat.

haec pocula non lavit.

sed Vilbia Rubriae fibulam ostendit.

Rubria fibulam avide spectavit.

soror fibulam tenebat.

After each student group has rewritten the sentences into a new paragraph, the new paragraphs can be shown on an overhead and the reasons for the choices can be discussed by the class. Of course, it is possible to focus the exercise by indicating which sentences are to be combined or by limiting the transformation to a single grammatical construction (e.g., relative clauses).

Text Completion

A common way of helping students focus on vocabulary, grammar, or cohesion is a gapped text that needs to be completed by the student. The following example focuses on transitions marking the chronology of the passage. Students choose from words and clauses at the bottom of the passage. The passage is adapted from the *Oxford Latin Course*, part 2, page 48.

Quintus et Marcus ad balnea procedebant. _____ advenerunt. intraverunt et circumspectabant. _____, Quintum reliquit et ad eum accessit. Quintus solus ad apodyterium discessit. vestimenta exuit et in armario posuit. _____ in tepidarium iniit et _____ in aqua tepida iacebat; _____ in calidarium iit; _____ in piscinam insiluit et _____ se exercebat. _____ ad apodyterium rediit vestimentaque quaesivit. sed _____, nihil inerat.

cum Marcus amicum quendam vidit   ubi armarium aperuit
aliquamdiu deinde denique mox paulisper primum tandem

A text completion task such as this asks the students to make decisions about the appropriate connectives to help the reader understand the temporal progress of the passage, yet they do not have to worry about creating content. And there is more than one way to complete the text. Depending on where one places *mox* and *tandem*, the location of *primum, deinde,* and *denique* will shift. In addition, student writers have some flexibility in where they choose to write *aliquamdiu* and *paulisper*. After students have completed the passage individually, it would be useful for them to compare their completed texts and the reasons for their choices with other students in the class so that they comprehend the range of possibilities for the temporal progression of the passage.

Guided Composition

Many texts in the ancient world are formulaic, especially inscriptions. Guided compositions help them become familiar with some of the formulae and discourse strategies of these texts. For example, after reading some examples of Pompeian election graffiti (e.g., Esler, Wallace), students are guided through a series of steps (1–8 here) to create an electoral endorsement of someone in the class, a character in the textbook, or a historical figure. Similar guided compositions could be done to show students how to write (and read) other formulaic texts, such as epitaphs, dedications, honorary inscriptions, or laws.

1. Candidate's name

2. Office, e.g., *quaestor, aedilis, duovir*

3. Descriptive phrase, e.g., *iuvenis probus* (an honest young man), *omni bono meritus iuvenis* (a young man deserving of every advantage), *verecundus adulescens* (a modest young man), *dignus rei publicae* (worthy of the city), *utilis rei publicae* (useful to the city)

4. *Oro vos faciatis* (I ask that you elect)

5. Reason for electing the candidate (optional), for example, *panem bonum fert* (he supplies good bread), *munerarius magnus* (great games-sponsor), *hic aerarium conservabit* (he will preserve the treasury)

6. Person(s) or groups endorsing the candidate, for example, *pomari* (fruiterers), *muliones* (muleteers), *tonsores* (barbers), *caupones* (inn-keepers), *discentes* (students), *spectaculi spectantes* (spectators), *pilicrepi* (ball-players), *seribibi* (latedrinkers) *universi, Macerio dormientes universi* (united sleepers in the market), *furunculi* (petty thieves)

7. Verb of asking or endorsing, for example, *rogant, facite.*

8. Final comment (optional), for example, *tales cives in colonia in perpetuo* (may there be such citizens in the colony forever), *(nomen) fac et ille te faciet* (name, elect him and he will elect you).

Examples:

Cn. Helvium Sabinum, omni bono meritum, aedilem dignum rei publicae, oro vos faciatis. D(ecimus) rogat. (Corpus Inscriptionum Latinarum 4.3535)

I ask you to elect Gnaeus Helvius Sabinus (a man) deserving every advantage (and) worthy of the city, aedile. Decimus asks (this).

Holconium Priscum duovirum spectaculi spectantes rogant. (Corpus Inscriptionum Latinarum 4.7585)

The spectators of the amphitheater ask for Holconius Priscus (as) duovir.

L. Ceium Secundum duovirum oro vos faciatis. Helpis (for Greek Elpis, "Hope") Afra rogat. (Corpus Inscriptionum Latinarum 4.2993)

I ask that you make Lucius Ceius Secundus duovir. Elpis Afra asks (this).

Creating *Ethos* and *Pathos*: Open-Ended Writing Assignments

While most controlled writing assignments focus on sentence-level syntax and larger discourse structures, the guided writing assignment that ended the previous section begins to show how important it is for a writer to choose a persona, to write from a point of view, and to understand his or her audience. In this section, I present some specific assignments asking students to utilize pictures, texts, and their imagination as a springboard for writing. These open-ended assignments encourage students to explore *ethos* and *pathos* while utilizing the knowledge of *logos* that they developed in various controlled writing assignments. I have found that they work best after students have been prepared through a variety of prewriting activities that have activated linguistic, cultural, and rhetorical frameworks appropriate for the assignment.[11]

Writing about Pictures, Maps, and Charts

Using pictures is an excellent way to provide focus for writing, and present at the same time culturally authentic situations. Students can develop writing skills at the word, phrase, sentence, paragraph, or discourse level, depending on the assignment and the ability of the students. The choice of pictures to use is as varied as the imagination allows: vase-paintings, wall-paintings, mosaics, portrait sculpture, relief sculpture, drawings and plans from language and art history textbooks. Many images are also available over the web.

Guided Tour

Find a plan of a Greek or Roman house and describe what happens in different rooms. The text could be written from the point of view of a family member giving a tour to a relative or friend, or to a business associate or client. The tour guide would not only describe the room but also make comments on what he or she thought about the people and activities in each room. There are many possibilities for varying the assignment, from changing the family member giving the tour (father, mother, sister, brother, wet-nurse, cook, etc.) to the person who receives the tour (distant relative, friend, a newly purchased slave, business associate, or client).

Eavesdropping

Using the same or a similar house plan, the writer could lead the reader around the house, the two of them eavesdropping on the occupants of each room. For example, the reader would "overhear" the cook giving orders to other slaves about how or what food to prepare, the father meeting with a business friend in a more intimate space, or children playing in the courtyard. The same activity could be used with plans of other social places such as a stoa, theater, or palaestra, or a bath complex, circus, or amphitheater.

Travel Brochure

Find a plan and picture of some public architecture or pictures of the sculpture that adorned it (e.g., the Parthenon, the Library of Celsus, the Baths of Caracalla) and ask students to write a travel brochure encouraging the reader to visit the monument or place. At some point in the description, students could paraphrase Pausanias, saying "it is well worth seeing."

Writing a Letter

Go to a local museum that has ancient portrait sculpture on exhibit or show in class a picture of a portrait sculpture. Imagining what they think of the person behind the portrait, students write a letter to the person portrayed, describing the qualities visible in the portrait and asking what the person's life was like or what a typical day was like. They might also add what life is like for the writer in the present. Writers could perform a similar task by writing a letter to one of the characters in a scene from mythology, asking why the divinity or hero acted the way he or she did. Students might also make comments, perhaps sympathizing with the character or expressing whether they think the character acted appropriately or not.

Working with Picture Sets (Based on Grabe and Kaplan 287)

Students can tell a story utilizing sets of pictures from a textbook or using ancient art that tells a story. Excellent resources for pictures include the drawings in both the *Cambridge Latin Course* and the *Oxford Latin Course*. For examples of narrative art in antiquity, one could choose all or a portion of the Parthenon frieze, the Gigantomachy on the Siphnian Treasury, Roman sarcophagi, frescoes from Pompeii, or a portion of the column of Trajan. If the pictures are simple enough, each student could write a story and then recount it to a small group. If more complicated, students could work in groups to write a story. Groups of students could also rearrange the picture sets to tell a different story. It may be useful to students doing this activity for the first time to offer them a set of questions in Latin or Greek that help lead them through the pictures; for example, Who is involved? When and where is the action taking place? What are the characters doing? What are they saying? What are the steps in the process? What motivates the characters to act the way they do? What is the outcome/climax of the story?

Comparison

Find two versions of a scene, either ancient or modern, from Greek or Roman mythology, for example, the quarrel of Achilles and Agamemnon, the meeting of Dido and Aeneas at Carthage, or the fall of Icarus. Divide students into pairs or groups with each group having one picture. After they have written a description, the rest of the class will have to guess which picture they are writing about.

Writing about Readings

Reading passages provide another catalyst for student writing. In addition, writing about reading passages offers students the opportunity to integrate the cultural content, discourse structures, syntax, and vocabulary contained in the reading into their writing. In the process, they master a wide range of literacy skills that are common to reading and writing. A few examples follow of ways that students can use writing to respond to readings.

Writing an Itinerary

After students have read a passage detailing the travels of Odysseus or Aeneas, or a fictional character in the textbook, a nice postreading activity is for the students to write a logbook or itinerary of the journey. In order to review the passage and keep in mind the order of the trip, students draw four columns on a piece of paper labeled *when? where? who?* and *what?* about each stage of the journey. Depending on their level of language proficiency, they might write phrases or complete sentences in Latin or Greek about each stage of the journey. Later, students might compare what they have written with other members of the class and then in turn read aloud to the rest of the class what they have written for one stage of the trip.

Who Am I?

After students have read stories with a large cast of characters, they could meet in small groups in order to write riddles for the rest of the class to solve. Each group writes in Greek or Latin three to five short statements about one or more characters, ending each set of statements with "Who am I?" For example, after reading the story of Theseus in *Athenaze*, chapter 6, they might write ὁ πατήρ μου ἐστί ὁ βασιλεὺς τῶν Ἀθηναίων. πλέω πρὸς τὴν Κρήτην. Βούλομαι γὰρ τοὺς ἑταίρους σῴζειν. ἡ Ἀριάδνη μοι βοηθεῖ. Τίς εἰμι; ("My father is king of the Athenians. I am sailing to Crete, for I want to save my companions. Ariadne helps me. Who am I?").

Point of View

Typically, narratives are told from a single point of view, either that of the protagonist or of a distant third-person narrator. Ask students to rewrite an episode from the point of view of a character whose perspective has not been adequately represented. For example, after students have read about Dido and Aeneas, let them choose an episode and retell it from the point of view of Dido or Anna or an anonymous Trojan or Carthaginian. Such an exercise offers students not only a chance to be imaginative but also a chance to deal with their attitudes toward the usually male or elite protagonist of textbook or of authentic ancient narratives. See chapter 5 for further suggestions about dealing with gender in the language classroom.

Writing a Letter

When a character, separated by some distance from his family, friends, or associates, hears some news about an important event, students can impersonate this character and write a letter detailing his or her feelings about the situation. In the *Oxford Latin Course*, chapter 30, for example, after students read Flaccus's letter to Quintus telling him about the betrothal of his sister, Horatia, and the death of the trusty family dog Argus, they can write a letter in response that details Quintus's feelings at hearing this news.

Create a Minidrama

Ask students to transform a narrative episode into a small dramatic scene. For example, after reading about a political assembly or a military triumph, students could compose a minidrama that includes at least five different characters (young and old, male and female, wealthy and poor, slave and free) commenting upon the arrival of Pericles or Caesar. After students compose their minidramas, they can then perform them for the rest of the class. Once again, such an assignment is an excellent opportunity for students to give voice to marginalized groups, and to reflect on the mechanics of power in the ancient world.

Writing a Summary

Another way that students can demonstrate their reading comprehension and combine reading and writing skills is by writing a summary of the passage in Latin. This is an especially useful exercise for a narrative that takes place over several chapters in a textbook, since it requires students to become aware of what the essential elements of the story are and then write them in a way that progresses smoothly from event to event. In the process, writers become more aware of how narratives are put together, learning about time markers, transitions, and point of view. For example, in *Athenaze*, chapter 11, Philip, the son of Dikaiopolis, becomes blind when hit trying to rescue a boy being bullied. When the doctor cannot heal him, he and his father begin the journey to Epidauros. In chapters 17–18 they arrive at Epidauros in order to be healed. The assignment may include the Philip story-thread throughout chapters 11–18, or it may focus only on Philip's stay in Epidauros. Either way, students should add to their summary with each new reading. Since the details are already in the text, the students need not compose completely new sentences but can instead base their summary on what is written in the text. As with most open-ended writing assignments, students should have a chance to share their summaries with their peers in order to receive feedback on the content and coherence of their narrative.

Imaginative Activities

Although reading passages and pictures, charts, and graphs offer something concrete that students may respond to, there are other activities that begin from students' imagination and intersect with linguistic knowledge.

Strip Stories

The teacher selects a story with clear transitional markers and then types the sentences, each on a separate line. After photocopying the story, individual sentences are cut and distributed to the class. Students, either individually or in small groups, reconstruct the story on the basis of clues in the text. This exercise helps students internalize the sequencing and cohesion devices used in Greek and Latin texts (adapted from Reid 192).

Chain Stories

Each student in the class writes the first sentence of a folktale, mystery, romance, or heroic tale and then passes it on to another student in the class. Each subsequent student (or small group) adds a sentence or two, striving for coherence and fun. At the end, stories are shared on screen, read aloud, or passed from student to student. Such an exercise develops creativity, as well as a sense of coherence and probability, and character and plot development. This exercise also helps students to learn while reading how to predict based on discourse cues, character development, and typical story-lines (Reid 192).

Writing Poems

Students, either individually or in small groups, create simple poems within a very structured framework, using vocabulary they have learned or words supplied by the instructor upon request. The first type of poem is the cinquain, which consists of five lines, constructed according to the following scheme:

Line 1: States a subject in one word (usually a noun)

Line 2: Describes the subject in two words (often a noun and an adjective or two adjectives)

Line 3: Describes an action about the subject in three words (often three infinitives, three participles, or a three-word sentence)

Line 4: Expresses an emotion about the subject in four words

Line 5: Restates the subject in another single word that reflects what has already been said (usually a noun)

Example:

Tree

Green branches

Growing, living, reaching

Your shade protects me

Peace. (Hadley 288)

A second type of poem is the anagram/acrostic/acronym poem. Students (or the instructor) choose a person, an abstract idea, or a metonym for a such an idea, such as Ἀριάδνη or Cloelia, οἶκος or domus, φιλία or amicitia, βῆμα or rostra. For each letter in the word, they write words or phrases that describe the idea. The finished poems can then be printed on paper that includes a picture that illustrates the poem.

A third type of poem is the Diamond Poem. In this activity, students place words in a visual display that moves from one extreme to another and produces a poem in a diamond shape:

Day

Bright Colorful

Light Warm Happy

Sun Yellow White Moon

Quiet Cool Dark

Shadow Black

Night

(Grabe and Kaplan 285–6)

Writing an Epitaph

After reading short examples of Greek or Roman epitaphs, students write an epitaph for a character encountered in the course of their reading. Writing epitaphs helps students not only master idioms of time and place but also understand ancient naming conventions, family relationships, and attitudes toward death.

Making the Audience Real: Responding to Student Writing

No writing is finished until it has been revised. No doubt Menander's comic script was revised throughout the rehearsal process: dialogue polished, jokes perfected, and speeches refined. One of the best ways to focus writers, to give them a purpose for writing, to help them develop *ethos*, *logos*, and *pathos* in their writing is to have them share their work with others. Second-language writers need feedback if they are going to improve their drafts, organize content, create coherence, and pay attention to language. They want feedback on form, but they also want people to respond to their ideas, stories, jokes, and descriptions as a real-world audience (Ferris; Reichelt and Waltner). They also need explicit instruction on how to revise their writing, since for many beginning writers, revision is a skill that they have not yet mastered in their native language (Berg; New). But all too often students receive comments only once during the writing process: when they hand their paper in to the instructor. The difficulty is, as Ann Raimes notes, if students receive feedback only at the end of the writing process,

> the teacher's response is to the finished product. The teacher can only judge and evaluate, not influence a piece of writing. Responding to a paper only at the end limits us to do the following:
>
> 1. Giving the paper a grade (A, B, C or 70, 80, 90 etc.);
>
> 2. Writing a comment: very good, needs improvement, careless;
>
> 3. Correcting errors.
>
> If we sometimes feel the futility of this enterprise, let us put ourselves in the position of a student who has worked very hard on a composition, looking up words in the dictionary, rereading, and checking. . . . What is the student to do now? What he does of course, quite often, is to groan, put the paper away, and hope he'll somehow get fewer "red marks" next time. (139–41)

But if writing is a process, then student writers need to receive feedback *before* their writing is evaluated. Readers (students and the instructor) can make suggestions, comment on content, indicate good points and areas for improvement at any of several stages in the writing process: prewriting, composing, revision, or editing. And if writing is a communicative act, then there should be multiple audiences for that writing, sympathetic and responsive, coaching, challenging, describing what they are reading and suggesting ways to improve it. In short, evaluating writing is only one aspect of responding to student writing. Response is a much broader concept, and it can come from numerous sources in a variety of settings. For example, Joy Reid (206) notes that response activities may include the following.

- Writers discussing their topics in small groups, and peers responding

- Students sharing a small section of their writings on the board or screen with students and teacher responding

- Teachers responding orally to students' questions either in class or in small groups

- Students interviewing each other about topic ideas, about their plans for an essay, or about their revision plans

- Writers annotating their own drafts, describing or labeling key features such as thesis statements, specific detail, transition devices, introduction techniques

- Teachers conferencing with students both during class and outside of class

- Peer review groups responding to each other's writing

Within each of these activities, teachers and students can respond to writers in five ways: praising, describing, asking for information, giving information, and making suggestions.[12] Each type of response helps student writers understand what to revise and how to do so. *Praise* helps them appreciate what they have accomplished well, whether it is a clever ending, good transitions, or effective choice of words. *Description* of the content of a text acts as a check for the writer: does the reader perceive what the writer intended? *Asking for information* is an excellent way for the reader and writer to interact and to spur the writer to add details and make ideas more explicit for the reader. *Giving information* is an opportunity that shows that the reader is interested and informed, responding to the writer and the text, without necessarily telling the writer what to do with the information. Finally, *making suggestions* is a potential way for the reader to act as coach or assistant. By varying the type of response, readers can demonstrate that they are more than evaluators, but rather involved with the writer's text as a sympathetic audience, interested reader, and supportive assistant. At the same time, writers recognize the importance of being attentive to one's audience, of organizing one's compositions for the maximum effect upon one's audience.

Peer Response Groups

Peer response is a crucial component in helping student writers improve. For writers, peer response groups provide a real and immediate audience for their writing. By listening to the comments of other students, writers get a sense of what works and what does not, what interests readers and what does not, what is clear and what needs more work. In addition, with guidance, peer response groups are able to assist the writer in revising the composition. In fact, research with ESL students has shown that student feedback can be more valuable than teacher feedback (Cumming; Jacobs and Zhang) and contributes to student writing in ways that teacher comments may not be able to (Tsui and Ng). At the same time, peer response helps student responders become more skilled at reading thoughtfully and with attention to detail. As a result, they begin to recognize strengths and weaknesses in their own writing. The strategies they discover for revising others' writing can be applied to their own compositions. Finally, peer response groups help develop skills in collaboration, problem solving, and negotiating meaning. Writers become more aware that texts cannot be read without awareness of one's audience.

In spite of all the advantages for peer response groups, students must receive instruction on how to respond productively, honestly, and tactfully to another's work.[13] At the beginning of a course, teachers can model peer response roles by showing safe essays (e.g., the teacher's work-in-progress or students' essays from a previous course). Students can also engage in discussion about their fears or misgivings concerning the peer review process and how the class can overcome these apprehensions. Finally, students can also be given guidelines or worksheets to follow when making their responses. For example, when responding to an early draft of writing, student response should involve neither evaluation nor error-hunting.

> Instead, members of effective response groups treat the papers they are examining as "works in progress" and recognize that their goal is to serve as a sympathetic reader suggesting methods for writers to use in improving their papers. Ideally a dialogue should be created between the writer and the other members of the group which clarifies the intent of the writer's essay and sharpens the way it is achieved. (Barron 24; cited in Reid 208)

Revising Guidelines

Peer review groups work more successfully if they have written guidelines for commenting on other students' work. Robert Mittan suggests a four-task exercise for peer review pairs or groups:

1. Offer a positive response to the writing ("What I liked best was . . .").
2. Identify the purpose of the writing ("The main idea is . . .").
3. Ask questions directed to the writer ("What do you mean here about . . .?").
4. Offer suggestions to the writer (an opportunity for open-ended comments). It is most helpful if the reader can be very *specific* and explain *why* these changes will be helpful to the reader.

As the term progresses, other questions may be added to the list. It is often useful to give the author the opportunity on the worksheet to ask the reader how to solve a particular problem or to get a second opinion on a specific point.[14]

Editing Checklist

Beginning language students want feedback not only on content but also on vocabulary, grammar, and syntax (Leki 1990). There are several ways for students to receive feedback on form. After students have revised and have reached the editing stage, student peer groups might receive an editing checklist that focuses on one or two points of grammar and syntax:

1. *Agreement*: Underline all the verbs. Then find the subject for each verb. Put a check next to the ones that agree with their verb. Circle the ones that don't.

2. *Appropriate case*: (a) Put a squiggly line under each direct object. Circle the nouns that are not in the accusative case but should be; (b) Bracket all the prepositional phrases. Write the case that the preposition should take. Circle the nouns that are not in the right case.

As students master these skills, editing handouts may focus on tense, mood, noun-adjective agreement, the gender, number, and case of the relative pronoun, or agreement of participles with their referent. An alternative to one student making all the suggestions for a single paper is to assign each member of a group a different color of pencil or marker and a different grammatical feature to check. For example, a student with blue checks subject-verb agreement, another with red checks adjective-noun agreement, a third with green checks case. Student editors simply circle or underline what they think needs to be examined by the author (Byrd).

Teacher Response

Teachers need not feel limited to written comments when responding to student writing. Teachers can respond to student writing in a number of ways: whole-class discussion of major points for revision, teacher demonstrations of revisions with specific student essays, miniconferences in class, one-on-one conferences away from class, and written comments on drafts.

An approach that I frequently use is to comment on student writing before it is turned in for a grade. I make comments on both content and form, but instead of teacher-correction of errors, I simply identify errors and then return the paper to the student for revision. Studies by Lalande and Fathman and Whalley, and others (summarized in Ferris) found that writing accuracy does increase with teacher feedback that simply marks the location of grammar errors. I typically circle the incorrect forms with few if any marginal comments to explain the error. Then students revise and turn the composition in for a grade. Although students do not catch every error, they successfully revise the vast majority of them. There are other, more involved ways to get students to attend to error, but I think that simplicity is probably best.

Response to writing completes the circle of *ethos*, *logos*, and *pathos* and takes us back to where we started. If writers receive feedback from a variety of readers, then the dialogue between writer, text, and reader begins to take place. As writers hear from readers, they have a context in which to create coherent text and have more motivation to learn grammar and syntax. If writers, moreover, engage in a sequence of activities before the final draft is turned in, they have time to develop ideas and to activate the linguistic, cultural, and rhetorical frameworks that are crucial for producing readable writing. At the same time they learn the very skills they need for becoming good readers. Finally, if writers have the opportunity to make choices about content, point of view, and style, they begin to enjoy composition and want to share their ideas. And it is in the process of producing the language that our students can reach higher levels of proficiency in Greek and Latin.

Writing does indeed have tangible benefits for beginning language students. The success of writing in beginning language courses hinges on three things: writers making choices, readers providing feedback, and teachers providing the structure to make the writing process work. It takes effort, but the result can be exhilarating as students begin to respond to ancient cultures, explore personae, collaborate with their peers, and work with language. As a result, our students are engaged in "the process of expression, interpretation, and negotiation of meaning" (Savignon). They become sensitive to all aspects of communicative competence—linguistic competence, cultural context, and strategic competence (Celce-Murcia, Dörnyei, and Thurrell)—and understand firsthand how form, meaning, and function are interdependent. In short, our students are learning to use Greek and Latin to communicate.

Notes

1. Two views of composition dominate our profession today. Ball and Ellsworth (1989; 1992) advocate the elimination of composition from the beginning language curriculum. According to this view, composition is an inefficient use of time, does not allow for step-by-step learning, has no practical use (who is the audience of a text written in a dead language, anyhow?), and has little connection with learning to read Latin and Greek, the primary goals of learning classical languages. Those who support composition (Gilleland; Newman; Pearcy; Saunders) consider it primarily as an *ancilla legendi*, a support skill that is crucial to developing the ability to read Latin or Greek. It helps students reinforce vocabulary and master the intricacies of Greek and Latin morphology and syntax, and at more advanced levels, it provides a way to understand ancient prose styles.

Even though these two views seem to be at odds with each other, they both maintain the same conception of composition. Both views tend to imagine composition as the translation into Latin or Greek of (not infrequently) decontextualized sentences or paragraphs from the textbook. I hope to offer a third approach, one that encourages beginning students to write to communicate and that integrates reading and writing—in addition to grammar and writing—in beginning language classes. Fortunately, others—Davisson for intermediate Latin students and Fogel for advanced students—are taking similar approaches to mine. Davisson stresses multiple drafts, while Fogel asks students to create meaningful discourse through the use of cohesive devices and to focus on themes such as narrative, rhythm, characterization of self and other, and audience.

2. Christopher Tribble (67–8) points out that writers need to know four types of knowledge to write effectively: content knowledge (knowledge of concepts involved in the subject area); context knowledge (knowledge of social context in which the text will be read, including the reader's expectations, and knowledge of the cotexts alongside which the new text will be read); language system knowledge (knowledge of the language system, e.g., lexis, syntax, that are necessary for the completion of the task); and writing process knowledge

(knowledge of the most appropriate way of preparing for a writing task). Compare these four types of knowledge with the components of communicative competence elucidated by Canale and Swain, Celce-Murcia et al., and others: background knowledge, sociolinguistic competence, discourse competence, grammatical competence, and strategic competence.

3. Significantly, this interaction and negotiation of meaning can be successfully accomplished through learners' interaction with either a proficient speaker or other learners (Pica et al. 1996).

4. For a summary of research on input, interaction, and output in language acquisition, see Gass and Selinker. On the importance of meaningful discourse, see chapter 1.

5. See Zamel 1992 and Spack for more activities that enhance reading through writing.

6. Just as writing a composition is a process, becoming a writer is a process. The Preliminary Proficiency Guidelines for Writing 2001 (Breiner-Sanders, Swender, and Terry) make clear what writers at novice and intermediate levels (most students in beginning language courses) are capable of doing at different stages in their development. Writing at these levels exhibits numerous errors, but is becoming more comprehensible to native and near-native speakers, demonstrates a wider range of genres and content, and reveals increasing mastery of a vocabulary, grammatical structures, and cohesive devices. In other words, the Guidelines point to the many ways that a student is becoming a better writer instead of focusing primarily on grammatical accuracy.

7. Black-figure hydria in the manner of the Antimenes painter, ca. 480 B.C.E., London, British Museum; drawing by Catherine Balme.

8. See Scott (ch. 5) and Reichelt and Waltner for other examples of writing assignments that help students at each stage of the writing process.

9. For a specific example of semantic mapping of ideas related to a Roman *comitia*, see Gruber-Miller 170. For more information about semantic mapping and other graphic organizers, see Grabe and Kaplan 311–3.

10. Most of the activities in this section on controlled writing fit the Proficiency Guidelines for Writing, novice level. Writers at the novice level can produce lists, short messages, and simple notes "to express themselves within the context in which the language was learned, relying mainly on practiced material" (Breiner-Sanders, Swender, and Terry 12).

11. Most of the assignments in this section conform to the Preliminary Proficiency Guidelines for Writing (Breiner-Sanders et al.) at the intermediate level: short, simple communications, compositions, descriptions, summaries, and narrations of paragraph length based on "personal experiences and immediate surroundings" (12). The Guidelines leave expository writing and more abstract and complex tasks for the advanced and superior levels. My experience indicates that students in beginning Latin or Greek can accomplish these tasks with appropriate preparation and attention to the process of writing.

12. Ferris et al. provide specific examples of each type (positive feedback, describing or giving information, asking for information, making a suggestion or request) of comment, including ways of hedging or softening the criticism as well as the importance of making the comments text specific. Although Ferris et al. are describing written comments, these types of comment are equally valid in a face-to-face discussion.

13. See Liu and Hansen 126–9 on additional ways to train students to engage in peer response and to make the classroom atmosphere conducive for peer response.

14. For more examples of revising worksheets, see Grabe and Kaplan 382–5. For an example of a step-by-step revision process that helps students develop a richer sense of Latin style, diction, and word order, see Davisson.

Works Cited

Ball, Robert J., and J. D. Ellsworth. 1989. "Against the Teaching of Composition in Classical Languages." *Classical Journal* 85: 54–62.

———. 1992. "Flushing Out the Dinosaurs: Against Teaching Composition II." *Classical Journal* 88: 55–65.

Balme, Maurice, and Gilbert Lawall. 2003. *Athenaze: An Introduction to Ancient Greek.* Bks. 1–2. 2nd ed. New York: Oxford University Press.

Balme, Maurice, and James Morwood, eds. 1996–97. *The Oxford Latin Course.* Pts. 1–3. 2nd ed. New York: Oxford University Press.

Barron, R. 1991. "What I Wish I Had Known about Peer Response Groups but Didn't." *English Journal* 80: 24–34.

Belanger, J. 1987. "Theory and Research into Reading and Writing Connections: A Critical Review." *Reading-Canada-Lecture* 5: 10–8.

Bereiter, C., and M. Scardamalia. 1987. *The Psychology of Written Composition.* Hillsdale, NJ: Erlbaum.

Berg, E. Catherine. 1999. "The Effects of Trained Peer Response on ESL Students' Revision Types and Writing Quality." *Journal of Second Language Writing* 8: 215–41.

Breiner-Sanders, Karen E., Elvira Swender, and Robert M. Terry. 2002. "Preliminary Proficiency Guidelines—Writing Revised 2001." *Foreign Language Annals* 35: 9–15.

Byrd, David R. 2003. "Practical Tips for Implementing Peer Editing Tasks in the Foreign Language Classroom." *Foreign Language Annals* 36: 434–9.

Canale, Michael, and Merrill Swain. 1980. "Theoretical Bases of Communicative Approaches to Second Language Teaching and Testing." *Applied Linguistics* 1: 1–47.

Carrell, Patricia L. 1987. "Text as Interaction: Some Implications of Text Analysis and Reading Research for ESL Composition." In U. Connor and R. B. Kaplan, eds., *Writing across Languages: Analysis of L2 Text.* Reading, MA: Addison Wesley, 47–56.

Carson, Joan G. 1993. "Reading for Writing: Cognitive Perspectives." In J. Carson and I. Leki, eds., *Reading in the Composition Classroom: Second Language Perspectives.* Boston: Heinle and Heinle, 85–104.

Celce-Murcia, Marianne, Zoltán Dörnyei, and Sarah Thurrell. 1995. "Communicative Competence: A Pedagogically Motivated Model with Content Specifications." *Issues in Applied Linguistics* 6: 5–35.

Chastain, Kenneth. 1976. *Developing Second-Language Skills: Theory to Practice.* 2nd ed. Chicago: Rand McNally.

Chiang, Steve Y. 1999. "Assessing Grammatical and Textual Features in L2 Writing Samples: The Case of French as Foreign Language." *Modern Language Journal* 83: 219–32.

———. 2003. "The Importance of Cohesive Conditions to Perceptions of Writing Quality at the Early Stages of Foreign Language Learning." *System* 31: 471–84.

Cumming, Alister. 1985. "Responding to the Writing of ESL Students." In M. Maguire and A. Pare, eds., *Patterns of Development.* Ottawa: Canadian Council of Teachers of English, 58–75.

Davisson, Mary H. T. 2000. "Prose Composition in Intermediate Latin: An Alternative Approach." *Classical Journal* 96: 75–80.

Ellis, Rod. 1999. *Learning a Second Language through Interaction.* Amsterdam: John Benjamins.

Emig, Janet. 1971. *The Composing Process of Twelfth Graders.* NCTE research report no. 13. Urbana, IL: National Council of Teachers of English.

Esler, Carol Clemeau. 1984. *Roman Voices: Everyday Latin in Ancient Rome.* Amherst, MA: NECN.

Fathman, Ann K., and Elizabeth Whalley. 1990. "Teacher Response to Student Writing: Focus on Form versus Content." In B. Kroll, ed., *Second Language Writing*. Cambridge, UK: Cambridge University Press, 178–90.

Ferris, Dana R. 2002. *Treatment of Error in Second Language Student Writing*. Ann Arbor: University of Michigan Press.

Ferris, Dana R., Susan Pezone, Cathy R. Tade, and Sharee Tinti. 1997. "Teacher Commentary on Student Writing: Descriptions and Implications." *Journal of Second Language Writing* 6: 155–82.

Flower, Linda. 1979. "Writer-Based Prose: A Cognitive Basis for Problems in Writing." *College English* 41: 19–37.

Fogel, Jerise. 2002. "Toward Beauty and Joy in Latin Prose Composition." *Classical World* 96: 79–87.

Ganss, George E. 1956. "A Historical Sketch of the Teaching of Latin." In *Saint Ignatius' Idea of a Jesuit University*. Milwaukee: Marquette University Press.

Gass, Susan, and Larry Selinker. 2001. *Second Language Acquisition: An Introductory Course*. 2nd ed. Mahwah, NJ: Erlbaum.

Gilleland, Brady B. 1991. "Elitist Professors and the Teaching of Prose Composition." *Classical World* 84: 215–7.

Grabe, William. 2001. "Reading-Writing Relations: Theoretical Perspectives and Instructional Practices." In Diane Belcher and Alan Hirvela, eds., *Linking Literacies: Perspectives on L2 Reading-Writing Connections*. Ann Arbor: University of Michigan Press, 15–47.

Grabe, William, and Robert B. Kaplan. 1996. *Theory and Practice of Writing*. New York: Longman.

Gruber-Miller, John C. 1998. "Toward Fluency and Accuracy: A Reading Approach to College Latin." In Richard A. LaFleur, ed., *Latin for the Twenty-first Century*. Glenview, IL: Scott Foresman–Addison Wesley, 162–75.

Hadley, Alice Omaggio. 2001. *Teaching Language in Context*. 3rd ed. Boston: Heinle and Heinle.

Harklau, Linda. 2002. "The Role of Writing in Classroom Second Language Acquisition." *Journal of Second Language Writing* 11: 329–50.

Hillocks, George. 1986. *Research on Written Composition: New Directions for Teaching*. Urbana, IL: ERIC Clearinghouse on Reading and Communication Skills and the National Conference on Research in English.

Jacobs, George, and Shuqiang Zhang. 1989. "Peer Feedback in Second Language Writing Instruction: Boon or Bane?" Urbana, IL: ERIC Clearinghouse on Languages and Linguistics ED306766.

Kauffmann, Ruth A. 1996. "Writing to Read and Reading to Write: Teaching Literature in the Foreign Language Classroom." *Foreign Language Annals* 29: 396–402.

Kitchell, Kenneth F., Jr. 1998. "The Great Latin Debate: The Futility of Utility." In Richard A. LaFleur, ed., *Latin for the Twenty-first Century*. Glenview, IL: Scott Foresman–Addison Wesley, 1–14.

Krapels, Alexandra Rowe. 1990. "An Overview of Second Language Writing Process Research." In B. Kroll, *Second Language Writing*. Cambridge, UK: Cambridge University Press, 37–56.

Krashen, Steven. 1984. *Writing: Research, Theory and Applications*. Oxford: Pergamon Institute of English.

Kucer, S. 1987. "The Cognitive Base of Reading and Writing." In J. R. Squire, ed., *The Dynamics of Language Learning*. Urbana, IL: ERIC Clearinghouse on Reading and Communication Skills, 27–51.

Lalande, J. 1982. "Reducing Composition Errors: An Experiment." *Modern Language Journal* 66: 140–9.

Leki, Ilona. 1990. "Coaching from the Margins: Issues in Written Response." In B. Kroll, ed., *Second Language Writing*. Cambridge, UK: Cambridge University Press, 57–68.

———. 1993. "Reciprocal Themes in ESL Reading and Writing." In J. Carson and I. Leki, eds., *Reading in the Composition Classroom: Second Language Perspectives*. Boston: Heinle and Heinle, 9–32.

Liu, Jun, and Jette G. Hansen. 2002. *Peer Response in Second Language Writing Classrooms*. Ann Arbor: University of Michigan Press.

Magnan, Sally Sieloff. 1985. "Teaching and Testing Proficiency in Writing: Skills to Transcend the Second-Language Classroom." In A. C. Omaggio, ed., *Proficiency, Curriculum, Articulation: The Ties that Bind*. Middlebury, VT: Northeast Conference on the Teaching of Foreign Languages, 109–36.

McLaughlin, Barry. 1990. "Restructuring." *Applied Linguistics* 11: 113–28.

McLaughlin, Barry, and J.L.C. Heredia. 1996. "Information Processing Approaches to Research on Second Language Acquisition and Use." In W. C. Ritchie and T. K. Bhatia, eds., *Handbook of Second Language Acquisition*. San Diego, CA: Academic Press, 213–28.

Mittan, Robert. 1989. "The Peer Review Process: Harnessing Students' Communicative Power." In D. M. Johnson and D. H. Roen, eds., *Richness in Writing: Empowering ESL Students*. New York: Longman, 207–19.

New, Elizabeth. 1999. "Computer-Aided Writing in French as a Foreign Language: A Qualitative and Quantitative Look at the Process of Revision." *Modern Language Journal* 83: 80–97.

Newman, J. K. 1990. "Composition: A Reply." *Classical Journal* 85: 344–9.

Nobuyoshi, J., and R. Ellis. 1993. "Focused Communication Tasks and Second Language Acquisition." *ELT Journal* 47: 203–10.

Pearcy, Lee T. 1998. "Writing Latin in Schools and Colleges." *Classical World* 92: 35–42.

Phinney, Ed, and Patricia Bell, eds. 1988–91. *The Cambridge Latin Course*. Units 1–4. North American 3rd ed. New York: Cambridge University Press.

Pica, Teresa. 1994. "Research on Negotiation: What Does It Reveal about Second Language Learning Conditions, Processes, and Outcomes?" *Language Learning* 44: 493–527.

Pica, Teresa, Lloyd Holliday, Nora Lewis, and Lynelle Morgenthaler. 1989. "Comprehensible Output as an Outcome of Linguistic Demands on the Learner." *Studies in Second Language Acquisition* 11: 63–90.

Pica, Teresa, Felicia Lincoln-Porter, Diana Paninos, and Julien Linnell. 1996. "Language Learner's Interaction: How Does It Address the Input, Output, and Feedback Needs of L2 Learners?" *TESOL Quarterly* 30: 59–84.

Raimes, Ann. 1983. *Techniques in Teaching Writing*. Oxford: Oxford University Press.

Reichelt, Melinda. 1999. "Toward a More Comprehensive View of L2 Writing: Foreign Language Writing in the U.S." *Journal of Second Language Writing* 8: 181–204.

———. 2001. A Critical Review of Foreign Language Writing Research on Pedagogical Practices." *Modern Language Journal* 85: 578–93.

Reichelt, Melinda, and Keri Bryant Waltner. 2001. "Writing in a Second-Year German Class." *Foreign Language Annals* 34: 235–45.

Reid, Joy. 1993. *Teaching ESL Writing*. Englewood Cliffs, NJ: Prentice-Hall.

Roca de Larios, Julio, Liz Murphy, and Javier Marín. 2002. "Critical Examination of L2 Writing Process Research." In Sarah Ransdell and Marie-Laure Barbier, eds., *New Directions for Research in L2 Writing*. Dordrecht: Kluwer, 11–47.

Roen, Duane H. 1989. "Developing Effective Assignments for Second Language Writers." In D. M. Johnson and D. H. Roen, eds., *Richness in Writing: Empowering ESL Students.* New York: Longman, 193–206.

Saunders, Anne Leslie. 1993. "The Value of Latin Prose Composition." *Classical Journal* 88: 385–92.

Savignon, Sandra. 1997. *Communicative Competence: Theory and Classroom Practice.* 2nd ed. New York: McGraw-Hill.

Scott, Virginia Mitchell. 1996. *Rethinking Foreign Language Writing.* Boston: Heinle and Heinle.

Silva, Tony. 1993. "Toward an Understanding of the Distinct Nature of L2 Writing: The ESL Research and Its Implications." *TESOL Quarterly* 27: 657–77.

Spack, Ruth. 1993. "Student Meets Text, Text Meets Student: Finding a Way into Academic Discourse." In J. Carson and I. Leki, eds., *Reading in the Composition Classroom: Second Language Perspectives.* Boston: Heinle and Heinle, 183–96.

Sternglass, M. 1986. Introduction to B. Peterson, ed., *Convergences: Transactions in Reading and Writing.* Urbana, IL: National Council of Teachers of English, 1–11.

———. 1988. *The Presence of Thought: Introspective Accounts of Reading and Writing.* Norwood, NJ: Ablex.

Stotsky, S. 1983. "Research on Reading/Writing Relationships: A Synthesis and Suggested Directions." *Language Arts* 60: 627–42.

Straw, Stanley. 1990. "Challenging Communication." In D. Bogdan and S. Straw, eds., *Beyond Communication: Reading Comprehension and Criticism.* Portsmouth, NH: Boynton/Cook, 67–89.

Swain, Merrill. 1985. "Communicative Competence: Some Roles of Comprehensible Input and Comprehensible Output in its Development." In S. Gass and C. Madden, eds., *Input in Second Language Acquisition.* Rowley, MA: Newbury House, 235–53.

Swain, Merrill, and Sharon Lapkin. 1995. "Problems in Output and the Cognitive Processes They Generate: A Step towards Second Language Learning." *Applied Linguistics* 16: 371–91.

Tierney, R. J., and P. D. Pearson. 1983. "Toward a Composing Model of Reading." *Language Arts* 60: 568–80.

Tittle, Matthew. 1996. "Russian Language Writing Activity Based on a Picture." *AATSEEL Newsletter* 39: 8–10.

Tribble, Christopher. 1996. *Writing.* Oxford: Oxford University Press.

Tsui, Amy B. M., and Maria Ng. 2000. "Do Secondary Writers Benefit from Peer Comments?" *Journal of Second Language Writing* 9: 147–70.

Ullman, B. L., Charles Henderson, Jr., and Norman E. Henry. 1968. *Latin for Americans.* 5th ed. New York: Macmillan.

Valdés, Guadalupe, Paz Haro, and Maria Paz Echevarriarza. 1992. "The Development of Writing Abilities in a Foreign Language: Contributions toward a General Theory of L2 Writing." *Modern Language Journal* 76: 333–52.

Wallace, Rex E. 2005. *An Introduction to Wall Inscriptions from Pompeii and Herculaneum.* Wauconda, IL: Bolchazy-Carducci.

Way, Denise Paige, Elizabeth G. Joiner, and Michael A. Seaman. 2000. "Writing in the Secondary Foreign Language Classroom: The Effects of Prompts and Tasks on Novice Learners of French." *Modern Language Journal* 84: 171–84.

Zamel, Vivian. 1983. The Composing Processes of Advanced ESL Students: Six Case Studies." *TESOL Quarterly* 17: 165–87.

———. 1992. "Writing One's Way into Reading." *TESOL Quarterly* 26: 463–85.

Selected Resources for Teaching Greek and Latin
An Annotated Bibliography

John Gruber-Miller

This bibliography does not claim to be exhaustive, but is intended as a starting point for language teachers who wish to explore specific topics in more depth. The works listed here are selected because they are good introductions to the topic, are accessible, and include practical activities for classroom use. This annotated bibliography is available at www.cornellcollege.edu/classical_studies/pedagogy/ and will be updated annually.

Places to Start

Introductory Textbooks

Celce-Murcia, Marianne, ed. 2001. *Teaching English as a Second or Foreign Language*. 3rd ed. Boston: Heinle and Heinle. Sections on teaching methodologies, the four language skills, teaching grammar, integrated approaches, learner needs, and ongoing teacher development. Each chapter includes activities for classroom use.

Hadley, Alice Omaggio. 2001. *Teaching Language in Context*. 3rd ed. Boston: Heinle and Heinle. A proficiency-oriented approach to language teaching, where proficiency is the goal of language learning, not the method. Reviews research on language learning, various teaching methodologies, and the importance of context in comprehending and learning a language. Additional chapters on the four skills, culture, testing, and designing the curriculum integrate research and specific classroom activities.

Ramírez, Arnulfo G. 1995. *Creating Contexts for Second Language Acquisition: Theory and Methods*. White Plains, NY: Longman. Presents communication-based, proficiency-based, and learner-centered approaches to second language instruction. Reviews second language acquisition research and integrates this research into chapters on student learning styles, culture, the four skills, and testing. Each chapter offers practical examples for increasing student language skills.

Shrum, Judith, and Eileen W. Glisan. 2000. *Teacher's Handbook: Contextualized Language Instruction*. 2nd ed. Boston: Heinle and Heinle. A great text for teaching a methods course. Argues that language introduced and taught in meaningful contexts develops learner competency, and that learning and development are as much social processes as cognitive processes. Incorporates the Standards into each chapter. Each chapter also offers teaching examples and case studies for readers to reflect on, providing examples from elementary, middle, and high schools and beyond. Finally, the role of sociocultural theory, especially Vygotsky's zone of proximal development, is integrated into each chapter's conceptual framework.

Research on Second Language Acquisition (SLA)

Brown, H. Douglas. 2000. *Principles of Language Learning and Teaching*. 4th ed. Englewood Cliffs, NJ: Prentice-Hall. Reviews research on how we learn languages (first and second) and how learner styles, personality, and sociocultural factors influence language acquisition; defines communicative competence, and summarizes various theories of second language acquisition. Less technical than Gass and Selinker.

Cook, Vivian. 2001. *Second Language Learning and Teaching*. 3rd ed. London: Edward Arnold. Geared to language teachers and teacher-trainees, the book begins with particular aspects of SLA—how we learn grammar, pronunciation, vocabulary, and writing–and gradually expands to larger issues: how learners process language by listening and reading, learner characteristics, language in the classroom and in society. The book ends with overall models of SLA and styles of language teaching. Intended audience similar to Brown.

Gass, Susan, and Larry Selinker. 2001. *Second Language Acquisition: An Introductory Course*. 2nd ed. Hillsdale, NJ: Erlbaum. More detailed introduction to second language acquisition. Chapters on the influence of first language on second language acquisition; SLA and linguistics; universal grammar; learners' interlanguage; input, interaction, and output; learner characteristics; the lexicon; and instructed second language learning.

Macaro, Ernesto. 2003. *Teaching and Learning a Second Language: A Review of Recent Research*. London: Continuum. Macaro writes this review of recent research with a teacher in mind. He includes chapters on theories, grammar, and methods, vocabulary, attitudes and motivation, reading, listening, oral interaction, and writing.

Mitchell, Rosamond, and Florence Myles. 1998. *Second Language Learning Theories*. London: Arnold. Written by an expert in second language teaching and a linguist with research interests in second language acquisition, the book surveys and critiques theories of second language learning, linguistic, psycholoinguistic, and sociolinguistic. The book is intended as an introduction to the field for students without substantial background in linguistics. Each chapter reviews a select number of empirical studies to illustrate the kind of research characteristic of the approach under discussion, the scope and nature of the language facts that are felt to be important, and the kinds of generalizations to be drawn.

History of Language Teaching and Language Teaching Methodologies

Kelly, L. G. 1969. *Twenty-five Centuries of Language Teaching: An Inquiry into the Science, Art, and Development of Language Teaching Methodology, 500 B.C.–1969*. Rowley, MA: Newbury House. The title says it all.

Kitchell, Kenneth F., Jr. 1998. "The Great Latin Debate: The Futility of Utility." In Richard A. LaFleur, ed., *Latin for the Twenty-first Century*. Glenview, IL: Scott Foresman–Addison Wesley, 1–14. A brief history of "how Latin has been taught, attacked, and defended at various crucial points in its history."

Larsen-Freeman, Diane. 2000. *Techniques and Principles of Language Teaching*. 2nd ed. Oxford: Oxford University Press. Explores language teaching methodologies from grammar-translation and the direct method to total physical response and communicative language teaching. Also includes more recent methodological innovations, such as content-based, task-based, and participatory approaches as well as strategy training, cooperative learning, and multiple intelligences. Readers are encouraged to reflect on their own beliefs and develop their own approach to language teaching.

Richards, Jack C., and Theodore S. Rogers. 2001. *Approaches and Methods in Language Teaching.* 2nd ed. Cambridge, UK: Cambridge University Press. A survey of the major foreign language teaching methodologies of the twentieth century, discussing the theory of language learning, goals, and classroom activities and techniques behind each approach.

Sebesta, Judith Lynn. 1998. "ALIQUID SEMPER NOVI: New Challenges, New Approaches." In Richard A. LaFleur, ed., *Latin for the Twenty-first Century.* Glenview, IL: Scott Foresman–Addison Wesley, 15–24. A review of how Latin has been taught since World War II.

Implementing National Standards

Abbott, Martha G., Sally Davis, and Richard C. Gascoyne. 1998. "National Standards and Curriculum Guidelines." In Richard A. LaFleur, ed., *Latin for the Twenty-first Century.* Glenview, IL: Scott Foresman–Addison Wesley, 44–58. Presents the historical context for the creation of the Standards, explains each of the Standards, and offers curriculum guidelines for Latin 1–2.

Gascoyne, Richard, et al. 1997. *Standards for Classical Language Learning.* Oxford, OH: American Classical League. Presents not only the five goals—Communication, Culture, Connections, Comparisons, and Communities—for learning Latin and Greek but also sample progress indicators for each level, fifteen classroom scenarios, plus FAQs about the Standards.

Phillips, June K., and Jamie Draper. *The Five Cs: The Standards for Foreign Language Learning WorkText.* Boston: Heinle and Heinle. Designed for self-study or teacher-training courses: each section asks the reader to analyze the Standards and relate it to his or her own teaching, create materials for the classroom, and reflect on the results. Also contains a summary of the Standards.

Phillips, June K., and Robert M. Terry, eds. 1998. *Foreign Language Standards: Linking Research, Theories, and Practices.* ACTFL Foreign Language Education Series. Lincolnwood, IL: National Textbook. Chapters on goals 1–4 plus a chapter entitled "Meeting the Needs of All Learners: Case Studies in Computer-Based Foreign Language Reading"; discusses primarily the theoretical underpinnings of the Standards with some practical applications.

Focus on the Learner

Learning Styles and Learner Variables

Claxton, Charles S., and Patricia H. Murrell. 1987. *Learning Styles: Implications for Improving Educational Practices.* ASHE-ERIC Higher Education Report no. 4. College Station, TX: Association for the Study of Higher Education. Reviews four approaches to learning styles of college students: personality, information processing, social interaction, and instructional methods. Includes techniques for applying one's knowledge on learning styles to improve student learning.

Ehrman, Madeline E. 1996. *Understanding Second Language Learning Difficulties.* Thousand Oaks, CA: Sage. This book is designed for classroom teachers to diagnose learning difficulties and begin to remedy those difficulties. It includes case studies that present readily identifiable, relatively easy-to-understand types of learners, addressing learning styles, affective factors, and learning strategies.

Ehrman, Madeline E., Betty Lou Leaver, and Rebecca L. Oxford. 2003. "A Brief Overview of Individual Differences in Second Language Learning." *System* 31: 313–30. Offers a brief, but broad overview of individual differences in language learning, focusing on learning styles, learning strategies, and affective variables, such as motivation.

Horwitz, Elaine K., and Dolly J. Young. 1991. *Language Anxiety: From Theory and Research to Classroom Implications.* Englewood Cliffs, NJ: Prentice-Hall. Includes a review of anxiety research; presents theoretical conceptualizations of language anxiety, empirical findings, students' perspectives, and teaching strategies for helping learners cope with anxiety.

O'Malley, J. Michael, and Anna Uhl Chamot. 1993. "Learner Characteristics in Second Language Acquisition." In Alice Omaggio Hadley, ed., *Research in Language Learning: Principles, Processes, and Prospects.* Lincolnwood, IL: National Textbook, 96–123. Provides a view of learning based on cognitive theory; describes learning strategies (metacognitive, cognitive, and social/affective), motivation, aptitude, and learning style; reviews empirical research; and discusses intructional implications.

Oxford, Rebecca L. 1990. *Language Learning Strategies: What Every Teacher Should Know.* New York: Newbury House. Offers practical recommendations for developing students' second language learning strategies, including detailed suggestions for strategy use in each of the four language skills.

Oxford, Rebecca L. 1996. "New Pathways of Language Learning Motivation." In Rebecca L. Oxford, ed., *Language Learning Motivation: Pathways to the New Century.* Honolulu: University of Hawaii, Second Language Teaching and Curriculum Center, 1–8. Presents a short overview of the history of language learning motivation research and discusses current efforts to expand the theory of language learning motivation.

Reid, Joy, ed. 1998. *Understanding Learning Styles in the Second Language Classroom.* Upper Saddle River, NJ: Prentice-Hall. Features sixteen chapters on such topics as introduction to multiple intelligence theory and second language learning, bridging the gap between teaching styles and learning styles. Additional chapters on how learning styles intersect with reading, writing, collaboration, technology, and LD. An appendix contains a compilation of instruments useful for identifying learning styles.

Feminist Approaches

Brantmeier, Cindy. 2001. "Second Language Reading Research on Passage Content: Challenges for the Intermediate Curriculum." *Foreign Language Annals* 34: 325–33. Summarizes research that passage content and gender has on reading comprehension and shows that passage content clearly influences one gender to be more successful than the other.

Calder, William M., and Judith P. Hallett, eds. 1996–97. Special issue: "Six Women Classicists." *Classical World* 90, 2–3: 83–197. Biographical articles on Abby Leach, Edith Hamilton, Gertrude Hirst, Elizabeth Haight, Gertrude Smith, and Mary White.

Chavez, Monika. 2001. *Gender in the Language Classroom.* New York: McGraw-Hill. Surveys and summarizes research on language learning and gender. Topics include gender and achievement, male-female interaction and behavior, motivation, beliefs, and learning styles.

Garrett, Alice. 2002. "Teaching Latin with a Feminist Consciousness." Classics Technology Center (CTCWeb). Available at http://ablemedia.com/ctcweb/netshots/lat101garrett1.html. Good place to start. Defines feminism and feminist consciousness; provides basic questions to ask to see if women are represented, and critiques three reading textbooks: *OLC, CLC, Ecce.*

McClure, Laura, ed. 2000. "Special Section on Feminist Pedagogy." *Classical World* 94, 1: 53–71. Includes articles by McClure on feminist approaches and the classics, Hoover on contextualizing learning with a case study of the *OLC* and Wheelock, Strange on a collaborative approach to teaching the *Somnium Scipionis*, and Gold on teaching and learning beginning Greek.

Rifkin, Benjamin, et al. 1998. "Gender Representation in Foreign Language Textbooks: A Case Study of Textbooks in Russian." *Modern Language Journal* 82: 217–36. Establishes a series of criteria for assessing the equity of gender representation in foreign language textbooks, and then applies the criteria to Russian textbooks.

Schmitz, Betty. 1985. *Integrating Women's Studies into the Curriculum: A Guide and Bibliography*. Old Westbury, NY: Feminist Press. Seminal work that identifies four categories for assessing the representation of women in elementary foreign language textbooks: exclusion, subordination, distortion, and degradation.

Multicultural Awareness and Diversity in the Ancient World

Chew, Kristina. 1997. "What Does *E Pluribus Unum* Mean? Reading the Classics and Multicultural Literature Together." *Classical Journal* 93: 55–81. Focuses primarily on literature in translation, but offers reasons and ways for increasing diversity in the classroom.

George, Edward V. 1998. "Latin and Spanish: Roman Culture and Hispanic America." In Richard A. LaFleur, ed., *Latin for the Twenty-first Century*. Glenview, IL: Scott Foresman–Addison Wesley, 227–36. Additional materials available at www2.tltc.ttu.edu/george/LatSpanWebsite/LatSpanMasterPage.htm. Offers arguments for adding Spanish to the Latin classroom. Provides overview of connections between Latin and Spanish along with practical activities and charts comparing the two languages.

Maiken, Peter T. 1991. "Latin as Minority Motivator." *Classical Outlook* 69: 11–4. Describes the multicultural Alexandria Project in Beloit, Wisconsin.

Students with Special Needs

Ashe, Althea. 1998. "Latin for Special Needs Students: Meeting the Challenge of Students with Learning Disabilities." In Richard A. LaFleur, ed., *Latin for the Twenty-first Century*. Glenview, IL: Scott Foresman–Addison Wesley, 237–50. Briefly describes why we need to accommodate LD students and why Latin may be a good language for LD students to study, and offers some basic ways to accommodate LD students: response journals, accountability logs, multisensory approach, vocabulary techniques, verb and noun charts, and testing accommodations.

Sparks, Richard L., Kay Fluharty, Leonore Ganschow, and Sherwin Little. 1995. "An Exploratory Study on the Effects of Latin on the Native Language Skills and Foreign Language Aptitude of Students with and without Learning Disabilities." *Classical Journal* 91: 165–84. Hypothesizes that LD students' native language skills improve when taught Latin with a multisensory approach.

Sparks, Richard L., Leonore Ganschow, Silvia Kenneweg, and Karen Miller. 1991. "Use of an Orton-Gillingham Approach to Teach a Foreign Language to Dyslexic/Learning Disabled Students: Explicit Teaching of Phonology in a Second Language." *Annals of Dyslexia* 41: 96–117. Explains a multisensory, structured language approach that adheres to the direct and explicit teaching of phonology. It emphasizes simultaneous writing and pronunciation so that students can "see," "hear," and "do" the language.

Collaborative and Cooperative Learning

Davis, Robert L. 1997. "Group Work is *not* Busy Work: Maximizing Success of Group Work in the L2 Classroom." *Foreign Language Annals* 30: 265–79. Useful overview of using group work, offering guidelines for implementing group work, and suggestions for specific activities within a communicative framework.

Fathman, Ann K., and Carolyn Kessler. 1993. "Cooperative Language Learning in School Contexts." *Annual Review of Applied Linguistics* 13: 127–40. Examines the major principles of cooperative learning and applies them to learning foreign languages.

Kessler, Carolyn, ed. 1992. *Cooperative Language Learning: A Teacher's Resource Book.* Englewood Cliffs, NJ: Prentice Hall Regents. The essays in part 1, "Foundations of Cooperative Learning," make the case that cooperative learning (CL) enhances interaction and communication in the classroom. Part 2, "Language through Content," shows how language is a tool for learning content. Part 3, "Focus on Teachers," compares teacher-fronted classrooms with student-centered CL. Sample minilessons are included in a number of chapters.

Oxford, Rebecca L., and Martha Nyikos, eds. 1997. Special issue, "Interaction, Collaboration, and Cooperation: Learning Languages and Preparing Language Teachers." *Modern Language Journal* 81, 4: 440–542. The lead article defines interaction, collaboration, and cooperative learning and presents the research behind each. Additional articles on interacting with authentic texts, computer-mediated collaborative learning, group dynamics and motivation, interactive listening, and collaborative learning in teacher education.

Whitman, Neal A. 1988. *Peer Teaching: To Teach Is To Learn Twice.* ASHE-ERIC Higher Education Report no. 4. College Station, TX: Association for the Study of Higher Education. Describes the use of students as teachers in higher education. Four sections discuss (1) the psychological basis for benefits of peer teaching; (2) types of peer teaching; and (3) strategies for implementing peer teaching at the institutional level and (4) classroom level.

Williams, Mark F. 1991. "Collaborative Learning in the College Latin Classroom." *Classical Journal* 86, 3: 256–61. Argues that collaborative learning in intermediate Latin can not only help students become "owners" of the subject matter and reinforce fundamentals of grammar and syntax but also help students make the jump from grammar and syntax to the great themes and values conveyed by the language. The article then offers an explanation and examples of three types of questions each group must answer: observation, interpretation, and application.

Foreign Language in the Elementary School (FLES)

Osburn, LeaAnn. 1998. "Latin in the Middle Grades." In Richard A. LaFleur, ed., *Latin for the Twenty-first Century.* Glenview, IL: Scott Foresman–Addison Wesley, 70–89. Describes characteristics of middle grade learners, different approaches to designing middle grade programs, and characteristics of effective instruction, sample activities, and resources for teaching the middle grades.

Polsky, Marion. 1998. "Latin in the Elementary Schools." In Richard A. LaFleur, ed., *Latin for the Twenty-first Century.* Glenview, IL: Scott Foresman–Addison Wesley, 59–69. Briefly surveys the history of K–6 Latin programs, provides an annotated list of textbooks available, and describes characteristics of younger learners.

Focus on the Language

Listening and Speaking

Abernathy, Faye, Jill Crooker, Margaret Curran, and David Perry. 1990. *The Development of Oral Skills in Latin with Visuals. A Supplementary Guide to the Syllabus Latin for Communication.* Draft copy. Albany: New York State Education Department. A wide variety of classroom activities.

Auden, H. W. *Greek Phrase Book.* London: Duckworth. Thousands of words and phrases organized by topic, each accompanied by citations from ancient authors. See Meissner.

Beach, Goodwin B., and Ford Lewis Battles. 1967. *Locutionum Cotidianarum Glossarum: A Guide to Latin Conversation.* 3rd ed. Hartford, CT: Hartford Seminary Press. A glossary of terms, culled from Plautus, Terence, Cicero's letters, Cato, Varro, Columella, Petronius, and Apicius, needed for daily situations, domestic, business, agricultural, and general daily life.

Littlewood, William. 1992. *Teaching Oral Communication: A Methodological Framework.* Oxford: Blackwell. Offers a framework for learning language that integrates grammar into a communicative methodology, and discusses a range of communicative activities that help learners internalize the language system so that they can eventually use language for authentic communication.

Meissner, C. 1981. *Latin Phrase Book.* Trans. H. W. Auden. London: Duckworth. More extensive than Beach and Battles; covers daily life as well as more abstract topics, such as the human life, the mind, emotions, virtues and vices, arts and sciences, and religion.

Peckett, C. W. E. 1992. "The Oral Method." *JACT Review* 11: 4–8. Explains how the oral method for teaching languages arose from the direct method; gives many examples of how to teach various grammatical constructions; guidelines for teaching Latin orally.

Strasheim, Lorraine. 1987. *Total Physical Response.* Amherst, MA: Classical Association of New England. Activities for Latin students that integrate movement and listening.

Traupman, John. 2006. *Conversational Latin for Oral Proficiency.* 4th ed. Wauconda, IL: Bolchazy-Carducci. Chapters arranged by topics, such as greetings, family, leisure activities. Each chapter includes model conversations at three levels of difficulty and topical vocabulary.

Wills, Jeffrey. 1998. "Speaking Latin in Schools and Colleges." *Classical World* 92: 27–34. Offers five simple oral activities for classroom use. Argues that adding some oral work in classical languages is useful because it reaches a greater number of students, it adds variety to the classroom, it reduces the affective filter, students recognize the usefulness of oral Latin, and it is often more efficient than writing.

Reading (Not Translation)

Barnett, Marva A. 1989. *More Than Meets the Eye. Foreign Language Reading: Theory and Practice.* Englewood Cliffs, NJ: Prentice-Hall. Reviews research on reading, both first and second language, and includes many activities for developing reading proficiency.

Carrell, Patricia L., Joanne Devine, and David Eskey, eds. 1988. *Interactive Approaches to Second Language Reading.* Cambridge, UK: Cambridge University Press. Articles that explore reading processes, especially the interaction of bottom-up and top-down processes in second language reading. Review of research, new case studies, and implications for instruction.

Devitt, Sean. 1997. "Interacting with Authentic Texts: Multilayered Processes." *Modern Language Journal* 81: 457–69. Links the two fields of second language acquisition and reading research and encourages several layers of interactive processes in reading authentic texts.

Dixon, Mollie. 1993. "Read Latin Aloud." *JACT Review* 13 (1993): 4–8. The benefits of reading Latin aloud to help students learn to read phrase by phrase and in Latin word order.

Grabe, William, and Fredericka Stoller. 2002. *Teaching and Researching Reading*. Harlow, UK: Pearson Education. Excellent summary of recent research on L1 and L2 reading and how it applies to teaching reading.

Hoyos, Dexter. 1993. "Reading, Recognition, Comprehension: The Trouble with Understanding Latin." *JACT Review* 13:11–6. Argues against the approach of decoding or disentangling of a Latin sentence; offers four basic principles for reading; then illustrates typical patterns in Roman prose: chronological order and logical arrangement. In addition, clauses and phrases are framed by the first and last words, words that define the essential structure of the group, in a kind of "arch" structure.

Hoyos, B. Dexter. 1997. *Latin. How to Read It Fluently: A Practical Manual*. Amherst, MA: Classical Association of New England. A more detailed version of Hoyos's approach to reading Latin in Latin word order.

O'Neal, William J. 1990. "Transitional Latin and the Gods." *Classical Journal* 85: 142–7. Describes the benefits of reading authentic texts about mythology that will help students of Latin make the transition from beginning to intermediate levels. In particular, discusses the style, syntax, and proclivities of the first Vatican mythographer (fl. 415 C.E.), second Vatican mythographer (Carolingian Age), and third Vatican mythographer (twelfth century C.E.).

Phillips, June K. 1984. "Practical Implications of Recent Research in Reading." *Foreign Language Annals* 17: 285–96. A great article. Reviews research and then applies it to the classroom with numerous suggested activities.

Writing

Carson, Joan G., and Ilona Leki, eds. *Reading in the Composition Classroom: Second Language Perspectives*. Boston: Heinle and Heinle. Review of research on reading-writing connections as well as the presentation of original research on cognitive and social issues pertinent to the relationship of reading and writing.

Grabe, William, and Robert B. Kaplan. 1996. *Theory and Practice of Writing*. New York: Longman. Reviews research on writing in both first and second languages, proposes a theory of writing, and provides many practical ways to teach writing at beginning, intermediate, and advanced levels.

Kroll, Barbara, ed. 1990. *Second Language Writing: Research Insights for the Classroom*. Cambridge, UK: Cambridge University Press. First half reviews current research on theoretical approaches to second language composition, process approaches to writing, responding to student writing, and connections between reading and writing. Second half reports on new studies that explore issues such as the effect of first language on second language writing, in-class versus at-home compositions, schema training, and feedback on student compositions.

Raimes, Ann. 1983. *Techniques in Teaching Writing*. Oxford: Oxford University Press. Chapters include techniques in using pictures, using readings, using all language skills, using controlled writing, teaching organization, and responding to student writing.

Reid, Joy. 1993. *Teaching ESL Writing*. Englewood Cliffs, NJ: Prentice-Hall. Includes chapters on research of both first and second language writing, syllabus design, student and teacher styles and strategies, sample assignments, and responding to and evaluating student writing.

Grammar in a Communicative Context

Celce-Murcia, Marianne, and Sharon Hillis. 1988. *Techniques and Resources in Teaching Grammar*. New York: Oxford University Press. Practical activities for introducing grammar into the classroom. Chapters on listening and responding, telling stories, drama, pictures, realia, and graphics, songs and verse, games and problem-solving activities, and text-based activities.

Deagon, Andrea Webb. 1991. "Learning Process and Exercise Sequencing in Latin Instruction." *Classical Journal* 87: 59–70. Recommends both variety and a gradual sequencing of language activities that develop automatic responses, keep anxiety levels low, and reinforce vocabulary and syntax within meaningful contexts. Includes examples of classroom activities.

Larsen-Freeman, Diane. 2001. "Teaching Grammar." In Marianne Celce-Murcia, ed., *Teaching English as a Second or Foreign Language*. 3rd ed. Boston: Heinle and Heinle. 251–66. Discusses a framework for teaching grammar that integrates form, function, and meaning.

Mahoney, Anne. 2004. "The Forms You *Really* Need to Know." *Classical Outlook* 81: 101–5. Analyzes the relative frequency of verb and noun forms in Greek and Latin literature in order to argue what forms beginning and intermediate students should concentrate on.

Ruebel, James S. 1996. "The Ablative as Adverb: Practical Linguistics and Practical Pedagogy." *Classical Journal* 92: 57–63. Argues that labels for the many uses of the ablative can be less than helpful for beginning students and shows the usefulness of teaching the ablative as a noun-phrase used as an adverb, answering the questions "how," "when," "why," or "where."

Seligson, Gerda, and Daniel J. Taylor. 1985. "Relief Is in Sight: Observations on Greek and English Grammar." *Classical Journal* 80: 157–8. Explains αὐτός, ἄν, uses of the optative, and sequence of moods.

Ur, Penny. 1988. *Grammar Practice Activities: A Practical Guide for Teachers*. Cambridge, UK: Cambridge University Press. Part 1 contains guidelines for the design of grammar activities and practical hints; Part 2 contains over 200 game-like activities for practicing English grammar (many can be adapted to Latin or Greek).

Vocabulary

Gairns, Ruth, and Stuart Redman. 1986. *Working with Words: A Guide to Teaching and Learning Vocabulary*. Cambridge, UK: Cambridge University Press. A practical guide for how teachers can select, organize, and teach vocabulary at all levels. The book is divided into three sections: words and their meanings, principles in teaching and learning vocabulary, and classroom activties.

Nation, I. S. P. 2001. *Learning Vocabulary in Another Language*. Cambridge, UK: Cambridge University Press. Offers a detailed survey of research on learning vocabulary, successful strategies for learning vocabulary, and tips for using class time efficiently in teaching vocabulary.

Rydberg-Cox, Jeffrey, and Anne Mahoney. 2002. "Vocabulary Building in the Perseus Digital Library." *Classical Outlook* 79: 145–9. Explains how to use the Perseus Vocabulary Tool to create specialized vocabulary lists for beginning, intermediate, and advanced students.

Other Issues, Other Resources

Second Culture Acquisition

Allen, Linda Quinn. 2004. "Implementing a Culture Portfolio Project within a Constructivist Paradigm." *Foreign Language Annals* 37: 232–9. Students identify stereotypes about the target culture and their own culture, do research, and then accept or reject the validity of the stereotypes. Students also demonstrate their own thinking process by explaining how their various sources of information led them to accept or reject their hypotheses.

Crawford-Lange, L. M., and D. L. Lange. 1984. "Doing the Unthinkable in the Second-Language Classroom: A Process for the Integration of Language and Culture." In T. V. Higgs, ed., *Teaching for Proficiency, The Organizing Principle*. ACTFL Foreign Language Education series. Lincolnwood, IL: National Textbook, 139–77. Advocates an approach that begins with culture and leads to language learning, asks students to understand culture within a larger framework, teaches cultural understanding as a process that helps students move from stereotypes to cultural awareness, and includes students' experiences and feelings about the culture.

Jourdain, Sarah. 1998. "Building Connections to Culture: A Student-Centered Approach." *Foreign Language Annals* 31: 439–47. Describes a three-phase model for addressing culture: information gathering, target-language communication, and discussion of cultural values. The student-centered focus helps students strengthen their research and communication skills; the teacher acts as a facilitator and guide.

Kramsch, Claire. 1993. *Context and Culture in Language Teaching*. New York: Oxford University Press. Explores the importance of cultural context in language teaching. Proposes a dialectic between the voices of the students, the text, and the target culture to help understand the multiplicity of voices to be negotiated and appreciated in teaching language and culture.

Moran, Patrick. 2001. *Teaching Culture: Perspectives in Practice*. Boston: Heinle and Heinle. A readable introduction to teaching culture that integrates teachers' voices and self-reflective investigations. Separate chapters on defining culture, cultural products, practices, and perspectives, cultural communities and persons, and the culture learning process.

Scott, Virginia M., and Julie A. Huntington. 2002. "Reading Culture: Using Literature to Develop C2 Competence." *Foreign Language Annals* 35: 622–31. Argues that literary texts, even at the beginning level, can contribute to students' knowledge and understanding of other cultures through affective learning and cognitive flexibility.

Storme, Julie A., and Mana Derekhshani. 2002. "Defining, Teaching, and Evaluating Cultural Proficiency in the Foreign Language Classroom." *Foreign Language Annals* 35: 657–68. Summarizes recent research, proposes a model of culture teaching, and makes suggestions for the evaluation of cultural proficiency

Testing and Assessment

Bachman, Lyle F., and Adrian S. Palmer. 1996. *Language Testing in Practice*. New York: Oxford University Press. Provides a conceptual framework and step-by-step processes for test making. Topics include the qualities of test usefulness; interrelationship of language testing, language teaching, and language use; performance testing; fairness in testing; and recognition that test scores are only one piece of information in making decisions about test-takers.

Bailey, Kathleen M. 1998. *Learning about Language Assessment: Dilemmas, Decisions, and Directions.* Pacific Grove, CA: Heinle and Heinle. Provides a practical analysis of language assessment theory and accessible explanations of the statistics involved; focuses on communicative language testing and alternative assessments for the classroom.

Delett, Jennifer S., Sarah Barnhardt, and Jennifer A. Kevorkian. 2001. "A Framework for Portfolio Assessment in the Foreign Language Classroom." *Foreign Language Annals* 34: 559–68. Guides teachers to establish the purpose and objectives, decide the contents, and create meaningful criteria for portfolio assessment.

Genesee, Fred, and John A. Upshur. 1996. *Classroom-Based Evaluation in Second Language Education.* Cambridge, UK: Cambridge University Press. Presents the context of second language evaluation (three chapters); understands "evaluation" to include classroom observation, portfolios, conferences, journals, questionaires, and interviews (three chapters); and discusses both objective-referenced or classroom-based and standardized tests (six chapters).

Technology

Bush, Michael D., and Robert M. Terry, eds. 1997. *Technology-Enhanced Language Learning.* ACTFL Foreign Language Education series. Lincolnwood, IL: National Textbook. Excellent collection of essays produced for ACTFL, offering essays on how to use technology to teach the four skills, using technology ranging from software and CDs to local area networks to the internet. Also includes chapters on evaluating technology resources, designing labs, and implementing technology.

Cameron, Keith, ed. 1999. *Computer Assisted Language Learning (CALL): Media, Designs, and Applications.* Lisse, Neth.: Swets and Zeitlinger. Articles on computer-mediated communication, user-driven and content-driven research and development of programs, authoring programs, CALL design, evaluation, sociocollaborative language learning, speech recognition, grammar checking, visual grammar, corpora of texts, and computer-assisted writing.

Crane, Gregory. 1998. "New Technologies for Reading: The Lexicon and the Digital Library." *Classical World* 91: 471–501. Discusses differences between printed sources and the internet in accessing lexical information while reading. In particular, notes how Liddell-Scott-Jones, *Greek-English Lexicon*, 9th ed. (Oxford: Oxford University Press, 1940) is transformed in hyperspace.

De Luce, Judith, Suzanne Bonefas, and Susan Bonvallet, eds. 2001. Special issue: Classics and Technology. *CALICO Journal* 18, 2: 207–403. Features a review of fifty years of classical computing, a description of a virtual classics department (Sunoikisis), articles on VRoma and Perseus, a collaborative project (high school and university) teaching Roman drama, Latin grammar drills, annotated intermediate Latin texts, and beginning ancient Greek.

Felix, Uschi, ed. 2003. *Language Learning On-line: Towards Best Practice.* Lisse, Neth.: Swets and Zeitlinger. Includes essays on optimizing web course design for language learning; servers, clients, testing, and teaching; engaging the learner; MOOs and virtual worlds as arenas for language learning; and using internet-based audio-graphic and video conferencing for language teaching.

Pennington, Martha C., ed. 1996. *The Power of CALL.* Houston: Athelstan. Reviews CALL research and how it fits in with other second language research, discusses networks, hypermedia, and concordancing in language teaching, and includes chapters on CALL and reading, writing, and spoken language skills.

Warschauer, Mark, ed. 1996. *Telecollaboration in Foreign Language Teaching*. University of Hawaii: Second Language Teaching and Curriculum Center. Focuses on the networked classroom, and utilizing hypermedia, the Web, e-mail, MOOs, and bulletin boards.

Teaching Greek

Genovese, E. N. 2001. "Linguatour: A Survey Course of Ancient Greek." *Classical World* 94: 385–8. Describes an eight-week short course introducing ancient Greek to mature adults.

Kitchell, Kenneth F., Jr., Edward Phinney, Susan Shelmerdine, and Marilyn Skinner. 1996. "Greek 2000—Crisis, Challenge, Deadline." *Classical Journal* 91: 393–420. Reviews the study of Greek in the United States, enrollments, textbooks, and curriculum goals, and asks how to improve the situation.

Reece, Steve. 1998. "Teaching Koine Greek in a Classics Department." *Classical Journal* 93: 417–29. Focuses on how to introduce *Acts of the Apostles* in the intermediate Greek curriculum.

Schork, R. J. 1995. "*Cebes' Tablet* as a Bridge-Text in the Greek Program." *Classical Journal* 91: 65–9. Touts the advantages of using *Cebes' Tablet*, a first-century allegory about the rocky road to true happiness, as an intermediate text that reinforces Greek grammar while reading an authentic text.

Winters, Timothy F. 2003. "Dedicated to Greek: Using Inscriptions in Elementary Greek." *Classical Journal* 98: 289–94. Offers specific suggestions for incorporating simple inscriptions into beginning Greek, such as the annual list of the Athenian war dead (*demosion sema* inscriptions) or dedications from the Athenian acropolis, as ways for integrating authentic texts into the classroom and stimulating discussions about Greek culture.

Professional Development

Organizations and Journals That Focus on Language Teaching

American Classical League (ACL): www.aclclassics.org/. Audience: Latin and Greek teachers, K–16; publishes *Classical Outlook*.

American Council on the Teaching of Foreign Languages (ACTFL): www.actfl.org/. Audience: all foreign languages, all levels; publishes *Foreign Language Annals*.

Association of Departments of Foreign Languages (ADFL): www.adfl.org/. Audience: college/university; publishes *ADFL Bulletin*.

Classical Association of the Atlantic States (CAAS): www.caas-cw.org/. Audience: Latin and Greek teachers, K–16; publishes *Classical World*.

Computer Assisted Language Instruction Consortium (CALICO): www.calico.org/. Audience: those who are interested in language teaching and technology; publishes *CALICO Journal*.

Classical Association of the Middle West and South (CAMWS): www.camws.org/. Audience: Latin and Greek teachers, K–16; publishes *Classical Journal*; sponsors the Committee for the Promotion of Latin.

Classical Association of New England (CANE): www.wellesley.edu/ClassicalStudies/cane/. Audience: Latin and Greek teachers, K–16; publishes *New England Classical Journal*.

Joint Association of Classical Teachers (JACT): www.jact.org/index.htm. Audience: Latin and Greek teachers, K–16; publishes *JACT Review*.

Teaching Materials, Bibliographies, Resources for Latin and Greek Teachers

Classics Technology Center on the Web. Ablemedia. ablemedia.com/ctcweb/index2.html. Contains teaching materials, learning resources, systems, and applications.

Edmunds, Lowell, and Shirley Werner. *Tools of the Trade for the Study of Roman Literature.* Rutgers University. classics.rutgers.edu/tools.html. A good resource for finding information about the ancient world; provides citations of books and databases; areas include dictionaries, reference works, collections, and more.

Kazmierski, Sharon. *Latinteach.* www.latinteach.com/. This website includes archives of Latinteach discussions as well as teaching guides, lesson plan ideas and projects, an extensive set of links, reviews of textbooks, and other material of interest to Latin teachers.

Latousek, Rob. *Software Directory for the Classics.* American Classical League. www.centaursystems.com/soft_dir.html.

Scaife, Ross. *University of Kentucky Classics.* www.uky.edu/AS/Classics/teaching.html. Features links to a wide variety of organizations, discussion lists, and internet resources.

Siegel, Janice. *Survey of Audio-Visual Resources for Classics.* www.stoa.org/avclassics/. Searchable database.

Svarlien, Diane Arnson. "Children's Books on the Ancient World: A Selective Bibliography." University of Kentucky Classics. www.uky.edu/AS/Classics/kidsklassics.html. A great list of books, both in English and Latin, that will appeal to children.

Searching for More Information

Liu, Alan. *The Voice of the Shuttle: Web Page for Humanities Research.* University of California, Santa Barbara. http://vos.ucsb.edu/index.asp.

Pantelia, Maria. *Electronic Resources for Classicists: The Second Generation.* University of California, Irvine. www.tlg.uci.edu/~tlg/index/resources.html.

Index

Culture
    compartmentalized, 14
    defined as products, practices, and
        perspectives, 14
    information about, to enhance compre-
        hension, 139–40
    see also Critical consciousness; Culture
        activities; Intercultural competence;
        Standards for Classical Language
        Learning, Culture goal; Underrepre-
        sented groups in the ancient world
Culture activities, 95–103, 144–50, 197–9,
    203–9

Decoding, grammatical. See under Reading
    processes, bottom-up
Dictionary, using the, 97–8. See also Glosses;
    Vocabulary
Disabilities. See Learning disabilities
Discourse competence, 20 n. 4
Discourse structure, 12, 140–1, 147, 193
Drills, ineffectiveness of, 20 n. 3, 124, 162–3,
    166

Error correction
    in communicative context, 167–8, 172
    in cooperative learning, 71
    in writing, 213
Exercises, classroom. See Activities, classroom

Feedback. See Responding to students
Feminist pedagogy, 86–109
    activities for the elementary Latin class-
        room, 94–109
    and classroom interactions, 91–3 (see also
        Cooperative learning; Peer teaching)
    and classroom materials, 90–1
    and critical consciousness, 15, 92
    and electronic resources, 93–4
    and liberation pedagogy, 92
    objectives of, 94–5
Form, focus on, 13
Friendship, Roman, 16

Games, classroom, 17, 36, 39
Garden-path sentences, 123
Gender. See Feminist pedagogy; Under-
    represented groups in the ancient
    world
Glosses, 141
Grammar activities, 80–1, 125–8, 200–3, 212–3
Grammar and syntax
    acquisition within a communicative
        context, 12–3, 164–5, 169, 177

author's choice of, 201–2
    explication of within the context of
        reading, 40, 77–9
    in prereading activities, 40–1, 139, 140–1
    teaching, 9–10, 12, 76–77, 184 n. 10, 186
        n. 14
    see also αὐτός; Conditions, future potential;
        Drills, ineffectiveness of; Error cor-
        rection; Form, focus on; Garden-path
        sentences; Imperfect tense; Meta-
        phrasing; Morphological ambiguity in
        Latin; Participles; Particles

High-risk foreign language learner, defined,
    50. See also Learning disabilities

Illustrations, using. See Pictures
Imperfect tense, 177
Individual differences. See Learning styles
Input. See Comprehensible input
Input vs. intake, 159
Instructor. See Teacher
Interaction, 163, 165–6, 184 n. 4. See also
    Language acquisition; Meaning,
    importance of
Intercultural competence, 15–16

Jigsaw activity, 80–81
Journals, student, 92, 95–7

Language acquisition, 12–13, 134–5, 162–4,
    183 nn. 2 and 4, 192–3
Latin, advantages for LD students, 55
Latin and Greek, advantages of, 3
LD. See Learning disabilities
Learner-centered approaches, 16–18, 34–42,
    59–64, 138, 150–1
Learning disabilities (learning difficulties,
    learning differences) (LD), students
    with
    defined, 53–4, 65 n. 3
    history of, in foreign languages, 51–3
    ideal instructor of, 59–61
    mainstreaming, 58–9, 61
    modified assignments for, 55–8, 60, 63
    recommendations for assisting, 61–4
Learning strategies, 42–5, 64, 80–1, 95, 170
Learning style inventories and questionnaires,
    42. See also Modern Language Apti-
    tude Test; Personality tests
Learning styles, 16–17, 27–34, 91, 159
    defined, 27
    diagnosing, 38–42
    as a factor of personality, 27, 42

and Latin instruction, 33–8
types of, 29–33
see also Learning strategies
Listening, 11–12, 136–44, 153 n. 9
difficulty for LD students, 53
prelistening, 138–42
and reading compared, 136–7
Lysias, 144–50

Marginalized groups in the ancient world.
See Underrepresented groups in the
ancient world
Meaning, importance of, 12, 124, 162–3, 184
n. 4, 192–3. *See also* Comprehen-
sible input; Comprehensible output
Meaning-based instruction, 10, 13, 124–5,
148–9, 162–3, 165–6, 184 n. 4
Memorization, 29–30, 33, 35–6, 43, 45, 53,
56–7
Memory, 120, 124, 162–3, 166, 170
Metaphrasing, 119–20, 126
Modern Language Aptitude Test, 54
MOO (Multi-User Domain Object Oriented),
11, 18, 82 n. 1
Morphological ambiguity in Latin, 5, 118–24
Multi-sensory structured language approach
(MSL), 53, 61. *See also* Orton-
Gillingham method

Natural Approach, 152 n. 2, 159, 162–5,
167–8
Natural, non-systematic preview of the language, 164–5

Orton-Gillingham (O-G) method, 54. *See also*
Multi-sensory structured language
approach
Output. *See* comprehensible output

Participles, 101–3
Particles, 140–1, 198
Peer teaching, 68–85
co-peer teaching defined, 70–71 (*see also*
Cooperative learning)
near-peer teaching defined, 70 (*see also*
Undergraduate teaching assistants)
peer response groups, 211–3
Performance
of texts, 11
of skits, 166, 177, 207
Personality tests
Gregorc Style Indicator, 27, 33, 41, 46 n. 1
Myers-Briggs Type Indicator (MBTI), 27,
33, 42, 46 n. 1

Pictures
drawing, 143, 199
illustrating vocabulary or a semantic field,
36, 37, 147–8
labeling, 142, 149
writing about, 197–8, 204–6

Read-and-speak method, 178–9
Reading
in a communicative context, 11
diagnosing unsuccessful strategies, 38–41
extensive reading as the goal of elementary
and intermediate Latin, 114–5
extensive vs. intensive, 116
and listening, 136–7
postreading, 128, 143–44, 149
and predicting content, 117–8, 125, 137,
142
prereading, 124–5, 138–42, 146–48
research, 114–6
sight, 80–81
strategies, 41, 140, 143
for Latin, 117–29
types of, 114–5
and writing, 193–4
see also Authentic texts; Communication;
Comprehensible input; Reading
activities; Reading processes; Standards for classical language learning,
standard 1.1; Translation
Reading activities, 41, 125–9, 144–50
Reading aloud, 57, 136, 142–3, 163–4
Reading processes
bottom-up, 115–26, 137
top-down, 115, 137–41. *See also* Schema
Responding to students, 167–9, 209–13. *See
also* Assessment; Learner-centered
approaches

Schema, 13, 137–9, 146–8, 193–4, 197–204
Scripts for conversation, 158–160, 166, 173
classroom transcript of a conversation,
170–3
sample scripts, 180–3
Semantic code, difficulty with, 53
Semantic field, 36
example of, 13
see also Vocabulary
Semantic mapping, 38, 142, 200
Speaking, 11
advantages, pedagogical, of speaking
Greek, 162–5
advantages, psychological, of speaking
Greek, 158–62